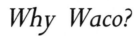

Why Waco?

Why Waco?

Cults and the Battle for Religious Freedom in America

James D. Tabor

and

Eugene V. Gallagher

UNIVERSITY OF CALIFORNIA PRESS

BERKELEY   LOS ANGELES   LONDON

University of California Press
Berkeley and Los Angeles, California

University of California Press, Ltd.
London, England

© 1995 by
The Regents of the University of California

Library of Congress Cataloging-in-Publication Data

Tabor, James D., 1946–
Why Waco? : cults and the battle for religious freedom in
America / James D. Tabor and Eugene V. Gallagher.
  p.   cm.
  Includes bibliographical references and index.
  ISBN 0-520-20186-8 (alk. paper)
  1. Koresh, David. 1959–1993.   2. Branch Davidians.
3. Waco Branch Dividian Disaster, Tex., 1993.
4. Cults—United States.
I. Gallagher, Eugene V.   II. Title.
BP605.B72T33   1995
299'.93—dc20   95-3553
                                                CIP
Printed in the United States of America
9 8 7 6 5 4 3 2 1

*For David P. Efroymson in friendship
and gratitude for a quarter century
of intellectual guidance
and
for Jonathan Z. Smith, who taught both
of us the importance of seeing ourselves in
the light of the other and the other in
the light of ourselves*

A cult is a religion with no political power.

TOM WOLFE,
In Our Time

CONTENTS

So thoroughly negative is the public perception of groups labeled as "cults" that any attempt to balance the picture may be seen as misguided, if not downright threatening, to the best interests of society. In the case of the Branch Davidians, the news media were saturated with reports of gun stockpiling, sexual misconduct, and child abuse. Despite the alarm and hostility provoked by such reports and by popularly accepted notions of "cults" in general, we believe that an accurate, truthful portrayal of David Koresh and his followers and of the events surrounding the siege of their community in Waco is essential for understanding contemporary religious life in our country. We must confront our fascination with and fear of "cults" if we are to view them in the wider context of our national commitment to religious tolerance—after all, the United States was founded by estranged minorities seeking religious freedom. Our intent is to examine with honesty and objectivity the questions raised by its title: Why did Waco happen and how can this American tragedy be avoided in the future?

ACKNOWLEDGMENTS

Writing this book was not an easy task, intellectually, emotionally, or physically. But we do think it was an important one. Without the help of many individuals we would not have been able to complete our research and writing, especially within the relatively short time allotted. We are particularly grateful to Clive Doyle, Wally Kennett, Sheila Martin, Janet McBean, Catherine Matteson, Woodrow and Janet Kendrick, and Rita Riddle for taking the time to relive painful memories and to enlighten us about the history, beliefs, and practices of the Mount Carmel community. We also thank Livingstone Fagan for having allowed us to read the early installments of his own exposition of Branch Davidian theology. David Thibodeau, who was inside Mount Carmel throughout the siege, gave us many unselfish hours of his time, trying to communicate to us what it was like. Marc Breault, even when we disagreed with him on specific matters, has been a gracious and extremely helpful source of information as well as a stimulating discussion partner. Mark Swett kindly shared with us his extensive collection of tapes and transcriptions of David Koresh's biblical material.

Phillip Arnold of the Reunion Institute in Houston, Texas, has been a valued conversation partner since the dramatic events at the Mount Carmel center began in February 1993. He has been particularly helpful in clarifying many difficult points of Branch Davidian theology and has contributed to the commentary in our appendix. James Trimm has also provided many theological insights and clarifications. Dick Reavis, who is writing his own book on Waco, graciously shared insights and material with us. We also thank our colleagues who have encouraged us in many ways in our work on this book, particularly Gordon Melton, Timothy Miller, Stuart Wright, and Catherine Wessinger.

The library of the *Waco Tribune-Herald* helpfully provided us with a full set of its stories about Mount Carmel from just before the initial BATF attack through its first anniversary. Morris Bowen, the court reporter at the trial of the eleven Branch Davidians charged with conspiracy to commit murder, was especially helpful in making transcripts of the trial available nearly as soon as he completed them. Diane Monte, Walter Kritemeyer, and Ashley Hanson assisted in tracking down some elusive bits and pieces that helped us put together our own mosaic of David Koresh and the Branch Davidians.

We gratefully acknowledge our extraordinary good fortune in having Douglas Abrams Arava as our editor at the University of California Press. His suggestions for revisions invariably made our presentation clearer, tighter, and more forceful. His sharp mind, good humor, and passionate interest made working with him a rare pleasure. We thank Marilyn Schwartz, our managing editor at the press, for seeing us through the long process from manuscript to final copy, and Rachel Berchten, our highly skilled copyeditor who worked so tirelessly to correct and improve our efforts. Finally, we thank the readers for the University of California Press who made many helpful suggestions, most of which we have tried to incorporate.

Jennifer Gallagher, Maggie Gallagher, and Cindy Driscoll in Noank, along with Lori Woodall and Eve and Seth Tabor-Woodall in Matthews—all conspired both to protect our time so that we could work in peace and to provide the necessary welcome distractions when we most needed them.

December 1, 1994

James D. Tabor, *Matthews, North Carolina*
Eugene V. Gallagher, *Noank, Connecticut*

ONE

What Might Have Been

THE FBI AGENTS CALLED to Mount Carmel center outside Waco, Texas, on February 28, 1993, can hardly be expected to have packed their Bibles. In retrospect, it would not have been such a bad idea. The news of the bloody shoot-out between agents of the Federal Bureau of Alcohol, Tobacco, and Firearms (BATF) and an obscure religious group known as the Branch Davidians, on the peaceful Sunday morning had been flashed around the world.[1] For months the BATF had planned a "search and arrest" assault on the group based on allegations that they possessed illegal firearms materials and were possibly converting AR-15 semiautomatic rifles into machine guns. At 7:30 A.M. an eighty-vehicle convoy, including two cattle trailers pulled by pickup trucks loaded with seventy-six heavily armed BATF agents, had made its way to a staging area a few miles from the rural Mount Carmel property. Shortly after 9:00 A.M. the assault began. The two cattle trailers drove rapidly up to the property, halted in front, and the BATF agents stormed the center. Over head two Blackhawk helicopters arrived simultaneously. Local newspaper and television people, who had been alerted to the raid, watched and filmed from a distance. On Saturday, the previous day, the *Waco Tribune-Herald* had begun to publish a dramatic front-page series called "The Sinful Messiah," which alleged that the "cult" and its leader, David Koresh, were guilty of bizarre sexual practices, child abuse, and paramilitary activities.[2]

Who fired the first shot that morning is disputed. David Koresh, the leader of the Branch Davidians, claimed that he went to the front door and shouted to the arriving agents, "Get back, we have women and children in here, let's talk," only to be cut off by a burst of gunfire.[3] The BATF claims that they tried to identify themselves, shouting to Koresh that they had a warrant, but were met with a hail of bullets.[4] Later, in the 1994 San Antonio trial of eleven Branch Davidians on charges of conspiracy to murder, it came out that the BATF had planned a "dynamic entry" with no realistic contingency for a peaceful serving of the search warrant.[5] A few minutes into the raid, the Branch Davidians called their local 911 number, demanding that the attack cease. By noon a cease-fire had been arranged. The BATF claims they were ambushed and outgunned by the Branch Davidians, who had known they were coming. The Branch Davidians maintain that their resistance was minimal and in self-defense, and that their 911 call demonstrated their nonconfrontational stance on that day. A standoff ensued, with Koresh and his followers inside refusing to surrender. Within hours the major television and print media had arrived, and the FBI was called in. For the next fifty-one days the situation at Waco dominated the news. David Koresh had instantly become a household name, and the public was hungry for information about this obscure thirty-three-year-old Bible-quoting Texan and his followers.

It all ended on Monday, April 19. Just after 6:00 A.M., two specially equipped M-60 tanks began to strategically punch holes into the Mount Carmel structure and insert CS gas in an effort to force the Davidians out. The wind was high that day, and most of the tear gas seemed to blow away. Over the next six hours the operation was stepped up, and four Bradley vehicles joined the tanks, firing 40 mm canisters of gas through the windows. A loudspeaker blared, "David, you have had your 15 minutes of fame. . . . Vernon [Koresh's given name] is no longer the Messiah. Leave the building now. You are under arrest. This standoff is over."[6] Around noon, smoke was seen coming from the second-story windows, and within minutes the thin frame building was engulfed in an uncontrollable fire, fanned by the gusty winds. The entire scene was carried live to the world over television satellite. Only nine Davidians were able to escape the fire. The bodies of most of the women and children were found huddled together in a concrete storage area near the kitchen, where they had apparently been trapped by falling debris.

The Waco operation turned out to be one of the most massive and tragic in the history of United States law enforcement.[7] In the initial raid, four BATF agents were killed and twenty wounded, while six Branch Davidians were fatally shot, with four others wounded.[8] The Branch Davidians inside the rambling Mount Carmel complex following the raid numbered approximately 123 persons, including 43 children. They were heavily armed and solidly behind their leader. On April 19, when it all came to a fiery end, 74 Branch Davidians were listed dead, including 21 children under the age of fourteen.[9] In the aftermath BATF director Stephen Higgins and five other high-ranking officials resigned from the agency.[10]

On the very evening following the initial Sunday raid by the BATF, Koresh, who had been seriously wounded, spoke several times by live telephone hookup over Dallas radio station KRLD and CNN cable television. Koresh began, in those gripping interviews, the first of hundreds of hours of explanations, based on his understanding of the biblical apocalyptic significance of the situation in which he found himself. His last direct communication with anyone other than government agents was an impromptu conversation with the station manager Charlie Serafin over KRLD radio at 1:50 A.M. the next morning.[11] In those live broadcasts Koresh offered the key to the Branch Davidians' biblical understanding of events. Unfortunately, neither the FBI agents in charge nor the myriad of advisers upon whom they relied could comprehend their perspective.

By that Monday morning, March 1, the FBI had already been called in and was in the process of taking over operations from the BATF. FBI Special Agent Jeff Jamar, from San Antonio, Texas, had taken command of the situation. The FBI fifty-person Hostage Rescue Team (HRT), a counterterrorist unit, was arriving. The situation was categorized by the FBI on this very first day of the siege as a "complex Hostage/Barricade rescue situation" even though the FBI recognized that many of the elements typically present in hostage situations were lacking. As the FBI itself later noted, "Koresh had made no threats, set no deadlines, and made no demands. Koresh and his followers were at Mount Carmel where they wanted to be and living under conditions that were only marginally more severe than they were accustomed to."[12] Nonetheless, negotiators and tactical personnel were called in, SWAT teams were put in place, and a method of dealing with the Branch Davidians was initiated, which was basically followed for the next fifty days—leading to the tragedy on April 19.

Listening carefully to what Koresh said in those live interviews over KRLD and CNN, a person familiar with the biblical texts could have perceived the situation in wholly different terms from the government's "hostage rescue." For the Branch Davidians, no one was a hostage. The only "rescue" they needed was from the government itself. In their view, the federal agents represented an evil government system, referred to in the book of Revelation as "Babylon." The idea of "surrendering to proper authority," as the government demanded throughout the next seven weeks, was absolutely out of the question for these believers unless or until they became convinced it was what God willed. As they saw it, their group had been wantonly attacked and slaughtered by government agents whom they understood to be in opposition to both God and his anointed prophet David Koresh. Their fate was now in God's hands.

The Waco situation could have been handled differently and possibly resolved peacefully. This is not unfounded speculation or wishful thinking. It is the considered opinion of the lawyers who spent the most time with the Davidians during the siege and of various scholars of religion who understand biblical apocalyptic belief systems such as that of the Branch Davidians.[13] There was a way to communicate with these biblically oriented people, but it had nothing to do with hostage rescue or counterterrorist tactics. Indeed, such a strategy was being pursued, with FBI cooperation, by Phillip Arnold of the Reunion Institute in Houston and James Tabor of the

University of North Carolina at Charlotte, one of the authors of this book. Arnold and Tabor worked in concert with the lawyers Dick DeGuerin and Jack Zimmerman, who spent a total of twenty hours inside the Mount Carmel center between March 29 and April 4, communicating directly with Koresh and his main spokesperson, Steve Schneider. Unfortunately, these attempts came too late. By the time they began to bear positive results, decisions had already been made in Washington to convince Attorney General Janet Reno to end the siege by force. As we will show, those officials briefing her had decided on the CS gas option and were determined to get her approval, despite her caution and better judgment.

In the KRLD radio conversations that first evening, the station manager urged Koresh to surrender and get medical attention. Since ten children had already come out, he was repeatedly asked whether he would allow more children to leave. In response, Koresh launched into a detailed message, quoting Scriptures and explaining his view of the situation. Most likely, his message was largely incomprehensible to the station manager and to much of the radio audience. Koresh was a master at his own form of biblical exposition and exegesis. From the theological perspective of the Branch Davidians, his message was highly systematic, rigidly consistent, and internally "logical"; to those unfamiliar with the prophetic portions of the Bible, however, the message, delivered in his typical nonstop style with lengthy quotations from the King James Version, surely must have seemed nonsensical. Among the many points he made in those initial conversations on KRLD, one stands out as particularly vital. "We are now in the Fifth Seal," he told his live audience—a cryptic reference to the book of Revelation.

The FBI negotiators spoke mostly with Schneider and Koresh in extended telephone conversations on the private line they had connected.[14] The Department of Justice report indicates that the conversations with Koresh were often two- or three-hour monologues in which Koresh attempted to teach them his biblical interpretations. Although the tapes of these "negotiations" have not been made public, the liberal samples quoted in the Department of Justice report give a fair idea of the style and content of Koresh's communications with the authorities. The FBI notes that his delivery of "religious rhetoric was so strong that they could hardly interrupt him to discuss possible surrender."[15] The report constantly laments that Koresh "refused to discuss any matters of substance" and merely insisted on "preaching" to negotiators.[16] What the authorities apparently never perceived is that Koresh's preaching was to him and to his followers, the *only* matter of substance and that a "surrender" could only be worked out through dialogue within the biblical framework in which the Branch Davidians lived.

In reading through the Department of Justice log of events, one detects early on a developing sense of frustration in dealing with Koresh. On March 5, the FBI agent in charge, Jeff Jamar, had summarized Koresh's position quite succinctly: "His stance is still that he's been told to wait, and when he gets the message to stop waiting, then we'll proceed from there." Indeed, on that same day, Jamar himself stressed that federal authorities were prepared to wait "as long as necessary to get Mr. Koresh and his followers out of the complex without violence, regardless of the time or expense."[17] This was in keeping with President Clinton's understanding that the FBI's philosophy was to "negotiate until the situation was resolved."[18]

Nonetheless, just over a week later, on March 15, the FBI agents in charge began to initiate an abrupt change in policy. Termed a "modified negotiation strategy," this new approach called upon the negotiators to be firm and to insist on peaceful surrender, but to refuse to listen any longer to what they now called Koresh's "Bible babble."[19] This shift in policy effectively sealed off any possibility of sympathetic communication between Koresh and the government negotiators. It deprived Koresh of the only means of communication he valued, namely his own biblical interpretation of what was unfolding. And just five days later—over one month before the April 19 fire—they began to discuss the CS gas option privately.[20]

At about the same time, the FBI began its "stress escalation" and harassment techniques. As early as March 9, a series of pressure tactics was initiated. For example, the electricity to Mount Carmel were temporarily, and later permanently, cut off. These tactics were expanded and intensified over the next few weeks. The pattern was that the FBI would demand that Koresh send out some of his people, the demand would be rejected, and the government would then retaliate with punitive measures. Searchlights kept the property brightly lit through the night, irritating noises and loud music were blared over large speakers, and vehicles and personal property of the Davidians were crushed or removed by armored vehicles. The FBI saw the situation as stalemated. They had little hope that Koresh would allow more children out. Those who were inside apparently intended to stay. All the while Koresh insisted that he would not exit until he received his "word from God."

As we mention earlier, Koresh and his followers had been labeled a "cult" and thoroughly "demonized" in a series of articles called "The Sinful Messiah" printed in the *Waco Tribune-Herald* beginning on February 27, just one day before the BATF raid. This series, based largely on charges by disaffected former Branch Davidians, painted a grim and bizarre picture of Koresh and his followers, echoing all the stereotypes the public had come to associate with unfamiliar groups or new religious movements that are pejoratively labeled "cults." Hungry for any "information" about this heretofore unknown religious group, all the major print, radio, and television media had snapped up this material the day of the February 28 raid. The FBI apparently shared and certainly tried to perpetuate the public perception of Koresh, charging that he was a power-mad, sex-crazed "con man" who constantly made up and changed the rules as things unfolded. They maintained that his word was completely unreliable, pointing to his broken promise to exit Mount Carmel on March 2, following the broadcast over radio of a fifty-eight-minute message he had recorded. After his default on March 2, two days after the BATF raid, however, Koresh stuck irrevocably to his position: God had told him to wait. No matter how hard the authorities pressed Koresh or his followers, demanding that they surrender and come out, the reply was the same: the group would not come out until Koresh received his "word from God." The potential horror of the situation was that if the group perceived itself to be "in the fifth seal," might they not unwittingly, or even willfully, orchestrate their own deaths in order to fulfill this prophecy of martyrdom?

Koresh talked most, almost incessantly, throughout the fifty-one days about the Seven Seals of the book of Revelation. Inseparable from his view of these Seven Seals was his understanding of himself as the unique messianic figure, sent by God to reveal the hidden meaning of the entire biblical prophetic corpus. This was clearly Koresh's primary theme. He would constantly challenge anyone, particularly the ministers and preachers of Christianity, to "prove him wrong" on the Seven Seals or to match him in expounding their hidden meaning.

In its opening chapters the book of Revelation describes a scene in which a mysterious book or scroll sealed with seven wax seals is introduced. The question is then raised: "Who is worthy to open this sealed book?" Koresh understood the sealed book to be the entire Bible, particularly the prophetic writings. Accordingly, to open the book is not only to explain it but also to orchestrate the events it sets forth, leading to the climax of human history, the end of the world. According to the book of Revelation, only one person can open this book, a figure called "the Lamb," whom Christians have always understood to be Jesus of Nazareth. Koresh, however, had an elaborate set of arguments to demonstrate that a figure other than Jesus was intended here, a second Christ, or Messiah, whom Koresh claimed to be. This second Messiah he found prophesied in many passages in the Bible, but particularly in the Psalms and in Isaiah, where he is called "Koresh," the Hebrew name for Cyrus, the ancient king of Persia who conquered Babylon. David Koresh, born Vernon Howell, claimed to be this special figure, sent before God's final judgment upon the world to open the Seven Seals of the book of Revelation and thus reveal to the world the full mysteries of the entire Bible.

When Koresh spoke about being "in the fifth seal" the day of the BATF raid, he was referring to his particular understanding of a sequence of events to unfold before the end, which he also connected to a host of related texts throughout the Bible. What is operating here is a series of interpretive dynamics, well known to scholars of Jewish and Christian apocalypticism, which have played themselves out countless times in the past twenty-five hundred years.[21] Biblical apocalypticism involves the interplay of three basic elements: (1) the sacred Text, which is fixed and inviolate; (2) the inspired Interpreter, who is involved in both transmitting and effecting the meaning of the Text; and (3) the fluid Context in which the Interpreter finds himself or herself. The Text functions as a "map" of things to come, setting forth an "apocalyptic scenario" of End Time events. Koresh's Text was of course, the entire Bible, particularly the books of Daniel, Revelation, the Psalms, Isaiah 40–61, and the Minor Prophets, which he had woven into a complex prophetic sequence of events that had deeply impressed his followers and convinced them he was a prophet himself.

Although the Text itself is fixed and unchanging, setting forth in advance what "must happen," there are two variables in this scheme of things, allowing for a high degree of flexibility. First, the Interpreter is interpreting the Text and the Context, or outside events. And further, outside events are always changing. In our view this was an important key to effective negotiations during the entire fifty-one-day standoff at Mount Carmel. The government largely controlled the Context, or outside situation, and therefore unknowingly possessed the ability to influence Koresh in his interpretations and thus in his actions. Unfortunately, the standard negotiation strategies and tactical maneuvers associated with complex Hostage/Barricade rescue situations confirmed Koresh in his initial perception of the events of February 28—that they were "in the fifth seal" and that the entire situation might well end tragically. In other words, the FBI unwittingly played the perfect part of Babylon throughout, validating in detail Koresh's interpretations of Scripture.

The Fifth Seal of the book of Revelation is chilling in its potential implications for the situation at Waco: "And when he had opened the fifth seal, I saw under the altar the souls of *them that were slain* for the word of God, and for the testimony which they held; and they cried out with a loud voice, saying, How long, O Lord, holy and true, dost thou not judge and avenge our blood on them that dwell on the earth? And white robes were given unto every one of them; and it was said unto them, that *they should rest yet for a little season, until their fellow-servants also and their brethren, that should be killed* as they were, should be fulfilled" (emphasis added). (Rev. 6:9–11) This Fifth Seal takes place shortly before the cosmic judgment of God, the great day of the Lord's wrath, which is to be revealed by a massive earthquake and various heavenly signs, introduced by the Sixth Seal (Rev. 6:12–17). In other words, it is the last major event leading to the end of human history. The text speaks of some of the faithful being slain, followed by a waiting period before the rest are killed. Koresh connected this with Psalm 2, which tells of a final confrontation between the "kings of the earth" and an anointed one, or "messiah." Based on this possible interpretation of events, the killing had begun on February 28. From the Branch Davidian point of view, those six who had been killed had died for no other reason than they were studying the Bible with David Koresh and thus were branded as part of a "cult"; they gave their lives "for the word of God, and for the testimony which they held," which is precisely what the book of Revelation prophesies. Accordingly, the group believed it was to *wait* for a "little season" until the rest would also be slain. The martyrdom of those remaining inside Mount Carmel would lead to the Sixth Seal, which would bring about the judgment of God on the world. As long as the Context outside continued to cause Koresh and his followers to believe that the fulfillment of this Fifth Seal was upon them, they viewed their impending death as inevitable.

It is obvious that Koresh himself was confused by the events that had transpired. His prophetic scenario did require fulfillment of this Fifth Seal, but Koresh had taught for years that it would happen in Jerusalem, in the land of Israel. Further, from their calculations of the End Time the group was expecting the final confrontation to come in 1995, not in 1993. Koresh had told his followers that, as the final Christ figure, he would inevitably be required, at some point, to die in a battle. The latter verses of Psalm 89, which Koresh mentioned on the day of the initial BATF raid, predict just such a fate for this Davidic figure. However, beginning in 1990, and particularly following the Gulf War in 1991, Koresh had speculated that at least a portion of these final events might take place in Texas rather than Israel.[22]

Koresh's uncertainty about whether or not the BATF raid presaged such a scenario offered the best hope for a peaceful resolution of the situation. In the February 28 KRLD radio conversation, the station manager asked Koresh how he felt about the BATF agents that had been killed and wounded. He answered emphatically, "My friend, it was *unnecessary*." He went on to say that the whole thing was regrettable, that innocent lives had been lost, and that he would have submitted to any governmental investigation of the weapons he had purchased. Indeed, nearly a year earlier, in July 1992, when BATF agents had questioned the Waco gun dealer Henry McMahon in their initial investigation of the Branch Davidians, Koresh had actually invited them to Mount Carmel to talk and later faxed copies of his arms purchase receipts to McMahon to assist him in responding to the BATF inquiry.[23] In the KRLD conversation Koresh described his cordial relationship with the local McLennan County sheriff Jack Harwell and other law enforcement officers, including the undercover BATF agent Robert Rodriguez, who had tried to infiltrate the group earlier that year. The 911 tapes, made on the same day, within minutes of the BATF raid, also reveal a panicked group inside Mount Carmel who desperately wanted the authorities to back off. On March 7 the group recorded a one-hour video of Koresh with his wives and children. In this video Koresh addresses the federal authorities in a most accommodating manner, stating his desire to resolve the situation peacefully, while still sharply blaming them for initiating the entire encounter. At the end of the tape he says, "Hopefully God will grant us more time."

These actions indicate that Koresh did not see the February 28 confrontation as an inevitable fulfillment of the final prophetic scenario that he had proclaimed to his followers in such detail. Some events did not match; the outcome was open ended and still to be determined. Yet he had been wounded, people had been killed, and he was now confronted by official agents of the United States government, whom Adventists had historically identified as the leader of the Babylonian system that Christ defeats in the book of Revelation (17–18). It is clear from conversations with surviving Branch Davidians who were inside Mount Carmel that the group feared that the overwhelmingly superior government forces might force their way in and kill them all at any moment. Koresh was convinced that the attack on February 28 was related to the final sequence of events foretold in the Bible, but, given these ambiguities, he was uncertain of what he was to do. Although the apocalyptic Text was fixed, like a script written in advance, the Interpretation and the precise Context were variable. Koresh was waiting because he believed that God had told him to do so and because he understood a waiting period to be required by the "fifth seal." In the meantime he was seeking his "word from God," which would clarify the ambiguities and uncertainties inherent in the changing outside situation.

On Friday, March 19, a significant event occurred that the group interpreted as the sign for which they had been waiting. The Branch Davidians were able to listen to local radio stations on transistor radios despite their electricity being cut off. Paul Harvey had mentioned a "guitar-shaped nebula" on his national radio news report. Koresh was extremely excited about this report, thinking that it might well be one of the "signs" from God that he was looking for. He discussed it with the FBI negotiators and later claimed that it was "his sign" sent by God to draw the world's attention to what was happening.[24] According to the Gospels, Jesus had predicted that shortly before the end such heavenly signs would appear.[25] The Davidians were particularly impressed that this comet had been described as having a guitarlike shape, since Koresh had always understood his role as a guitar player in his rock band to be an integral part of his prophetic mission. The surviving Davidian David Thibodeau, who was the drummer in the band, reports that Koresh and all the Davidians were deeply moved by what they understood to be the clear correspondence between this rare heavenly sign and their situation.[26] Obviously, Koresh and his followers were anxious to see some indication from God, some supernatural manifestation, that would confirm them in the course they had taken. This also comes out in the series of letters Koresh sent out during the final week of the siege. In his last letter he actually predicts an earthquake to occur in the Waco area. These elements of his thinking indicate that the situation was much more flexible than one might have supposed and that Koresh's insistence upon waiting for a word from God suggested fluidity and open options rather than intransigence.

Phillip Arnold and James Tabor offered their services to the FBI on March 7.[27] As biblical scholars they specialized in the history of biblical apocalyptic interpretation and were generally familiar with Adventist groups although neither had ever heard of David Koresh and the Branch Davidians before February 28. They studied carefully the fifty-eight-minute tape that Koresh had released on March 2 and began many hours of theological conversation over the telephone with Livingstone Fagan. Fagan had been sent out of Mount Carmel by Koresh on March 23 to act as a theological spokesperson for the Davidians; he was now being held in jail in Waco on charges stemming from the February 28 BATF raid. He holds a graduate degree in theology and is an articulate defender of Koresh's teachings. Tabor and Arnold began to grasp the details of Koresh's teachings. Their intentions in approaching the FBI were twofold: First, they offered to help the negotiators to interpret the complexities of books like Daniel and Revelation, as understood by the Branch Davidians. But even more important, they wanted to communicate with Koresh directly, offering him sympathetic and informed response to his apocalyptic interpretations. Their goal was to build upon the ambiguity that they knew he already felt about his situation. Fagan had stressed to them that from the Davidian viewpoint the outcome of the crisis was completely opened-ended and undetermined. According to Fagan, what would transpire depended on how the government authorities responded to Koresh's efforts to communicate his biblical faith. Fagan saw the Mount Carmel siege as a kind of spiritual trial, or test, for our culture, to determine whether or not we would listen to God's final messenger. Tabor and Arnold hoped to build on this point with Koresh, emphasizing that given his interpretation of the Bible, right or wrong, one might not necessarily understand the standoff at Waco as a fulfillment of the penultimate End Time scenario. It was clear that Koresh desperately wanted the FBI to recognize his skill and wisdom in the Scriptures. His preaching to the negotiators was a monologue, because none of them was equipped to discuss the many texts that Koresh brought up and no substantive dialogue ensued.[28]

In early March, Arnold had done short interviews over Dallas radio stations KRLD and KGBS, discussing the book of Revelation and its relevance to how the Branch Davidians understood the situation at Mount Carmel. These broadcasts had attracted the attention of Koresh and Schneider who were able to listen on their battery-powered transistor radios. On March 16, they made a formal request that they be allowed to discuss the Bible with Arnold. The FBI denied their request but allowed tapes of the radio interviews with Arnold to be sent into Mount Carmel.[29] Encouraged by this positive response, Arnold and Tabor began to formulate a more carefully worked-out plan to communicate with Koresh. Ron Engleman, host of a daily talk show over station KGBS, had shown sympathy toward the Branch Davidians from the day of the initial BATF raid. His program was faithfully followed by those inside Mount Carmel.[30] On April 1, Arnold and Tabor spoke on Engleman's show and discussed in some detail the prophetic technicalities of the Waco situation as it might be viewed by the Branch Davidians. Although this program took the form of a dialogue between Arnold and Tabor, it was deliberately pitched for the ears of Koresh and his followers and was designed to show that someone outside was listening and capable of discussing the book of Revelation on a level the Davidians could appreciate. David Thibodeau, who was inside, remembers that this program created a very favorable response.[31] Around this time Arnold had also spent many hours with Dick DeGuerin, Koresh's attorney, who was meeting daily with Koresh inside Mount Carmel. DeGuerin reported that Koresh wanted most to discuss the Bible, and Arnold tried to lay out for him the religious framework of his client. On April 4, just before Passover, the FBI allowed a tape of this radio discussion to be taken into Mount Carmel by Dick De-Guerin and given directly to Koresh. This was the last face-to-face contact anyone from the outside had with those who died inside Mount Carmel.[32]

On April 14, following the eight-day Passover celebration of the Davidians,[33] and just four days before the FBI gas attack and resulting fire, Koresh received his long-awaited "word from God." According to survivors of the fire, he had spent the prior Passover week in deep prayer and meditation, seeking an answer to his question as to what God expected him to do. On that day, a Wednesday, Koresh released a letter addressed to his lawyer, Dick DeGuerin, which would be his final communication to the outside world. In it he joyfully announces that the group will come out as soon as he finishes writing his basic message on the Seven Seals and sees that it is delivered to Arnold and Tabor. In part the letter reads:

> I am presently *being permitted* to document, in structured form, the decoded messages of the Seven Seals. Upon completion of this task, I will be *free of my "waiting period."* I hope to finish this as soon as possible and to stand before man to answer any and all questions regarding my actions.
>
> This written Revelation of the Seven Seals *will not be sold,* but is to be available to all who wish to know the Truth. The Four Angels of Revelation are here, now ready to punish foolish mankind; but, the writing of these Seals will cause the winds of God's wrath to be held back a little longer.
>
> I have been *praying so long* for this opportunity; to put the Seals in written form. Speaking the Truth seems to have very little effect on man.
>
> I was shown that as soon as I am given over into the hands of man, I will be made a spectacle of, and people will not be concerned about the truth of God, but just the bizarrity of me in the flesh.
>
> I want the people of this generation to be saved. *I am working night and day to complete my final work* of the writing out of these Seals.
>
> I thank my Father, He has finally *granted me the chance* to do this. It will bring New Light and hope for many and they will not have to deal with me the person.
>
> I will demand the first manuscript of the Seals be given to you [Dick DeGuerin]. Many scholars and religious leaders will wish to

have copies for examination. I will keep a copy with me. As soon as I can see that people like Jim Tabor and Phil Arnold have a copy *I will come out* and then you can do your thing with this beast.[34] (Emphasis added.)

This letter is invaluable as a reflection of Koresh's personal piety and his apocalyptic way of thinking. He speaks of receiving permission to write out his message of the Seven Seals. In his understanding of things, this point is of supreme significance. Indeed, as he now saw it, the time had arrived, at long last, for the mysteries of the book of Revelation, which had been revealed to him in 1985, to be given to the world. In Revelation 10, an angelic figure is told to "seal up" and not write the mysteries of seven "thunders," which are equivalent to the events of the Seven Seals. Yet this figure has in his hand a "little book," and he is given all the "mystery of God as declared to the prophets." This messenger, whom Koresh claimed to be, is subsequently told, "You must prophesy *again* before many people, nations, and tongues, and kings" (emphasis added). Arnold and Tabor had discussed this passage in detail in their April 1 tape. They knew that he claimed to be this very figure in Revelation 10. They pointed out to him that, although his name was now a household word and he had been on the cover of *Time* and *Newsweek* and he was mentioned hourly in CNN news reports, all the public knew about him were the charges of child abuse, sexual molestation of minors, and a myriad of other bizarre practices widely reported by the media. The figure in Revelation 10 has a "little book," which apparently contains the sealed message; yet at some point this messenger is told to go to the world at large with the message. Arnold and Tabor had stressed that no one outside Mount Carmel understood his central claim—the meaning of the Seven Seals. His letter clearly responds to the major points they had raised in that tape. He now wanted to separate what he calls the "bizarrity [*sic*] of me in the flesh" from his message of the Seven Seals, and he was ready to "stand before man to answer any and all questions" regarding his behavior.

The FBI apparently failed to recognize that according to this letter, Koresh had finally received his word from God. He clearly says that his "waiting period" will be over once he completes this manuscript on the Seven Seals. The FBI immediately responded to this latest breakthrough with ridicule. They joked about Koresh, the high-school dropout, writing a book and labeled Koresh's "word from God" nothing more than another "delay tactic" to prolong the agony of the siege for his own purposes. The daily chronology log in the Department of Justice report does not even mention this letter of April 14; it merely notes that "David had established a new precondition for his coming out."[35] The Arnold-Tabor audiotape is never mentioned either. From the Department of Justice report, it appears that nothing was working, that all negotiations had failed, and that the government had one alternative—the CS gas attack. In fact, the only strategy that seemed promising was that of a dispassionate, reasoned dialogue based on the prophecies of the Bible, coupled with the legal arrangements for surrender worked out by the attorneys DeGuerin and Zimmerman.[36] Unfortunately, by that time the government authorities on the ground in Waco were exasperated and had already decided to move with force. Although some in the FBI's inner circles of advisers argued for continued negotiation and more time, on the whole the government did not trust Koresh and considered him insincere and manipulative.[37] Koresh had promised to come out on March 2 when the authorities agreed to have his fifty-eight-minute "message" played over radio but had gone back on his word. Subsequent indications that he would soon exit proved unfounded. This latest letter was seen as another ploy. The FBI asked Murray Miron of Syracuse University to examine this and four other letters sent out the previous week. Miron concluded that the letters bore "all the hallmarks of rampant, morbidly virulent paranoia."[38] In fact, the other four letters consisted mostly of scriptural quotations related to Koresh's understanding of the situation. If Miron had had any training in Scripture, or in the long history of apocalyptic interpretation, he would have recognized that those texts were a kind of code mapping out the perspectives of the group in biblical language. Miron so seriously misunderstood this vital April 14 letter that he apparently thought the mention of the names Tabor and Arnold had to do with book rights, as if they were literary agents and

Koresh were interested in cutting a deal with them, despite the fact that Koresh insists that his manuscript is not to be sold. The FBI summary of Miron's findings on this "fifth letter" echoes this serious failure to comprehend the situation: "With regard to the fifth letter, Dr. Miron noted that the letter appeared to be a ploy designed to buy more time for Koresh. Dr. Miron noted that Koresh's discussion in the letter of mundane issues such as book rights, and his ability to contact his lawyer after he 'comes out,' were future oriented and therefore inconsistent with typical suicide precursors such as self-blame, guilt, or despair. After analyzing all five letters, Dr. Miron concluded on April 15, 1993 that he did not believe 'there is in these writings any better, or at least certain, hope for an early end to the standoff.' "[39] This influential analysis was submitted just three days before the fire. The official opinion was now fixed: Koresh was a determined, hardened, manipulative, and paranoid adversary who had no intention of delivering himself. This appears to have been a serious misreading of the Mount Carmel situation. It is doubtful that Miron had the competence to judge or evaluate this type of biblically based material.[40] From Koresh's worldview, the April 14 letter is "rational" and consistent, reflecting the Branch Davidians' unfluctuating understanding of the situation. For seven weeks Koresh had said, consistently and incessantly, he would not come out until he received his word from God. Then he wrote that he had received that word and that he was coming out. All the legal issues related to a surrender had been worked out by DeGuerin and Zimmerman prior to Passover, which began on April 5. Koresh repeatedly told them that he was coming out, but that he had first to resolve what course he should take from his own religious perspective and faith.

What is doubly tragic is that Attorney General Reno was apparently never told about this April 14 breakthrough, nor shown this crucial letter. The Department of Justice report reveals that meetings were held in Washington throughout the week prior to the Monday, April 19, CS gas assault on Mount Carmel.[41] The FBI was pressing for permission to go in with force. Reno was very hesitant and kept asking whether there was any other way. She repeatedly asked, "What are the arguments for waiting?" A crucial meeting was held with the attorney general on April 14, the very day Koresh released this letter, to discuss the effects of CS gas on children.[42] Toward the end of that week, as deliberations in Washington continued, Reno decided to go ahead with the FBI plan but then reversed herself on April 16, requesting more information. The FBI not only supplied her with the religiously uninformed analysis of Miron but also, on April 17, they presented her with a memorandum from Park Dietz of the UCLA School of Medicine, which also concluded that Koresh was a con man, that further negotiations were hopeless, that he was not coming out, and that he was likely involved in the continued sexual abuse of the children inside. Reno was finally persuaded and gave permission for the CS gas operation. From her account to the media the day of the fire, clearly this unsubstantiated charge of child abuse, more than any other factor, pushed her over the edge. Later that week the Department of Justice issued a "clarification" stating that in fact they had no evidence of child abuse during the fifty-one-day siege. Indeed, Texas Children's Protective Services had thoroughly investigated the child abuse charges in 1992 and dismissed them for lack of evidence.[43] Apparently, Reno was not apprised of this information. There is also no indication anywhere in the Department of Justice report that the attorney general was ever shown the videotapes the Branch Davidians had made and sent out during the siege, which included interviews with many of the adults and their interactions with the children. If she had viewed these tapes, her perceptions of the Davidians might have been humanized, and she would have seen Koresh's relaxed and normal interaction with his children. Even in the official Department of Justice report, the FBI maintains that "historical evidence suggested that Koresh had engaged in child physical and sexual abuse over a long period of time prior to the [B]ATF shootout on February 28."[44] The evidence was technically hearsay coming from disaffected former Davidians and, whether true or not, was passed on as undoubted fact.

On April 19, the day of the fire, Jeff Jamar, the FBI agent in charge at Waco, emphatically stated on CNN's *Larry King Live* and ABC's *Nightline* that the FBI had incontrovertible evidence, based on classified government surveillance techniques, that Koresh had *not* begun his manuscript on the Seven Seals and had no plans to do so.[45] When he was specifically questioned about the April 14 letter and Koresh's promise to surrender, he insisted that, based on this undisclosed evidence, Koresh's latest claim was merely a further attempt to delay surrender and manipulate the authorities. The Department of Justice report makes it clear that the FBI had already decided *weeks before* that they were going ahead with the CS gas attack and that they were not to be deterred. Their only obstacle was convincing Attorney General Reno. By a highly selective presentation of the evidence, and through a reliance upon the one-sided opinions of their two outside "experts," the FBI prevailed. When Dick De-Guerin told Jeff Jamar about the April 14 letter, Jamar was apparently concerned about not tipping him off regarding the upcoming plan to go in with force. He told him, "We've got all the time it takes"; yet he was aware that on that very day meetings were being held in Washington to plan the Monday assault.[46]

We now know that Koresh was working on his manuscript, which he considered his divinely sanctioned task and opportunity. He worked on it as late as Sunday evening, the night before the April 19 assault, completing his exposition of the First Seal. Those in Mount Carmel were excited and pleased by his progress, fully convinced that they would soon be able to come out peacefully.[47] Ruth Riddle, a Branch Davidian who survived the fire, served as his stenographer and typist that weekend. On the day of the fire, she carried out a computer disk in her jacket pocket, containing what Koresh had written up to that point. A substantial piece, it runs about twenty-eight manuscript pages; it reflects Koresh's personality in its style, content, and passion.[48] At the end of the document, he quotes the book of Joel and then offers his commentary: " 'Blow the trumpet in Zion, sanctify a fast, call a solemn assembly. Gather the people, sanctify the congregation, assemble the elders, gather the children, and those that nurse at the breast; let the bridegroom go forth from his chamber, and the bride out of her closet [Joel 2:15, 16].' Yes, the bride is definitely to be revealed for we know that Christ is in the Heavenly Sanctuary anticipating His Marriage of which God has spoken. Should we not eagerly ourselves be ready to accept this truth and *come out of our closet and be revealed to the world* as those who love Christ in truth and in righteousness?" (emphasis added). Koresh had found his text for the situation at hand. As he then understood events, as always through the lens of the biblical prophets, the group was to come out and be revealed to the world. This does not mean he had given up his apocalyptic scenario or his view of himself as the Koresh/Christ who would in the end confront and defeat Babylon. He surely believed that God would bring about the final confrontation in the future. He had come to understand that his immediate task was to communicate his message to the world, after which he would surrender and allow God's will to unfold.

The only effective way to communicate with Koresh was within the biblically based apocalyptic "world" he inhabited, taking advantage of the inherent flexibility that the situation at Mount Carmel presented. Of course, no one can ever know if Koresh would have honored his pledge to come out once the manuscript was finished, but whether he would have or not, the outcome could not have been more terrible. To the FBI he was a con man using religion to cover his need for dominance and pleasure. To the psychiatrists he was psychopathic, suffering from delusional paranoia. Such perceptions, whether valid or not, obscured the only positive means of dealing with Koresh and his followers. Although the FBI has charged that Koresh constantly went back on his word, contradicting himself and willfully breaking his promises, the Department of Justice's highly detailed log reveals otherwise: Koresh and his followers were utterly consistent from March 2 onward. They had been told to wait by God; they would not come out until Koresh received his word from God telling them what to do. No amount of pressure or abuse would move them from this path. The final tragedy is that, when Koresh finally got his "word" on April 14, no one with any understanding of the religious dynamics of the situation had access to those making the decisions that week in Washington.

Who or what caused the fire on April 19 remains a matter of controversy. The government claims that the evidence shows the fire was deliberately set on orders from Koresh.[49] The survivors vehemently deny this. First, they insist that, according to their beliefs, suicide is a serious sin. Further, they maintain that most of the women and children who died were trapped by the fire in the concrete storage vault and could not escape.[50] They report that before noon that day Koresh himself had led them there for their safety to escape the gas, urging the women to protect with wet blankets the children who were too young to wear gas masks. These Davidians maintain that it is inconceivable that Koresh would allow his followers—not to mention his own wives and children, whom he deeply loved and treasured—to die in this way. Whatever the truth, the actions by the government on April 19 were inexcusable, particularly given the positive turn in the situation the week before. The entire fiasco was unnecessary. What is doubly tragic, as this book will demonstrate, is that the government, including the president and the attorney general, the media, and the general public have not begun to comprehend what went wrong at Waco in the spring of 1993 and its implications for religious freedom in our society.

TWO

Moving to Mount Carmel

WHO WERE THE 130 BRANCH Davidians living at Mount Carmel in the spring of 1993, how had they come there, and why did they choose to stay even if remaining there might lead to death? The public was never shown the human side of the Waco story, despite the fact that during the siege the Branch Davidians made and released three one-hour videos in which many of them talked on camera, trying to communicate something about themselves and their convictions. Perhaps fearing that these tapes would produce a sympathetic reaction from the American public, the FBI chose not to release them to the media. The official Department of Justice report notes that those who spoke on these videos appeared calm, assured, thoughtful, and articulate. The report concludes, "The abiding impression is not a bunch of 'lunatics,' but rather of a group of people who, for whatever reason, believed so strongly in Koresh that the notion of leaving the squalid compound was unthinkable."[1]

A few statistics begin to convey some important elements of the human side of this story. In the spring of 1993 the Mount Carmel community numbered approximately 130 persons, which included 42 men, 46 women, and 43 children aged sixteen or younger. Some members of this group had lived on the Mount Carmel property since the 1950s. However, most were recruited in the 1980s and early 1990s from throughout the United States, including Hawaii, and a dozen other countries, among them, Britain, Canada, Australia, Israel, Mexico, Jamaica, the Philippines, and New Zealand. In fact, at least half were foreign nationals, with one-third of this group from Britain. Over half of the community members were people of color: about forty-five were Black, and another twenty-five were either Asian or Hispanic. Often, they came with families. For example, Zilla Henry, a fifty-five-year-old nurse from England, took her five children with her, aged nineteen through twenty-three. Her husband had rejected Koresh's message and refused to make the move to Texas. Wayne and Sheila Martin, a couple in their forties, moved to Mount Carmel with their five children. A graduate of Harvard Law School, Wayne was a law librarian at the University of North Carolina when he became attracted to Koresh's message. Livingstone and Evette Fagan also came from England with their two young children, along with Livingstone's mother, Doris, aged sixty. Livingstone had been a lay minister in the Seventh-Day Adventist church with an advanced degree in theology from Newbold College, an Adventist institution.

The Branch Davidians also owned a house in Pomona, California, which served as a kind of West Coast base of operations. Donald Bunds, an affluent California design engineer, and his wife, Jeannine, a nurse, had become devoted followers of Koresh in the 1980s and helped support the California recruitment efforts. Their daughter, Robyn, later bore Koresh a son, and the entire family lived in Texas at various times although Robyn and her son, as well as her mother and her brother, David, finally left the group. Jeannine, who was fifty years old at the time, was one of the first married women whom Koresh took as one of his sacred wives.

This rich mix of race and culture was a direct reflection of the demography of the Seventh-Day Adventist church, from which the vast majority of these Branch Davidians came. Although there are only 750,000 Seventh-Day Adventists in the United States, there are over seven million of them worldwide.[2] Throughout the 1980s Koresh and some of his more enthusiastic and skilled supporters had made many trips outside Texas to recruit new followers, especially in California, Hawaii, England, Israel, Canada, and Australia.

Koresh's evangelistic methods were not primarily intended for the general public. His foremost mission, which was to be fulfilled in two stages, was to bring a message to the Seventh-Day Adventist church. Initially, his followers believed that Koresh would be instrumental in drawing out a highly select group, whom God was directly choosing to join their little band. The group's members would become the select martyrs of the Fifth Seal and receive the major responsibilities of rulership in the coming Kingdom of God. In the second stage, he would be a general witness to the Adventist church as a whole, in order to prepare the way for the 144,000 worthy ones who would be spared in the coming great conflagration, as foretold in Revelation 7. Identifying himself with the seventh and final "angel," or messenger, of the book of Revelation, he believed that his mission was to "save" as many as he could reach with his message. Given this philosophy Koresh concentrated a great deal of personal attention on a single potential convert. For example, David Thibodeau, a musician living in the Los Angeles area, met David Koresh and Steve Schneider in a music store on one of their California trips. He recalls that Koresh studied intensely with him in one-on-one sessions, devoting a tremendous amount of time and energy in taking him through the complexities of the Branch Davidian biblical teachings.[3] Thibodeau eventually became the drummer in Koresh's band and moved to Mount Carmel, where he took up permanent residence. This method of concentrated personal study with selected interested individuals became standard with Koresh. No person was unimportant to him since he viewed anyone who showed interest as among those that God was choosing for a special mission.

The Branch Davidians maintained a large mailing list and regularly sent out tapes and literature expounding Koresh's teachings.[4] Koresh would address these tapes to "Branches, Davidians, and Adventists" worldwide. He focused on what he called the "seventh angel's message," which he claimed to deliver to them.[5] In these teachings, there was a constant emphasis on the "wonderful messages of truth" and the "understanding God has given in regards to the writings of the prophets."[6]

Koresh traveled throughout the United States and abroad, and met with small groups that gathered to hear his message, often in a home of a sympathetic follower or potential recruit. Marc Breault and Steve Schneider, both of whom had graduate theological training in Seventh-Day Adventist universities, were particularly effective in drawing in new members. Breault, who was from Hawaii, had been recruited in early 1986 in California on one of Koresh's frequent West Coast visits.[7] A man of many talents, a computer wiz, and a musician, he was trained in biblical studies. Breault ended up playing keyboards in Koresh's band and became his closest and most trusted confidant. Later that year Breault went to Honolulu, his hometown, and was able to interest his best friend, Steve Schneider, and Steve's wife, Judy, in Koresh and his message. Schneider was teaching comparative religion at the University of Hawaii at the time. He and his wife later moved to Mount Carmel, where he became one of Koresh's most articulate and skilled spokespersons. On a single trip to England in 1988 Schneider was able to make over twenty converts, many of whom eventually visited or came to live permanently at Mount Carmel.

Believing that God might choose to include anyone in the select group, Koresh welcomed all who would hear his message; however, with few exceptions those he convinced were of Seventh-Day Adventist background. Initially, the group's proselytizers attempted to interest these people in hearing Koresh, who was said to have great wisdom and skill in expounding the entire Bible, particularly the Old Testament prophets and the book of Revelation, in a way that none could equal. Koresh's entire efforts rested on the fundamental presupposition, sacrosanct through 150 years of Adventist history, that humankind was living in the last days, and that God's true people would be guided by the voice of a living prophet. The crux of the Davidian claim was that no one could have the wisdom and skill that Koresh had in the Scriptures unless God had inspired him or her. Koresh viewed the parent body of Seventh-Day Adventists as apostate and corrupt, pointing to the way in which they now courted the favor of the "Babylonian" churches of Christendom at large. Historically, the Adventists had been a separatist tradition that claimed to have the exclusive truth in contrast to other churches, which were viewed as apostate. However, in the last half of the century Seventh-Day Adventists had been welcomed and accepted by the mainstream evangelical Christian world, losing much of their "cultic" or sectarian status. Koresh saw himself as one sent by God to warn them and call them back to their original distinctive and separatist stance.

Koresh believed that his select group, the "Branches" as he called its members, was being offered the opportunity to be among those who would reign with Christ at his right hand in the Kingdom of God. This special promise was constantly held out to those Adventists who would heed God's final messenger.

As one might expect, Koresh's evangelistic efforts were not always successful. He regularly met sharp opposition from the local Adventist clergy and often from dissenting listeners in his study sessions. A tape survives of one such session held in South Carolina in 1987. Steve Schneider, Koresh's right-hand man is present. Several of those listening to Koresh constantly interrupt him, raising contradictory points and arguments particularly centering on just how one is to verify the claims of a living prophet who believes God speaks directly to him. Both Koresh and Schneider become increasingly frustrated and defensive at this resistance to their efforts. They are anxious that Koresh be able to demonstrate his exegetical skills and demand that the carping and petty questioning cease. The main doubter, a woman named Lori, keeps asking Koresh whether she can learn this truth directly from her Bible without his guidance.

KORESH: Now let me, now let me say this . . . Now, silence please, okay? Because we have to get in order now, okay? I have the floor, okay? I've come all this distance . . . Okay, if you would like to know, let's start from the beginning. In 1985 I was in Israel. Okay? And since that time, that I was in Israel, there is not a Bible scholar or theologian that can put the truth down now.

Lori and a few others continue to interrupt, and Koresh never really gets to launch into his message. At one point she asks:

LORI: But what I'm saying is if I go home and I read Zechariah 2 again, if I go home . . .

KORESH: You will get nothing from it.

LORI: But no, listen. When I go home and I take this to the Lord and I say is this right you just told me, I can't test it?[8]

Koresh denies to the group that they can truly understand the Bible on their own without a living prophet. He quotes Amos 3:7: "Surely the LORD will do nothing, unless he reveals his secret to his servants the prophets." He takes the group to Joel 2:23 which speaks of an early and later "rain," which in Hebrew is the word *teacher*. So, he concludes, a later or *final teacher* is to come, who will be necessary for proper understanding. After more than an hour, the questioning ends with Lori walking out and saying, "I'm sorry, I just can't stay, I'm sorry." The door slamming shut can be heard on the tape; there is silence for a minute; then Koresh continues with his exposition.

Nonetheless, many did listen and anyone receptive to the message Koresh preached was urged to visit Mount Carmel to hear more. Rita Riddle, who is in her thirties and lived at Mount Carmel, reports that people were always coming to and going from the Mount Carmel property.[9] According to her description, anyone who wanted to listen to Koresh teach the Bible was welcome. Groups would arrive from around the country and abroad, and stay as long as they could afford to be away from home. Particularly during the week-long festivals of Passover and Tabernacles, in the spring and fall of each year, she reports, the numbers at Mount Carmel would often swell to over two hundred. Rita first became interested through her brother, Jimmy, in the early 1990s. Koresh met her at her home in Asheville, North Carolina, when he came through that part of the country with her brother, making visits and holding study sessions with those who were interested. Rita says that although she had been raised an Adventist, she did not consider herself particularly the "religious" type. She recalls that first meeting: "So I finally got a Bible and he started giving us his study. I was supposed to have gone into work. It was about 7:30 when we started and at 10:00 I called work and told them I wasn't coming in that night. And I kept David up all night. From there one thing led to another. . . . I've read this a hundred times. I saw this but I didn't see it. And I studied more, you know I'm still looking for things to find to fight with him. But really I couldn't because he would always go back and tell us, 'Look, don't look at me, what does this say? You just read it?' . . . I just saw that he had the ability to do what nobody else had ever done. I learned more with him in one night than I had learned in a lifetime of going to church." [10]

Rita began to travel regularly between North Carolina and Texas, attending the group's festivals of Passover and Tabernacles, and later went to live permanently at Mount Carmel. When asked about what "pulled" her to that decision, she replied: "How David taught. That's it. Because we realized that because he was teaching Seven Seals . . . other than what David taught, nothing. As a matter of fact, Texas, I hated it. The first time I flew here I was supposed to stay seven days, I made it three . . . so basically the reason everyone was there was not because we liked the state. . . . It was strictly what David taught. . . . And like I said, after being around him and having the experience of being around him, then we know that he had the ability to do that [expound the entire Bible through the interpretation of the Seven Seals of the book of Revelation]. So if the Bible is true, then what he taught is correct. If not, then there is no God." [11] What Riddle reports is confirmed by all the Davidians we have interviewed. [12] They often make the point that if David is a false prophet or a charlatan, then the Bible itself is unreliable. This is the measure of their conviction that what he had shown them in the texts of Scripture was unrivaled in their experience. The twenty-two adults, most of whom died in the April 19 fire, who were interviewed on video tape on March 8 inside Mount Carmel, say much the same thing when asked what led them to become part of the group. Each in his or her own way tells of being drawn to the group because of the way in which David Koresh expounded the Scriptures. They speak of being "in the message," or "coming into the message," referring to their individual acceptance of Koresh's claims about himself.

Livingstone Fagan first encountered Koresh in his native England in the summer of 1988 when he was pursuing his master of arts degree in theology. He recently reflected on that initial encounter: "David visited the campus, conducting some unscheduled studies on the nature of God and Salvation. Shortly before he concluded, I had opportunity to hear a couple of his studies. This was for approximately three hours in total. During that short time, I had perceived more significant biblical truths than I had done the entire eight years I had been involved with organized religion." [13] Fagan visited Mount Carmel later that year and continued to listen to Koresh teach the Bible. He describes his growing interest: "My interest continued to develop. It is important to note that we were dealing with an highly intelligent and systematic enquiry into the text of Scripture. After spending four weeks in the United States I returned home to England. I made several additional trips to Mt. Carmel, of varying duration, prior to April, 1992. At each visit the subject of study intensified. By April, 1992 I felt it necessary to return to America on an extended stay, in order to keep pace with the truths being revealed. This may not be understood by all, but the concept of a continuing revelation of truth is entirely biblical." [14]

Those who held such convictions were urged to move to Mount Carmel so they could experience the detail and depth of Koresh's Bible studies and thus prepare themselves for their special role. Indeed, whether one would actually make such a move—giving up career, employment, and property, and leaving friends and relatives—became both a test and sign of membership in the select group. Livingstone Fagan was one of many who came with his entire family, including his mother.

The absolute center of life at Mount Carmel was the Bible studies that Koresh conducted for the group. He claimed that those who lived at Mount Carmel were exposed to his deeper teachings, which had never been revealed before. [15] Within the group there was a sense that God was beginning to reveal more and more truth and understanding, and Koresh and his followers speak of this with joy and exhilaration. The Davidians thought themselves to be on the absolute edge of God's latest revelation regarding all the matters that would pertain to the final events of history and their own vital participation therein—and it was all being expounded to them through the mouth of David Koresh. The tapes that survive of the Bible studies during the late 1980s and early 1990s are full of references to the "wonderful truths" that God is progressively revealing:

KORESH: This last Passover season was a very special Passover season for those who have been following the spirit of truth since the message first came, since 1983. And there . . . [have] been those who have been allowed by God to come and be partakers of this wonderful truth even after that time. The subject matter which we are fixing to deal with is very important. It is the most important subject matter since the foundation of the world.[16]

Catherine Matteson, who is in her seventies, reports that people living at Mount Carmel did not like to be sent into town for errands or business for fear of "missing something" that Koresh might be teaching that day.[17] Catherine has been a Branch Davidian for over twenty-five years and worked as a personal assistant to Lois Roden long before David Koresh appeared on the scene. After meeting Koresh in 1981, she says she watched him develop and personally witnessed his transformation beginning in 1985, when he received his calling as a prophet. "He greatly matured," she said; "in fact at the very end he was more mature than any man I have ever met in my lifetime."[18] She recalled the long Bible studies: "He gave prolonged Bible studies, yes. But I'll tell you something, lots of times, maybe he would say, 'I'm tired of giving Bible studies to you guys. I wish you would learn [to give] Bible studies.' So everyone would hang around. And he'd say, 'What is it that you want? More Bible study?' And everyone would run and get their Bibles and come down. We might sit there for 15, 19 hours, 10 hours, 6 hours. It would depend. It was never a bore. He could have been a professional entertainer, the best this world has ever seen. He could entertain. He would have us in stitches. We'd sit there for hours. It was just great being around him."[19]

The group normally met morning and evening for their Bible studies and their twice daily communion service of bread and wine. Although there was much work to do—providing daily meals for over one hundred people, schooling the children, and maintaining the property—community life revolved around Bible study with Koresh. After 1989 the men and women lived in separate quarters, and a disciplined form of communal living was practiced. Livingstone Fagan commented on this: "For many years Mt. Carmel was a place where people came from many parts of the world, for serious pursuit of the Scriptures. The Center had been graced by the presence of a succession of inspired teachers. . . . As a matter of fact, the way Mt. Carmel was organized was really no different from a monastery. The prototype to your modern day theological seminary. The basic difference being Mt. Carmel was concerned not with a theory of religion and God, but, rather, the reality. We were deadly serious about God."[20]

Those at Mount Carmel believed that their eternal salvation depended upon their adherence to the message Koresh taught and, indeed, to Koresh himself as the bearer of that message. In a private Bible study taped in 1986 Koresh tells his followers: "The message of Cyrus [Koresh], the angel that ascends from the east, that same person who is also compassed with iniquity and infirmity, that same person is going to be able to stand before Christ and explain to Christ why we are so bad the way we are. Let's face it, we are bad. . . . You see Cyrus can explain to God why we are because Cyrus is just like all of us but this is God's righteousness. *You reject Cyrus, you reject God*" (emphasis added).[21] The Davidians believed that they were involved in a transforming process at Mount Carmel, in which their acceptance of the revelations coming through Koresh was essential to their relationship to God. As God's messiah, Koresh could actually intercede in their behalf and represent them sympathetically before God. They saw their position as one of great privilege, much like the small group of early followers of Jesus, but also as one of fearful and awesome responsibility. Particularly during the 1990s the group came to believe that they were part of something very special

and that major events were impending that would usher in the fulfillment of the prophecies that Koresh had been teaching. Koresh
constantly taught them that they must be purified, fortified, and
prepared in body, mind, and spirit. They saw themselves as an elite
corps that God had chosen for a special perfection and an extraordinary responsibility of rulership in the coming Kingdom of God. Fagan comments on this: "As a center for serious biblical studies, Mt.
Carmel was designed for purposes of wholistically transcending this
present artificial and sensory based consciousness. . . . Mt. Carmel
was designed of heaven for purposes of accomplishing the above
transcendence. . . . By these experiences, the residents at Mt. Carmel
were able to hear God's word, while blocking out the artificial noise
of humanity. This is what the government labelled brainwashing,
and the judge at our trial termed fanaticism! No, the truth is, it is
the world that is brainwashed." [22]

When the government engaged the Davidians in the 1993 Waco
standoff, their minds and hearts were firmly rooted in the 150 years
of Adventist history that they claimed to most faithfully represent
and in the veracity of the Bible itself, as they had come to understand
it through their prophet and teacher, David Koresh. They saw themselves as a family, as God's true people, in solidarity with all the
prophets, disciples, and martyrs through the ages who had stood firm
for truth against a benighted society. Given this perspective, there
was no possibility that they would leave the compound in response
to any kind of pressure from "those wicked people," as Anetta Richards, Koresh's Jamaican nurse, called them. Even the fourteen adults
sent out by Koresh during the siege went out at his request for various purposes, but none of them really wanted to leave. [23] The Branch
Davidians firmly believed that the outcome was destined and that
their duty was faithfulness to God based on their understanding of
the Scriptures as revealed to Koresh, whom they were convinced was
the final prophetic messenger to the world.

THE ORIGINS OF THE MOUNT CARMEL COMMUNITY

The Davidian adventists, as distinct from the Branch Davidians who
came later, originated in 1929. Their founder, Victor Houteff, was

born in Bulgaria in 1886 and immigrated to the United States in 1907.[24] In 1918, at thirty-two, he became a Seventh-Day Adventist and later settled in Los Angeles, where he worked as a salesman. Although he had only a third-grade education, he was an avid student of the Bible, and in 1928 he began an intensive study of biblical prophecy. He began to develop two interrelated teachings, both out of keeping with orthodox Seventh-Day Adventist doctrine, which would eventually lead him into sharp conflict with the denomination's mainstream.

The first precept had to do with the 144,000 "servants of God" mentioned in Revelation 7. According to the text this select number is "sealed" by an angel from the east shortly before the final plagues of judgment fall upon the earth. Ellen G. White, the nineteenth-century Seventh-Day Adventist prophet, understood this group to be the Adventists themselves, who were drawn to the message she and her associates had proclaimed and in accordance with her message purified themselves in conduct and faith to await the Second Coming.[25] However, in Houteff's day the Seventh-Day Adventists counted a membership of nearly half a million worldwide, and he felt they had become lethargic, self-satisfied, and complacent, and were increasingly succumbing to "worldly" influences. In fact, he identified the Adventists of his day with the "lukewarm" Laodicean church of Revelation 3:14–22, which he interpreted to represent the state of things among God's people immediately prior to the end. Houteff believed that his divinely appointed task was to purify the church from within and to gather together this remnant group of 144,000 just before the coming of Christ. Although he accepted Ellen G. White as a prophet, he did not believe that God had revealed to her the entire message for the last days. He insisted that her call for purification applied to the Adventists themselves in his day. Houteff believed that he was to fulfill the role of this "angel from the east" and that God had chosen him to be a prophet to the Adventists in order to bring them a fuller biblical message. Although Koresh recognized Houteff as his legitimate predecessor, he subsequently took for himself this role of the "angel from the east" who gathers the select, which became the core of Koresh's messianic identity.

Houteff's second insight was potentially even more disruptive to the parent Adventist body. Houteff concluded that the biblical prophets clearly taught that the Kingdom of God was to be a literal, physical, millennial rule on earth, centered in Palestine. His intention was to actually lead the purified group of 144,000 to the ancient land of Israel, where he believed they would meet Christ at his return. He insisted that texts like Isaiah 2 and 11, which foretell the reign of the Messiah, were to be understood according to their most literal meaning. In contrast, Ellen G. White and other Seventh-Day Adventists taught that the Kingdom of God was a spiritual phenomenon and they would spend the millennium in heaven with Christ, while the earth lay desolate, awaiting the creation of a new heaven and earth following the final Day of Judgment.[26]

In 1929 Houteff began to present his ideas in Sabbath school classes in the local Seventh-Day Adventist church in Los Angeles. He was an enthusiastic and lively teacher with the ability to communicate his conviction that God had spoken to him through the Scriptures. Although many members were interested and wanted to hear more, the elders of the congregation were alarmed, considering his message heretical. They subsequently barred him from further teaching. That same year he began to publish his findings in a periodical he called *The Shepherd's Rod*. Houteff attracted a number of followers who aggressively spread his teaching to other Adventists. After a hearing with Seventh-Day Adventist officials in 1934, he was officially removed from the church rolls.[27] Although Houteff had never intended to separate from the mother church, after he was forced out, his movement officially took the name Davidian Seventh-Day Adventists. The name "Davidian" referred to the sect's distinctive teaching about the imminent restoration of the "Davidic" messianic kingdom in Palestine, much along the lines of traditional Judaism. Houteff saw himself as the seventh and final link in a long chain of reformers, each of whom had restored a crucial doctrine to the true biblical faith: Luther (Faith); Knox (Holy Spirit); Wesley (Grace); Campbell (Baptism); Miller (Second Coming); and White (Sabbath). Accordingly, his mission was to bring the teaching of the literal Kingdom to God's remnant Adventist people. As time went on and opposition from the main body stiffened, Houteff began to view the Seventh-Day Adventists as a "heathen" apostate group, in contrast to his own small band of followers, whom he identified as the "remnant" true church. All his efforts were concentrated on drawing out the "faithful" from their ranks.[28] He applied the blistering words of the biblical prophets against the "false shepherds" of ancient Israel to the ministry and leadership of the Seventh-Day Adventist church. Clearly, in the 1990s Koresh was trying to carry out, in a modified way, the same task that Houteff set for himself in the 1930s.

Despite Houteff's insistence on an actual kingdom in Palestine, his interpretive method, much like that of Koresh, his ultimate successor, involved a curious mixture of a literal reading with that which was "spiritual," or symbolic. In some cases Houteff applied prophecies of the Hebrew Bible that addressed ancient Judah or Jerusalem of the sixth century B.C.E. directly to the Adventist church, as the present "people of God"; whereas in other cases he took references to the land of Israel to mean modern Palestine. For example, the regathering of the tribes of Israel and Judah to the land and their subsequent purification, which Isaiah, Jeremiah, Ezekiel, and most of the other prophets predict for "the last days," Houteff clearly applied to the church, quoting Ellen G. White in support.[29] However, he insisted that these Christian "Israelites" were not truly Gentiles but actually members of the "lost tribes" scattered among the nations.[30] Accordingly, they would actually go to Palestine and join their Jewish brothers, who would finally accept Jesus as Messiah. This constant blending of literal and symbolic readings left room for an infinite amount of "play" and adjustment of interpretation as events unfolded. This method allowed every line, every word, every symbol in the entire Bible to serve, on some level, as a coded indicator for the contemporary situation, often directly addressing Houteff and his group. Even in cases where a text had an obvious historical fulfillment or point of reference, it could always have a "double" hidden meaning, revealed only through the "Spirit of prophecy." Koresh employed precisely the same methods in his own exposition of the Scriptures, often to the utter bafflement of the FBI negotiators.

In May 1935 Houteff moved his group to Texas, where they had purchased a remote 189-acre tract outside Waco. Although the original pioneer group numbered only twelve, Houteff was fired with faith regarding his mission. Houteff named the fledgling settlement Mount Carmel.[31] By the end of the year their number had grown to thirty-seven, and they had finished several buildings. They expected the return of Christ within a year or so, at which time they would quickly gather the 144,000 and move to Palestine. Houteff likened the Mount Carmel property to the camp of the ancient Israelites, a kind of staging area where they could prepare and purify themselves before their entrance to the Promised Land. During these Depression years, the group lived a sparse communal life, striving to become self-sufficient. At one point they even created their own paper and cardboard "currency," and an academy was established for the children's education. Bible studies were held each night, and there were three services on the Sabbath. Members report that Houteff was a spellbinding teacher, who used a chapter-by-chapter method of Bible instruction. George Saether, a member of the group in those days, remembers Houteff as stern with his members but extremely hard-working and unpretentious.[32] In 1937, now fifty-two, Houteff married Florence Hermanson, the seventeen-year-old daughter of two of his dedicated followers.

The mission of the group was urgent, singular, and clear-cut: to reach Adventists worldwide with the Houteff Davidian message. Although the move to Palestine did not materialize as expected, throughout the 1940s the group carried on an astoundingly ambitious program of proselytization. Houteff was a prolific writer who constantly turned out tracts and articles. The group had put together a huge mailing list of more than 100,000 Seventh-Day Adventist addresses. They had their own print shop, and at one point George Saether remembers that they were sending out 48,000 tracts every two weeks.[33] In 1952 Houteff sent out thirty field workers with the goal of meeting every Seventh-Day Adventist family in the United States and Canada. Six new Chevrolets had been purchased for this mission. The group also sent representatives to England, India, the West Indies, and Australia. Although their mailing list swelled from these efforts, and they stirred up a lot of interest and opposition, those joining them at Mount Carmel were few. These efforts were financed by selling off portions of their land, which they had expanded over the years to 375 acres.

In February 1955 Victor Houteff died at age sixty-nine. His followers were devastated since most had been convinced he would take them to the land of Israel before the return of Christ. Despite some disputes among factions, Houteff's wife, Florence, took charge of the group. In December 1957 the Davidians sold their property for $700,000 and relocated nearby on 941 acres near the tiny community of Elk, nine miles east of Waco. They paid $85,000 for this new piece of land and called it New Mount Carmel. With their abundant cash they built eighteen houses, farm buildings, and a large dairy, saving the rest for their future exodus from the United States. This was the plot that Koresh and his followers later occupied.

Florence Houteff was very concerned that the expected events that would usher in the Kingdom of God, which at the time the Davidians had awaited for twenty years, had not come about. She became convinced that the end would begin during the 1959 Passover season. She called upon Davidians and Adventists around the world to gather at Mount Carmel in anticipation of that date. Her expectations and actions parallel those of David Koresh thirty years later. During the movement's fifty-year history, there is continuity in the successive leaders' emphasis upon actually moving to the Mount Carmel property and there awaiting the final events.

By April 1959 about nine hundred Davidians had gathered at the New Mount Carmel center. Many had quit their jobs, sold their property, and actually moved to the community, while others had driven long distances to see what would happen. A giant tent was erected for mass meetings. Expectations were high all day Wednesday, April 22. Some expected Victor Houteff to be resurrected from the dead and lead them to Palestine. Others awaited an announcement that war had broken out in the Middle East. As the days passed, the group began to dwindle. Many who had made a permanent move stayed for a time, but in the years that followed, disputes over leadership took their toll. David Koresh was born that same year on August 17, 1959, at a time when the Davidians had reached their lowest point. Mrs. Houteff moved to California and became inactive. Throughout the early 1960s rival factions battled in court for control of the property. Eventually a faction led by Ben and Lois Roden managed to take possession of Mount Carmel and hold it. By that time parts of the property had been sold, leaving only seventy-seven acres, and most of the cash the group had accumulated had been exhausted in legal fees. Less than fifty people still lived at Mount Carmel by the mid-1960s.[34]

THE BRANCHES TRIUMPH

Ben and Lois Roden from Odessa, Texas, had visited Mount Carmel off and on through the 1950s when Victor Houteff was still living. In October 1955 they came to stay, bringing with them Perry Jones, a new convert to the Davidian faith. Ben Roden claimed that he had received a revelation that he was the anointed "Branch" spoken of by the prophet Zechariah (3:8; 6:12) and that his task, as the Davidic figure, was to organize the theocratic Kingdom in preparation for Christ's return. Significantly, prefiguring the subsequent claims of Koresh, Roden appropriated for himself both a title and a role that Christians have traditionally assigned to Jesus Christ. He also taught that other "Branches" would be associated with him, based on John 15:1–3, where Jesus tells his followers: "I am the vine, and you are the branches."

The Mount Carmel group appears to have thrived through the 1970s. The group had always observed the Sabbath on Saturday, but the Rodens introduced the observance of such annual biblical festivals as Passover, Pentecost, and the feast of Tabernacles as well. They continued to publish and distribute their pamphlets around the world, appealing to Adventists in particular to accept the Houteff message of the literal Kingdom, along with the Roden revelation that the theocratic rule of the "Branch" had already been inaugurated. The Rodens traveled widely, particularly to Israel. At one point Lois Roden lived in Israel for three years. They continuously urged their followers worldwide to emigrate to Israel and prepare for the final events, another idea that David Koresh continued to promulgate when he took over the group in the late 1980s. Four years after Ben Roden's death in 1978, his wife, Lois, was able to obtain permission from the Israeli authorities to have his body buried on the Mount of Olives in Jerusalem.

In 1977 Lois Roden had received a revelation regarding the Holy Spirit as a feminine figure.[35] Over the next few years, while leading the group at Mount Carmel, she emphasized the restoration of the feminine aspect of God based on her interpretation of the Bible. She delved into Greek and Hebrew, became a prolific writer, and began to publish a magazine called *SHEkinah,* which is a feminine Hebrew word for the manifested presence or "Spirit" of God.[36] Lois Roden taught that the Messiah, as New Adam, fully embodies the female aspects of the Divinity. On her trips to Israel she had discussed some of her ideas on the nature of God with Jewish rabbis, and her writings show some familiarity with Jewish mystical and theosophic notions regarding the Godhead. Although many Davidians balked at this latest "new light," Lois Roden maintained the loyalty of a core of dedicated followers such as Perry Jones, the Australian Clive Doyle, Catherine Matteson, and Woodrow and Janet Kendrick—all who were to become dedicated followers of Koresh. She continued her heavy travel schedule, constantly speaking and giving lectures throughout North America and abroad. While she was away from Mount Carmel, things did not always go smoothly. Her son, George Roden, a somewhat eccentric character by any measure, was beginning to assert himself as the true successor of his father.

In 1981 David Koresh, then known as Vernon Howell, joined the Branch Davidians at Mount Carmel. Howell had been baptized two years earlier into the local Seventh-Day Adventist church that his mother attended in Tyler, Texas. Growing up, Koresh had two passions, the Bible and his electric guitar. He had memorized large portions of the Scriptures as a teenager and often challenged the local church establishment on their knowledge of doctrines. Although he was fiercely loyal to the historic Adventist movement, he believed that the church had become corrupt and compromised its original prophetic mission. His mother reports that he spent hours in prayer, crying and begging God to send his people a living prophet who could lead them in the right path.[37] Koresh was eventually removed from the membership roll of the Tyler church for causing dissension. He visited Mount Carmel in the summer of 1981 because he had been told that the group was led by a prophet who claimed to receive revelations. Koresh accepted the teachings of Lois Roden with enthusiasm, and in turn she was impressed with his knowledge of the Scriptures and his sincerity. Not surprisingly, her son, George, became increasingly jealous of Koresh as a potential threat to his own claims of leadership. George Roden charged that Koresh was having sex with his mother, who was at the time sixty-seven years old. A close friend of Lois Roden's, Theresa Moore, even claims that the two were "married" in a private nonlegal wedding ceremony before a 1983 trip to Israel together.[38] Marc Breault, who did not join the group until 1986, maintains that Koresh talked openly of this and did not try to hide it, asserting that their relationship fulfilled the prophecy of the prophetess having a child by a prophet (Isa. 8:3) although Lois did not conceive. His story is confirmed by all the sources.[39] When asked about this charge on camera by an Australian film crew in 1992, Koresh jokingly sidesteps the question, remarking that if he "had gotten a seventy-year-old woman pregnant then he must be God after all."[40] By 1983 it was obvious that Lois favored Koresh and recognized him as her successor. He was openly claiming to have received the "seventh angel's message" mentioned in Revelation 10:7, a text that was used as the foundation for Koresh's messianic identity. In January 1984 Koresh legally married Rachel Jones, the fourteen-year-old daughter of longtime Branch Davidian Perry Jones, who was one of those killed by the BATF in the February 28 raid. Lois Roden was understandably hurt and openly confessed her sexual relationship with Koresh in a Bible study session at Mount Carmel. Some witnesses report that she suffered a near breakdown and at one point even claimed to be pregnant by Koresh.[41] Understandably, the two were never close thereafter. Lois Roden died in November 1986 and was buried beside her husband on the Mount of Olives.

In 1984 George Roden's confrontation with his rival began to intensify.[42] Roden had taken to wearing a .357 Magnum pistol on his hip to the Bible study meetings and often threatened Koresh and those who backed him, effectively splitting the group. He also suffered from Tourette's syndrome, which causes a person to swear compulsively and fall into fits of rage. Koresh and his new wife, Rachel, now pregnant with Cyrus, their first son, had gone to Israel in January 1985. It was on that trip that Koresh claimed to have received his definitive message, which involved his distinctive mission as a messianic "Cyrus" figure. Roden took advantage of his absence to intimidate and threaten those loyal to Koresh. Despite Koresh's return, Roden was able to gain control of the mailing lists, call for an election, and take full control of the Mount Carmel property by June 1985. He renamed it Rodenville, expelling all dissidents by force. Koresh and forty of his followers retreated to a small piece of property in the pine woods near Palestine, Texas. Ironically, this "exile" proved to be a time of growth for them, despite the primitive conditions in which they lived. Both Marc Breault and Steve Schneider, two of Koresh's most talented followers, joined the group in 1986. These were the years of some of the dissident group's most successful recruitment of Adventists worldwide, and Koresh, to judge from the tapes of Bible study sessions that survive from that period, was in full form as a teacher, greatly buoyed by the revelations he claimed to experience since his most recent visit to Israel. During this period Koresh also began to openly teach the group that his special prophetic, messianic role in God's plan would require him to take more than one wife. In the spring of 1986 he announced his nonlegal "marriage" to fourteen-year-old Karen Doyle, whose father, Clive Doyle, was a long-standing member of the group. Rachel, Koresh's first wife, was reportedly upset at first but later had a dream in which she heard God telling her husband to "do something terrible," so that she came to accept this as God's will. Apparently, later that same year Koresh secretly "married" Michelle Jones, Rachel's twelve-year-old sister, who subsequently bore him three daughters. In 1987 Koresh took at least three additional wives, the Californian Robyn Bunds (aged seventeen), the Australian Nicole Gent (aged sixteen), and the Hawaiian Dana Okimoto (aged twenty)—all of whom later had children by him.

In November 1987 one of the most bizarre episodes in the history of the Branch Davidian movement took place. George Roden dug up the body of Anna Hughes, a Davidian who had died at eighty-four and had been buried for twenty years on the Mount Carmel property. He put the casket in the chapel and challenged Koresh to a contest to see who could raise her from the dead. Koresh asked the McLennan County sheriff to arrest Roden for corpse violation but was told he would need to bring proof. Koresh and seven of his loyal followers tried to sneak onto the property to take a photo of the corpse. They were dressed in camouflage fatigues and heavily armed. A forty-five-minute gun battle ensued, each side blaming the other for firing first. Roden was wounded slightly in the hand. Koresh and his men were charged with attempted murder, and surely one of the strangest trials in Waco history was held in April 1988. The jurors found the others not guilty but were split over the question of Koresh's guilt. The judge declared a mistrial. Six months later George Roden was charged with the murder of a fifty-six-year-old man in an unrelated incident. He was found not guilty by reason of insanity and was sentenced to an indeterminate stay in the state hospital in Vernon, Texas. In the meantime Koresh came up with the money to pay the back taxes on the Mount Carmel property, and his group returned triumphantly and began to rebuild.[43]

AN "OLD" NEW RELIGIOUS MOVEMENT

Although the Seventh-Day Adventist church long ago repudiated the theology of Victor Houteff and the Rodens, and more recently has even more emphatically attempted to distance itself from Koresh and what took place at Waco, it is a fact that Koresh was an Adventist from start to finish.[44] Only through an understanding of Adventist history can one ever hope to accurately comprehend Koresh within a meaningful context. The media and the federal government were satisfied with the generic label "cult" leader, as if Koresh somehow existed outside time and place. However, such a superficial identification not only fails to do justice to the long and complex history of the Millerite-Adventist-Davidian tradition but also underlies the authorities' misunderstanding of Koresh.

Like Houteff and Ben Roden before him, Koresh had been formally removed from the official rolls of the Seventh-Day Adventist denomination. However, from their viewpoint, this very opposition made them more "Adventist" than ever. They saw themselves in the critical, prophetic role of men like Isaiah, Jeremiah, Hosea, and Micah, not to mention Jesus himself, who had stood against their own established religious tradition and been persecuted for it. And they argued continually that they represented a theological vision that was actually more loyal to the founder William Miller and the prophet Ellen G. White than that of the apostate parent body.

The historical roots of David Koresh, the Branch Davidians, and the events at Mount Carmel in 1993 actually reach back 175 years to upstate New York. In 1818 William Miller, a twenty-six-year-old Baptist farmer living in Low Hampton, New York, reached the conclusion that the Second Coming of Christ would occur "about the year 1843."[45] Two years earlier, Miller, who had served as a captain in the U.S. Army during the War of 1812, had begun an intensive verse-by-verse study of the Bible using his King James Version and a concordance. He was determined to understand the Scriptures as completely as possible, allowing the Bible to harmonize and interpret itself. He particularly focused on biblical prophecies and delved deep into the books of Daniel and Revelation.[46] Miller subsequently launched what is arguably the largest indigenous religious movement in the history of the United States.[47] The Branch Davidians and Koresh, their latest prophet, must be viewed in this wider context. The group has a long and rich history, and its fundamental approach to Scripture, as well as general world view, is a familiar and important part of the landscape of American religious history.[48]

Beginning in 1831 Miller addressed any gathering available to him, whether pulpit, camp meeting, public hall, or club meeting, often speaking to crowds of several thousand.[49] Over the next twelve years he reported that he spoke at 4,500 gatherings to an estimated total of 500,000 persons.[50] Miller expected the return of Christ sometime between March 21, 1843, and March 21, 1844, based upon the biblical Jewish year which began in the spring. On February 27, 1843, a spectacular blazing comet appeared in the sky and was clearly visible in both southern and northern hemispheres for weeks, even in broad daylight. It was the most brilliant comet of the century. Since Jesus had predicted such "signs in the heavens" immediately preceding his return, thousands were motivated to listen more closely to the growing band of Millerites.[51] On March 2, 1843, the *New York Tribune* carried a full front-page story on the phenomenon, which was sharply critical of the growing movement.

The basic principles of biblical interpretation that Miller employed and advocated are quite similar to those used by Koresh and his Adventist forebears, as well as many other fundamentalist Christians. Miller saw his exegetical work as highly systematic and rigorously logical. Two aspects of his basic interpretive agenda are particularly relevant to our understanding of the Branch Davidians.[52] First, he insisted that "scripture must be its own expositor" and one must not rely upon human creeds and the "traditions of men" in arriving at the truth.[53] This "democratization" of biblical studies has proven to be of incalculable influence in the development of American religion and was one of the major assumptions of the Branch Davidians.[54] Second, Miller insisted that although the biblical prophets used figures of speech and symbolic language to convey their message, the historical fulfillment of their words was always literal and exact. This meant that one must search past history, compare it with the text, and thereby determine if this or that prophecy had come about. According to this method, if a given text has not yet been fulfilled, then it would surely come about, even to the smallest detail, at some point in the future. Koresh heavily relied on this argument, insisting to his followers that if certain prophecies did not come to pass, then the Bible would be shown to be a "lie."[55]

The March 21, 1844, date passed without incident. Although disappointed, the Millerites were hardly disillusioned. Miller saw the delay as a final test of faith and wrote to his friend Joshua Himes, "I expect every moment to see the Saviour descend from heaven. I have now nothing to look for but this glorious hope."[56] As early as February

1844, Samuel Snow, an associate of William Miller's, had begun to defend the idea that Miller's calculations for the coming of Christ more properly pointed to the fall rather than the spring of that year. He had reset the date for Wednesday, October 22, based on the Karaite Jewish reckoning for the Day of Atonement.[57] This new date electrified the movement since in ancient Judaism Yom Kippur, the Day of Atonement, was the very day the high priest would exit the Temple sanctuary after having cleansed the sins of the people.[58]

Throughout the spring and summer of 1844 the Millerites grew in influence and numbers while the opposition of the establishment clergy and mainstream press intensified. Both before and after the unfulfilled expectations of a Second Coming in 1844 enemies charged that the Millerite faith promoted insanity and fanaticism. A good deal of slander was directed against William Miller himself.[59] Most of the major Christian denominations were postmillennial in their orientation and did not accept this premillennial date setting.[60] The Millerites had begun to apply Revelation 18:2–4 directly to their situation: "Babylon the great is fallen, is fallen. . . . and I heard another voice from heaven, saying, *Come out of her,* my people, that you be not partakers of her sins, and that you receive not of her plagues" (emphasis added). They labeled their entire opposition, both religious and political, "Babylon" and urged those who believed Miller's Second Coming message to separate from the churches and all those who scoffed at them.[61] Although Miller and his followers never intended to set up a new denomination, increasingly the "Adventists," as they were beginning to be called, were holding their own meetings in town halls and homes around the country, considering themselves the "remnant" of God's faithful people in the last days. One hundred and fifty years later, in Waco, Texas, David Koresh and his followers were carrying on this tradition in a slightly adapted form when they labeled the religious and political establishment as "Babylon" and gathered together in the expectation that their own particular scenario of the imminent end was unfolding.

Historians conservatively number the hard-core Millerites at around fifty thousand on October 22, 1844, but many thousands of others must have taken Miller's view seriously enough to prepare for the Second Coming in their own individual ways without formally joining the movement. Most believers spent the day in gatherings around the country, waiting for the sudden heavenly appearance of Christ in the clouds. Observers report that a spirit of bliss prevailed. When Christ failed to return on the expected date, the "Great Disappointment," as it came to be known, left Adventists around the world deeply disillusioned.[62] However, Miller maintained his faith in God, in the Bible, and even in the essential validity of his understanding of the prophecies until his death in 1849 at the age of sixty-eight. In August 1845 he published his *Apology and Defense,* which recounted his life and experiences in the movement. Although he admits that he was wrong on the precise dating, he continued to affirm that the return of Christ was imminent and, most significantly, claimed that his work was a direct fulfillment of Revelation 14:6–7, where the first of three angels appears to proclaim to the world that "the hour of his judgment is come." Adventist theology is subsequently built around this idea of a sequence of "end time" messages, symbolized by these angelic messengers, with which Adventists associate the key events in their own history.[63] Koresh always insisted that Miller indeed *was* this first angel, but claimed that he, himself, was the seventh and final messenger, which he found mentioned in verses 17–20 of the same chapter. Thus Koresh had inherited and built upon the precepts of the Millerite movement; and he saw William Miller as having begun the work of unlocking the "seals" that had been put on the book of Daniel and the entire biblical prophetic corpus. Although the Branch Davidians were a small, sectarian group, they stand firmly within the Millerite-Adventist tradition and it is impossible to properly understand them outside this broader context.

By the end of 1845, a tiny group of Millerites centered in Washington, New Hampshire, began to advocate the observance of the seventh-day Sabbath, that is, keeping Saturday rather than Sunday as a holy day of rest based on the fourth of the Ten Commandments. They argued that Sunday was a pagan, Roman Catholic corruption of the original biblical faith. This Sabbatarian group was led by Joseph Bates, James White, and Ellen G. Harmon, whom White married in 1846. They argued that Miller had been right about his date but wrong about the event and that Christ had entered the inner room of the heavenly Temple on that day in preparation for his final work of judgment. At an undetermined time in the future he would return visibly to judge the world.[64]

The observance of the seventh-day Sabbath reflected a central doctrine of these Adventists. Joseph Bates, the theologian of the group, contended that the three messenger angels in Revelation 14 seemed to echo precisely the Millerite-Adventist-Sabbatarian experiences. He concluded that the message of the first two angels, that the hour of judgment had come and that Babylon was to fall, had been fulfilled by Miller and his associates prior to 1844. However, the third angel's message, which contained a warning against participating in the false religious system of Babylon and a blessing for "keeping the commandments of God and the faith of Jesus," Bates directly associated with their seventh-day Sabbatarian message (Rev. 14:9–12).[65] Thus, as early as 1847, the fundamental pillars of the Seventh-Day Adventist movement were in place among this group: the teaching regarding the arrival of the time of judgment in 1844; the seventh-day Sabbath; and the acceptance of ongoing prophetic gifts and revelations. What is of particular note is that the group was able to "find itself" within the text of Revelation 14. These Seventh-Day Adventists, led by James and Ellen G. White and Joseph Bates, began to understand that their main mission and calling was to spread these three angelic messages, and they understood themselves to be actually fulfilling the task of the third angel, preparing the way for the return of Christ.[66] From the religious perspective, this is perhaps the crucial dynamic in understanding Koresh and what happened at Waco.

Other than the observance of the seventh-day Sabbath, the most distinguishing characteristic of the Seventh-Day Adventist movement is its teaching regarding the "Spirit of prophecy" and what Ellen G. White referred to as "present truth" or "new light."[67] "Present truth" means truth for the time, which is *progressively* revealed to God's remnant people in the last days. This notion of an unfolding, dynamic increase in "truth" and "light" as the coming of Christ approaches is essential for understanding the Branch Davidians and Koresh. They considered themselves heirs of William Miller and Ellen G. White, whom they always honored highly, while setting forth subsequent revelations that had been given to them. Viewing themselves as the true heirs of the movement, despite their small numbers within the larger Adventist movement, they felt that they were carrying on the living voice of the "Spirit of prophecy" whereas the larger body of the official Seventh-Day Adventist church was apostate and dead to new truth. Koresh and his predecessors reasoned that God had surely not abandoned his people since Ellen G. White's death in 1915, particularly as the return of Christ drew closer. In that sense their claim to "present truth" and ongoing revelation was quintessentially "Adventist," rather than anomalous or aberrant. To be "in the message," as the Branch Davidians put it, was to be a faithful follower of what God was *presently* revealing to his servants the prophets. Koresh's strongest appeal to his followers was his ability to convince them, from the text of the Bible, that he had received further "light" regarding the full meaning of the prophetic word and its continuing application to their lives.

David Koresh constantly quoted "Sister White," as he affectionately called Ellen G. White, and reminded his followers often that she had exhorted them to "patiently wait and watch to receive further light."[68] Seventh-Day Adventists have always focused on the three angelic messages of Revelation 14 for their self-understanding and identity. They believe that William Miller fulfilled the role of the first two angels by proclaiming that the "end times" had arrived and that "Babylon" was ready to fall. They maintain that Ellen G. White had brought the third angel's message by calling for a return to the seventh-day Sabbath and by forsaking the paganized customs of the mainstream Christian church (Rev. 14:9–12). Koresh accepted this understanding and fully claimed this history as his own. This was not a minor point with him, and it comes out constantly in his Bible study sessions. However, Koresh argued that there were seven messengers, not just three, in the book of Revelation. If Ellen G. White was the third, he pointed out, then there must be four others to come. He identified the fourth with Victor Houteff, who in 1929

began to teach that there would be a literal, earthly Davidic Kingdom of God in Palestine. The fifth angel or messenger he understood
to be Ben Roden, who, around the year 1955, restored the observance
of such biblical festival days as Passover, Pentecost, and the feast of
Tabernacles. The sixth messenger was recognized in Lois Roden,
who in 1977 began to teach that the Holy Spirit was feminine, recovering a vital "lost" aspect of the understanding of God. Koresh saw
himself as the seventh and last prophet. In accord with his 1985 revelation regarding Koresh/Cyrus as the final Christ figure, Koresh's
own teachings drew upon those of his predecessors, from Miller
through Lois Roden. The Branch Davidians were, with very few exceptions, "former" Adventists who felt that by accepting "present
truth" as taught by Koresh, they were showing a loyalty to both God
and their tradition. They felt highly privileged to be participating in
the latest events that God was revealing through his prophets just
prior to the close of human history. They were particularly attracted
to the breadth of truth they felt they had received through all seven
of these "messages."

As Koresh explained it to his followers, when Ellen G. White died,
the Seventh-Day Adventists lost their living prophetic voice, the
"Spirit of prophecy" that had guided them since 1845. For seventy
years God left them alone without a prophet or new revelation until
Koresh's revelatory experience in Israel in 1985.[69] Although they experienced incredible numerical growth, spiritually, they withered and
died and slowly fell away from even the truths they had. According
to Koresh, over those decades they increasingly sought the favor of
the more mainstream evangelical Christian churches that observed
Sunday as the Sabbath, ate pork, kept "pagan" holidays such as
Christmas and Easter, and generally followed a "worldly" lifestyle.
That same year Koresh attended the General Conference of the
Seventh-Day Adventist church, which was held in New Orleans. He
tried to communicate his revelation, but as a "nobody" removed
from church rolls, not even an official delegate to the convention, he
was barred from even entering the main hall and addressing the
group. Later, he likened himself to that "angel from the east," of
Revelation 7, who came from a far country to "seal" the true servants

of God. However, like the "servant" figure in Isaiah 53, he had been "despised and rejected," "one from whom we hid our faces." After all, Koresh reminded his followers, did not Isaiah indicate that this "servant" of the last days would say, "He has made my mouth like a sharp sword, in the shadow of his hand *he has hid me*" (emphasis added). (Isa.49: 2) In other words, as Koresh understood these texts, the servant would not be recognized at first.[70] Koresh assured his followers that his message would not go forth in a powerful and influential way to the world until a decisive point in the future when they would be confronted by the government, which he identified as "Babylon." In the meantime he understood that his immediate mission was to work with that tiny group of breakaway Adventists, the Branch Davidians in Waco and elsewhere in the world, who would accept these messages of the last four angels. Given this interpretation, in the 1990s the Mount Carmel community and its final historical role made it the center of the universe for the Davidians.

THREE

Unlocking the Seven Seals

AT ONE POINT IN THE live KRLD radio interview with the wounded Koresh on February 28, the day of the initial BATF raid, the station manager, Charlie Serafin, asked, "Are you getting enough to eat, David?" In characteristic style he replied, groaning in pain, "Well, yes, although I am a ravenous bird from the east, I'm not eating too much, I'm sipping a little orange juice, I'm okay." Understandably, this obscure reference to Isaiah 46:11 surely went past Serafin, but for Koresh and his followers, who lived and breathed the Scriptures, such a way of thinking and talking had become second nature. Indeed, their identification of Koresh as this prophetic "ravenous bird" is a vital part of their theology and explains much of their behavior before and during the fifty-one-day siege. Koresh and his followers lived within a coded world of biblical language that created for them a sacred context they perceived to be concrete, systematic, and reliable. Those "outside" had few, if any, clues to comprehending this world, so that the most technical and vital aspects of the group's understanding of Scripture simply became "mumbo jumbo" and "Bible babble." Koresh and his followers repeatedly pleaded this point with the Federal negotiators: "You don't understand who we are, you don't understand our message." Koresh's primary concern throughout the entire fifty-one days was this "message" and how it might be communicated.

Why did Koresh's followers find his message so convincing? Why were they willing to stay with him until the end, even unto death? Many sensational allegations about Koresh were made from the day the Waco story broke: that he claimed to be God or Jesus Christ, that he beat children, that he had sex with minors and married women, and that he exercised a powerful and mysterious control over his followers. In his last communication Koresh himself used the phrase "the bizarrity [sic] of me in the flesh." Few professional Hostage Rescue Team agents, or even journalists and television reporters interested in the lurid aspects of a fascinating story, would have been willing or able to connect such reports to any kind of a biblical message. Yet Koresh's followers uniformly claim that they moved to Mount Carmel because of Koresh's abilities and insights in the Scriptures.

Accordingly, only in retrospect, by trying to grasp the essential outlines of the message Koresh brought, can "outsiders" comprehend the dynamics of what went on at Waco. The sources for such an analysis by scholars of religion are abundant but difficult to bring together. Although Koresh did not publish much, there are a few tracts and booklets in addition to his final incomplete manuscript, as well as recordings of some of his Bible study sessions, both formal and informal. However, the most important source is the testimony of his surviving students, most of whom still believe and live by the message.[1]

OPENING THE SEVEN SEALS

The one element of Koresh's teaching consistently reported in the media is his claim to be able to "open the Seven Seals" of the book of Revelation. As we have explained, the Davidians understood the sealed book to be the entire Bible. Koresh often said he had been sent both to "explain and to do the Scriptures." In other words, the Davidians believed that opening these seals involved not only explaining their mysterious meaning but also bringing about the events they prophesied. Therefore, to "open a seal" was ultimately to usher in its actual accomplishment on earth. Koresh felt God had given him the task of actually carrying out the major events that would lead to the consummation of history, which is part of the dynamics of "opening the seals." Not only does opening them bring understanding and insight, it also effects events that lead to the culmination of history as carried out by this mysterious "figure" mentioned throughout the Prophets. According to the Davidian interpretation, the seals were to be realized in history on two levels: first in the life of Koresh and his followers and later, in a more grand and manifest way, universally. In that sense the Davidians expected them to have a type of "double" fulfillment. In other words, opening the seals involved two things: God's plan of salvation through Koresh, the second Christ figure, and the final events of the end of history. It was this complicated interpretive mix that formed the core of Davidian theology.[2]

Koresh claimed to be that Lamb of Revelation 5, who takes and opens the sealed book. Christians have traditionally understood this as a clear and exclusive reference to Jesus Christ, but Koresh argued otherwise. He pointed out that the entire book of Revelation, though revealed by Jesus Christ and written by John in the first century, was only to be understood and accomplished shortly before the end of history. The opening verses of the book say it was given to "reveal to his servants things which must shortly come to pass" and that "the time is at hand." As Koresh explained it, since the end was, in fact, not imminent when the book was written in the first century, this could only refer to a time far into the future from that of Jesus of Nazareth, when the events described in the book would be "at hand." Otherwise, following Branch Davidian interpretation, the failure of a single prophecy to be fulfilled would render the entire Bible invalid. Therefore, according to Koresh, the book of Revelation would remain closed and sealed until the appearance at some future point of a "Lamb" who would open and ultimately usher in the fulfillment of all its prophecies. The book closes with the statement by Jesus, "Surely I come quickly," which, as Koresh pointed out, would make Christ a liar if his return was to have taken place in the first century. In other words, the Davidians believed that the entire book is written from the standpoint of a later time, a kind of proleptic message for the last generation, which Koresh believed had arrived in his own lifetime.

Koresh did understand himself as a "Christ" figure but not as the historical person Jesus. In his view, Jesus was also "Christ." The English word *Christ,* taken from the Greek *christos,* comes from the Hebrew word *messiah,* a title, not a proper name, that is commonly used in the Old Testament for all the kings and priests of Israel. Koresh believed that just as God sent Jesus as a "Christ" to his generation to accomplish a certain mission, a final manifestation of another such Christ figure would also appear prior to the end of time.[3] Thus, the Branch Davidians understood the term "Christ" as a dynamic reality, not a static historical figure. They believed it referred to the manifestation of the "Word of God" (John 1:1) through a human agent, who in this way becomes the anointed Son of God. Koresh claimed to have that same "Spirit of Christ" that is called in the book of Revelation the "Spirit of prophecy" and that descended upon Jesus of Nazareth at his baptism (Rev. 19:10). In some of his tapes, he attempts to explain this metaphor of the Lamb, whom he believed in a certain sense also referred to Jesus Christ, by using the formula "the Lamb has a Christ, the Lamb sends a bird with a message." By this, he could affirm Jesus as the Lamb but at the same time acknowledge another future manifestation.

Koresh relied chiefly on the Psalms to show that such a manifestation of "Christ" was not limited to Jesus in the first century. In Psalm 110:4 a descendant of David, king of ancient Israel, is addressed as "a priest forever after the order of Melchizedek." This mysterious figure of Melchizedek, a contemporary of Abraham two thousand years before Jesus, is spoken of in the New Testament as a pre-Christian "Christ": "Without father, without mother, without descent, having neither beginning of days, nor end of life; but made like unto the Son of God, remains a priest continually. Now consider how great this man was, to whom even Abraham gave tithes of all he had" (Heb. 7:3–4).[4]

This point was extremely important to Koresh's theology. If such a figure had appeared two thousand years before Jesus, then it would not be surprising that one would appear two thousand years after. In support of this view, Koresh quoted one verse in the book of Revelation more often than any other: "In the days of the voice of the seventh angel [or messenger], when he shall begin to sound, the mystery of God should be finished, as he declared to his servants the prophets" (Rev. 10:7). Since 1983 Koresh had claimed to be this final seventh messenger. The text speaks of a definite time, the "days of the seventh messenger," which Koresh argued was an unequivocal reference to the last times, not to the time of Jesus. Over the next decade everything he said about himself was tied to this fundamental self-understanding: that all the "mysteries" of the Prophets had been revealed to him. In other words, he saw himself as God's final "Word" to the world.

Such a view of Christ is not unknown in the history of Christianity. The Ebionites, who were the original Jewish-Christian followers of Jesus in the first century c.e., appeared to hold a view quite similar to this.[5] They believed that the "Christ Spirit" had appeared in numerous forms through the ages in figures like Enoch, Noah, Abraham, Isaac, Jacob, and Moses. As they expressed it, "the Christ [True Prophet] from the beginning of the world is hastening through the ages."[6] Of course they held that Jesus of Nazareth at his baptism received this "Christ Spirit" in a fullness that made him unique. He was the "beloved son" whom God chose as Messiah. This view came to be called "Adoptionism" because it postulated that Jesus was a fully ordinary human being who was *adopted* as Son of God. Psalm 2:7, in which God declares to his anointed (Christ), "You are my Son; this day have I begotten you," was very important to such groups. This Adoptionist perspective, in various forms, has been part of Christianity through the ages though the more classic view of the Trinity became the orthodox position of the mainstream Christian churches. However, the Ebionites and other Adoptionists did not believe any further "Christs" would appear after Jesus. For such groups he was the final and ultimate manifestation of the phenomenon.

Koresh focused particularly on Psalms 40 and 45, both of which speak of a Davidic Christ figure. He attempted to show, using a verse-by-verse interpretation, that these chapters could not refer to

Jesus and therefore must apply to a subsequent and final "Christ." For example, Psalm 40:7 introduces a figure who speaks in the first person: "Then said I, Lo, I come: in the scroll of the book it is written of me, I delight to do your will, O my God, yes, your law is within my heart." From a Christian perspective, one might easily understand this to refer to Jesus. However, as Koresh so often pointed out, in verse 12 the same figure laments: "My iniquities have taken hold upon me, so that I am not able to look up, they are more than the hairs of my head: therefore my heart fails me." Few of his mostly former Seventh-Day Adventist students would dare to apply such a notion to Jesus, who was understood to be perfect and sinless. Koresh would drive this point home: who is this mysterious figure, he would ask, one who is written about in a "scroll of a book," but who is a "*sinful* messiah"?

Psalm 45 was even more crucial to his understanding of this final Christ. He deals with it extensively in his manuscript on the Seven Seals written shortly before the April 19 fire. The Psalm speaks of a kingly figure who rides triumphantly on a horse, conquering his enemies. This figure is clearly addressed as a Son of God, and he is "anointed with the oil of gladness" above his fellows, thus made a "Christ" (v. 7). Yet this Christ goes on to marry virgin daughters and have children, and those children "become princes in all the earth" (vv. 9–16). Koresh would rhetorically ask his students, "Did Jesus marry many virgins, did he have children who subsequently ruled the earth?" Koresh directly identified this figure of Psalm 45 with the opening of the First Seal in Revelation 6: "And I saw, and behold, a white horse; and he that sat on him had a bow; and a crown was given to him; and he went forth conquering and to conquer" (v. 2). In other words, fulfilling his beliefs, the events prophesied in the book of Revelation would begin to unfold with the appearance of this figure on the white horse, this "Christ" who would usher in the time of the end by both revealing and effecting these events.

This kind of detail, as technical as it may appear, actually convinced the Davidians that Koresh alone was teaching the Bible in its full and manifest meaning. Revealing the Seven Seals had to do with explaining the hidden meanings of the book of Revelation. As

Koresh was fond of saying, "Every book of the Bible meets and ends in the book of Revelation."[7] Their understanding was that the scroll or book, which God holds in his right hand in the heavenly throne scene of Revelation 5, is nothing less than the complete Bible itself. In their view, the entire Bible, not merely the book of Revelation, was sealed and hidden from full understanding until the time of the seventh messenger, who would open it all and proclaim it to the world. Accordingly, when Koresh claimed to be able to "explain the Seals," which to him was the only real test of his legitimacy, he was asserting his ability to weave together the entire Bible, from Genesis to Revelation, into a coherent whole, explicating every verse, even every line, in context.[8]

A RAVENOUS BIRD FROM THE EAST

David Koresh was born Vernon Howell, on August 17, 1959, in Houston, Texas, to Bonnie Clark, a fifteen-year-old unwed mother. Thirty-one years later, in August 1990, he had his name legally changed to David Koresh in a Pomona, California, court. According to the court petition, he requested the name change because he was an entertainer and wished to use the new name for publicity purposes. He had actually taken the name from his Bible for reasons that went far beyond entertainment.

At twenty-five, Koresh had a profound "experience" while visiting Israel in January 1985, which proved the pivotal, defining moment of his life. He often referred to this event, even mentioning it during the KRLD radio conversation with Charlie Serafin the day of the initial BATF raid. Prior to that 1985 experience he seemed a devout, earnest, precocious student of the Bible with roots in the Seventh-Day Adventist church. After the ninth grade, he had dropped out of Garland High School in the Dallas area and supported himself by carpentry work. In 1981, when he was twenty, he made his way to the Mount Carmel center outside Waco and attached himself to the Branch Davidians living there, led at that time by Lois Roden.

Before this revelatory event in 1985, Koresh emphasized, he was nothing, he knew nothing, and he was a wandering "bonehead" with no real understanding of his purpose. However, those who knew him at that time confirm that he was already well versed in the Bible and had a special interest in prophecy, particularly the book of Revelation. A year prior to the 1985 Israel trip, in a letter to George Roden, he expressed his profound interest in the seventh messenger mentioned in Revelation 10:7, who would receive the final message, but he clearly said that the message hasn't come yet.[9] A survivor of Mount Carmel, Catherine Matteson, aged seventy-eight and still a faithful Branch Davidian, was there at the time. She said that prior to 1985 Vernon often told the group that the "full message" was coming, but it hadn't arrived yet. When he returned from Israel in February 1985, Catherine remembered, everything about him had totally changed. He told her and others that he had now received the full message and that the mystery of all the Prophets, as indicated in Revelation 10:7, was beginning to unfold. In fact, one can hear a marked difference in the existing tapes of his Bible study sessions before and after 1985. In the earlier materials Koresh clearly knows the texts of the Bible well, but his teaching is routine and tends to be rather straightforward, even dull at times. In the later materials he is full of energy and shows great skill in weaving together many dozens of complicated images and concepts. Koresh called his new teaching the "Cyrus message."

Cyrus, king of Persia, who is mentioned in Isaiah 45, conquered the ancient kingdom of Babylon in 539 B.C.E. These Babylonians had taken the Jews into captivity in 586 B.C.E. and were thus perceived by the Jews as a cruel and ruthless enemy. In the first verse of Isaiah 45, Cyrus is called the "anointed one" or "messiah" of Yahweh. From a strictly historical point of view this language is not particularly surprising. The term "messiah" is used for a variety of figures in the Hebrew Bible and basically means "one chosen or appointed for a special mission." For example, in Psalm 105:15 even the patriarchs Abraham, Isaac, and Jacob are called "anointed ones," or "messiahs." The word in Hebrew literally means "one anointed" and originally referred to a ceremony in which oil was poured over the head of a priest or king, consecrating him for special service. In Leviticus 4:3 the ancient Israelite priests are called "messiahs," or "anointed ones," and in 1 Samuel 10:1 oil is poured on the head of Saul, first king of Israel, making him a "messiah." Since "messiah" is translated as *christos* in Greek, or "christ," one could accurately say that Cyrus is here called a "christ."

In this passage in Isaiah (chap. 45) Cyrus is the divinely sanctioned conqueror of Babylon, the empire that has oppressed God's people. One of the major themes of the book of Revelation is the "fall of Babylon" (chap. 17) despite the fact that ancient Babylon had long since disappeared when the book was written in the late first century. The early Christians cryptically referred to the Roman Empire as "Babylon" (1 Pet. 5:13). Therefore in terms of biblical symbolism based on the myth of the Tower of Babel and of Babel as the first world kingdom to oppose the rule of God (Gen. 11), the name "Babylon" comes to refer to the dominant system of corrupt human government in whatever period or age. When the book of Revelation is interpreted in this futurist perspective, one is always waiting for a final manifestation of "Babylon." The Davidians, like many evangelical Christians, identified the dominant political, economic, and military might of the West as the most likely candidate for the "Babylon" of Revelation. Koresh argued that no one could credibly maintain that the ancient Persian Cyrus fulfilled all the texts that run through this section of Isaiah (chaps. 40–54).[10] He argued that "Koresh," the Hebrew name for Cyrus that he had taken, was actually a surname according to Isaiah 45:4 and as such belonged to all of his followers. This group as a whole is called the "firstfruits" in Revelation 14:4. This agricultural image refers to the first portions of a field that were dedicated to God in the spring and summer barley harvest. In fact, the feast of Pentecost is actually called the feast of "firstfruits" (Lev. 23:15–21). However, even before the firstfruits were gathered in ancient Israel, there was the offering of the "wave sheaf," a single sheaf of the firstfruits of the barley harvest (Lev. 23:10–11).[11] Koresh taught his immediate followers, those who had come to Mount Carmel and were learning the meaning of the Seven Seals from him since 1985, that they were indeed this preliminary "wave sheaf" offering and thus would come to the truth before the larger group of the 144,000. All the students of the Seven Seals who had accepted Koresh's message considered Koresh their last name.[12] They understood themselves to be one family drawn from all the nations of the world but united in their opposition to modern Babylon, which they identified as the dominant political, social, and economic system of the Western world, particularly as represented by the United Nations led by the United States.

What Koresh experienced in Israel in 1985, as he described it, was a sudden and complete insight into the full role of this Koreshian messiah figure, also called the "Servant" and "Shepherd" of God (Isa. 44:26–28). He began to find this final figure, this new conqueror of new Babylon, on nearly every page of the Prophets of the Bible, particularly the later chapters of Isaiah (40–66).[13] He said that this revelation came to him as a direct voice, the voice of God himself, much like Moses received at the Burning Bush.[14] The voice stayed with him and began to teach him, through his reading, all the hidden and cryptic meaning of the Scriptures. Apparently, he also thought he had undergone some kind of ascent to the heavens in which he was shown certain mysteries, somewhat akin to the Jewish *merkabah* mystics.[15] He believed that this event had transformed him into a virtually "new creation" in which his body and soul had been mysteriously remade into a new person. Koresh said he never really needed to study the Bible after that; he would go through it, read it, expound it, and the meanings would simply "fall into place." His favorite text in this regard, which he often quoted, was Isaiah 50:4: "The Lord Yahweh has given me the tongue of the learned, that I should know how to speak a word in season to him that is weary; he wakes me morning by morning, he wakes my ear to hear as the learned." Koresh claimed that this often happened to him: he would hear the voice and receive some new insight or some further refinement of the meaning of the biblical texts. At other times, he said, he would simply see "pictures in his head" and vividly describe them to his listeners.[16] He emphasized that he lacked education, that he was dyslexic, and that it would be impossible for him to have received this vast understanding of Scripture unless God had given it to him. The Davidians believed that the Scriptures, particularly the words of prophecy, reflect the very Mind of God. In other words, the written

Word of God and the Mind of God are in perfect harmony, the former a reflection of the latter. Accordingly, they expected that when the final seventh messenger arrived, he would be given this Christ Spirit, which is the very Word of God once again inhabiting flesh. This messenger would understand all the mysteries of the entire biblical revelation; in fact, one might even say that this Christ figure had written the Scriptures, in the sense that the Spirit that inspired the prophets of old would be working without restriction in a final chosen figure.[17]

As Koresh searched section after section of Isaiah, Daniel, Micah, Nahum, and all the other prophetic writings, which most Christians would surely find obscure, he found many references to this figure, a specific messenger who would appear in the last times and reveal all the mysteries of God.[18] Although some of these texts had been previously applied by Christians to Jesus of Nazareth, Koresh attempted to demonstrate to his followers that the historical Jesus did not fulfill this role in the first century and that it remained for a second or final manifestation of the Spirit of Christ, which he claimed to have received in its fullness in 1985. Even Isaiah 53, whose verses describe the suffering and death of this servant figure, which Christians have taken as a clear reference to Jesus, Koresh applied to his later Christ figure, namely himself. He focused on one verse in particular: "He shall see his seed, he shall prolong his days" (v. 10). "Could this be Jesus?" he would ask his students. "Did Jesus have children? Did Jesus live to see his seed?" From here he would go back to Psalm 45, which speaks of another messiah who does marry virgins and has children who rule the earth: none other than the rider on the white horse.

Such arguments and methods would not necessarily convince all hearers, nor even those potential converts who professed belief in the Bible. More traditional Christians could work through these materials and continue, by the use of allegory, to apply them to Jesus. One might claim, for example, that Isaiah 52:10 speaks of the "spiritual" offspring of Jesus Christ, that is, those who believe in him, not his literal "seed." Koresh actually used a method employed at least as early as the Christian apologist Justin Martyr in his debate with

Trypho the Jew in the second century C.E. Jews who objected to faith in Jesus as Messiah would simply point out all the acts predicted by the prophets that he failed to accomplish. Christians would reply one of two ways: Jesus has, in fact, done these things, but in a spiritual, symbolic way; or, he will do them at his Second Coming. Koresh's appeal would only work with those convinced that the texts must be understood in a literal way. In promulgating such ideas, he had actually adopted a basic Jewish polemic developed for centuries by the rabbis that insists that Jesus did not fulfill the messianic prophecies and that "another" was to come. However, Koresh, unlike the rabbis, nonetheless affirmed and validated the role of Jesus as Christ in his time and place. The Branch Davidians were a Christian group in that they believed in Jesus Christ though they preferred to call him by his Hebrew name Yeshua. They believed he was the Son of God, the Lamb, and the Savior of the world, and they took Holy Communion twice a day. Like all Adventists they believed that Christ was in the heavenly sanctuary. But they also believed that he had sent his Lamb, his servant, his messiah—this "bird from the east"—who would usher in the Kingdom of God through the most concrete means as spoken by these prophets. They found a duality running throughout the Scriptures in this regard. The star of David, with its two triangles, one pointing up toward heaven, and the other down toward earth, was a fitting symbol of the Davidic Branch idea. The Christ in heaven was thus linked to the Davidic Christ on earth.

GUNS AND SEX

The most sensational reports the public heard about Koresh and his followers described a stockpile of weapons and his multiple wives, some of whom were allegedly girls as young as twelve and others said to be married to his male followers. It is somewhat difficult to separate fact from gossip, slander, and pure fiction, but there seems little doubt that in both of these areas Koresh should have been properly investigated and allowed to offer a defense. Instead, the BATF raid created a crisis situation, and from March 2 on, just two days after the BATF raid, Koresh was not permitted to speak to the public again. The FBI had cut all phone lines to Mount Carmel except for the two connected to their own negotiators. As we will show in the following chapters, the public had to rely solely on one-sided media reports and tightly controlled daily press briefings orchestrated by the FBI and BATF agents in charge at the scene. At no point during the siege was anyone allowed to hear the Branch Davidians themselves defend their beliefs and conduct.

The surviving Davidians claim that their huge stock of weapons was part of a legitimate business run by Paul Fatta, Mike Schroeder, and David Koresh. Fatta and Schroeder regularly attended the large gun shows held frequently throughout Texas and were constantly turning over large quantities of material for short-term profits, generating thousands of dollars per year in support of the communal life of the Davidians. They say that much of this material was kept boxed and often remained in its shipping packing. Despite the fact that on the very morning of the Sunday BATF raid Fatta and Schroeder left the property at sunrise for some routine trading at one of these shows, the Davidians unequivocally deny that the group as a whole was involved with, or even interested in, guns. They point out that Steve Schneider, Koresh's right-hand man during the siege, detested guns, as did the Harvard-educated lawyer Wayne Martin.[19] David Thibodeau, one of the survivors of the April 19 fire, says that the "gun business" was strictly a fascination of Koresh and a few others such as Mike Schroeder and Paul Fatta. As an American citizen Koresh, like many fellow Texans, cherished the right to own legal arms. In his March 7 videotaped interview he forcefully made the point that the government had no right to storm his home violently and that he had the right to defend his family by all necessary force in such circumstances: "I don't care who they are. Nobody is going to come to my home, with my babies around, shaking guns around, without a gun back in their face. That's just the American way." Apparently, under Texas law, he was correct. When the eleven Branch Davidians were on trial in San Antonio in the spring of 1994, Judge Walter Smith told the jury in no uncertain terms that under Texas law a citizen had the right to use armed force in self-defense, even against law-enforcement agents, if in his best judgment those authorities were exercising improper force in carrying out their duty.[20] Without question Texas is very much a "gun" state, with sixty-eight million registered weapons among a population of only seventeen million.[21] Indeed, some observers have jokingly made the point that by Texas standards the group of 130 was actually under-armed on the day of the siege.

Nonetheless, by Koresh's own admission there was obviously more involved. When asked about the weapons by Charlie Serafin in the KRLD interview on the day of the BATF raid, Koresh defended them as part of the biblical understanding of the group. He quoted Jesus, who had told his disciples at the Last Supper shortly before he was arrested, "But now, he that has a purse let him take it, and likewise his money, and he that has no sword, let him sell his garment and buy one" (Luke 22:36). In Koresh's view, the first coming of Christ was in meekness and humility. Jesus allowed himself to be arrested and killed; he did not resist. However, shortly before his death he announces that this approach of nonresistance is to come to an end and actually instructs his followers to buy weapons. Later that evening, as described in another Gospel, when Jesus is on trial before the Roman procurator Pontius Pilate, he is asked specifically about his kingdom; and he replies: "My kingdom is not of this world: if my kingdom were of this world, then would my servants fight, that I should not be delivered to the Jews: but *now* my kingdom is not from here" (emphasis added). (John 18:36) Koresh quoted this passage often, even beginning his final manuscript on the Seven Seals with it. He would emphasize that in both these verses Christians have completely ignored the small word "now," which signals a change of policy in this regard. The Second Coming of Christ was to be with power and involve a lot of violence. The book of Revelation is clearly the most violent book in the Bible. Texts like Zechariah 14 and Ezekiel 38 describe a scene of carnage when the followers of God finally confront their enemies in the last days. The policy of nonresistance, according to Koresh, was reversed at the death of Jesus and only applied to his self-sacrifice for the sins of humankind during his lifetime. The more general, biblical position, from the Old Testament through the book of Revelation, Koresh maintained, is that the active and forceful opposition to evil is not only permitted but expected and required by God's people. With such beliefs, the Mount Carmel community felt it was wrong to be pacifist. In God's timing they expected a great war to take place in Palestine, in which they would fight alongside the Israelis against an invading United Nations force. They were taught not to actively initiate violence until that final confrontation; but if attacked or persecuted, they were permitted in self-defense to resist evil with force. As we pointed out in the first chapter, on the day of the initial BATF raid Koresh said he deeply regretted the loss of life on both sides and blamed the government for beginning the violence, which he declared was completely unnecessary.

Since Koresh's position on self-defense is probably shared by millions of Americans, whether Christian or otherwise, it is much easier to explain than his views on sex. The sexual practices of the Branch Davidians involved a strange mixture of celibacy and polygamy. Neither is unknown in the history of Judaism and Christianity, but a combination of the two is rare. We find the practice of celibacy, for example, among the ancient Essenes, the early Christian Gnostics, certain Anabaptist groups, the Cathars, the Shakers, and of course, the Roman Catholic priesthood and religious orders. According to biblical texts, polygamy was common in ancient Israel, and it has been practiced by Mormon groups in our own century.

During the Mount Carmel standoff Koresh was quite open about his many "wives" and children. In the March 7 videotape, which the group sent out from the Mount Carmel center, Koresh affectionately introduced all twelve of his children on camera and several of his wives—all of whom died in the fire. Two of the women were pregnant at the time. In the videotape he also held up photos of several additional children born to "wives" who had left the group.[22] He had not always been so forthcoming. He realized that the practice of polygamy itself, not to mention his sexual relations with girls as young as twelve or thirteen, could cause him serious legal problems. In January 1992, when he granted an interview to the Australian television show *A Current Affair,* he is asked point blank by Martin King:

KING: How many wives do you have?

KORESH: One

KING: One wife?

KORESH: One wife. I've always had . . .

KING: Have you committed . . .

KORESH: Have I committed adultery? Is that what you're fixing to ask me?

KING: Have you committed adultery?

KORESH (laughing): No, I don't commit adultery.

KING: Are you telling me the truth?

KORESH: I am telling you the truth. I don't commit adultery.[23]

Clearly, Koresh is being evasive here. It was technically true that he only had one legal wife, Rachel, whom he had married in 1984. However, at the time he was speaking, there were at least six or seven other women living at Mount Carmel who had even borne him children and whom he certainly considered his "wives" in God's eyes. Further, although he might not have defined his sexual relations with the married women of the group as "adultery" since he had "dissolved" all their marriages in 1989, his answer on camera is clearly intended to mislead. For example, everyone at Mount Carmel knew that Mayanah, Judy Schneider's infant daughter, had been fathered by Koresh and that Jeannine Bunds, wife of follower Donald Bunds, had a sexual relationship with Koresh. Koresh was so fearful that the outside authorities would invade his private world and possibly take his children away that he even arranged sham "marriages" for his wives with selected male members. David Thibodeau was married to Michelle Jones, Greg Summers to Aisha Gyarfas, Jeff Little to Nicole Gent, and so forth. Thibodeau admits these "marriages" were never consummated and that it was understood that they were only for "appearance' " sake. He even wrote letters to Michelle as if he were her "real" husband, which she could keep for evidence if anyone ever tried to question the legitimacy of their "marriage." Koresh justified this duplicity because he knew that the outside world would not understand or sympathize with what he was doing. However, among his followers, he openly discussed these sexual activities and justified them theologically.

Using various Old Testament examples such as Abraham, Jacob, and King David himself, Koresh defended his practice of taking more than one wife. However, according to Koresh and his followers, there was something much more mysterious involved in these unions. All the survivors agree that these special children of David Koresh's were central to the group's understanding of its special role in the divine plan.

In the summer of 1989 Koresh began to share a startling "new" revelation with his followers. First, those who were married were to separate from their mates and no longer live together or have sexual relations. And second, his children, both present and future, were to occupy an exalted status in the coming Kingdom of God that would be set up in Israel. This new teaching was referred to as the "New Light" revelation.

Koresh insisted on the policy of celibacy on both practical and biblical grounds. The apostle Paul had written his own followers that the time was coming when "they that have wives will be as though they had none" (1 Cor. 7:29). Convinced that this apocalyptic time was near, Paul had strongly advised celibacy. Paul wrote that "the form of this world is passing away," referring to the normal male/female realities of the physical creation (1 Cor. 7:31). The early Christians believed that a "new creation" was taking place, where there would no longer be marriage and the distinctions of male and female would pass away (Luke 20:35; Gal. 3:28; 2 Cor. 5:17). Jesus himself had spoken of those who "become celibate for the sake of the Kingdom of God," and by most evidence he lived such a nonsexual life (Matt. 19:12). In Revelation 14:4 the select group of 144,000 who follow the Lamb are celibate. Koresh declared that such a time had arrived. He also appealed to Isaiah 2:19–22, which seems to describe an apocalyptic scene parallel in many ways to that quoted above from Revelation 6:15–17: "And they shall go into the holes of the rocks, and into the caves of the earth, for fear of the LORD, and for the glory of his majesty, when he arises to shake terribly the earth. . . . *Cease you from man,* whose breath is in his nostrils; for wherein is he to be accounted of" (emphasis added). To "cease" from man was understood as a message to the faithful just prior to this awesome time of judgment: they were to turn from the normal human pattern of life in anticipation of the new creation.

On the basis of Genesis 1:26–27, the Branch Davidians believed that Adam, when first created, embodied both male and female, but was later split into two. In the new creation this breach would be healed, and the two would become perfectly one again. Human sexuality, in the meantime, is a temporary and disappointing expression of that original union. No one really finds the right mate in this life, Koresh told his followers, but in the Kingdom of God all will receive his or her true lost "self," whether male or female, for whom each longs. In an unpublished manuscript written since the Waco events, the Branch Davidian theologian Livingstone Fagan puts it in this way: "This wall of separation exists between all men, even a man and woman in a marital union, which is not really marriage as God perceives it. This is more aptly evident during sexual intercourse. Neither party really feels each other. The man does not know what the woman is feeling, nor the woman, the man. They feel how they are affected by the contact between themselves. This condition of being trapped in one's self, both mind and body, is the problem of all problems facing man. We are truly separated and isolated from each other. We are lonely yet created to be twain." [24]

Koresh begins his Seven Seals manuscript with his own esoteric, thirteen-stanza poem about two birds, "he" and "she," who only find union at the "marriage of the Lamb" when the completeness of Eden is restored to the earth. The most representative lines of this poem, titled "Eden to Eden," are:

> Search forth for the meaning here,
> Hidden within these words

'Tis a song that's sung of fallen tears,
Given way for two love birds.

Love birds yet not of feathered creed
Shot down for gambled play,
And caged a far distance betweenst themselves
For the hunter felt it best that way.

. . . .

And now we see the hunter man,
Robbed without a prey,
The evil which he sought to do,
Caused the birds to pass away.

For loneliness and solitaire,
Is death to every soul.
For birds of God were meant to pair,
The two to complete the whole.

. . . .

For with Adam and his spirit Eve,
To share the kingdom fair;
But when they sinned they lost their crown
In exchange for shame to bear.

So Eve travailed and brought forth death,
And passed the crown to all;
For each to learn the lesson here,
The kingdom of the fall.

. . . .

For in the Christ, we've seen a bride,
The water mixed with blood,
The wife with cloven tongues of fire,
Of whom the Christ has loved.

And now He's back to sing His song,
The life of every spring,
And love birds gather, each one with mate,
For the marriage of the King.

The title "Eden to Eden" signifies that the followers of the Lamb
will be united with him in a future marriage, each thereby recover-

ing his male or her female self that was lost in the Garden of Eden. Writing extensively of this marriage feast in his Seven Seals manuscript, Koresh understands his role as a final manifestation of Christ, the messenger from the east, who will "seal" or designate this select group, which will be the vanguard of the new Edenic state (Rev. 7:1–5).

According to Koresh, sexual life was fine in past ages; indeed, it was necessary for the propagation of the species. However, just before the end time, those who have purified themselves for the new creation and for the Kingdom of God must separate themselves from this passing, obsolete state of life. Celibacy was hard for the other Davidians to accept, to put it mildly. Some left the group at this point, including Marc Breault and his new bride, Elizabeth Baranyai, who both became avowed opponents of Koresh because of these new teachings and practices. Even Livingstone Fagan, whose wife and two children lived with him at Mount Carmel, initially had great trouble accepting this teaching.

However, like the apostle Paul in 1 Corinthians 7, Koresh stressed the practical aspects of this doctrine. He discussed with the group how much sex functioned as an intrusion upon human life and actually inhibited close friendships between men and women, casting them into modes of deception and hypocrisy. Once in a Bible study session Koresh had one of the women stand and lift up her dress, exposing her legs and underpants. He told everyone to look at her for a moment, then asked how many of the men had been aroused or distracted although they had no legitimate reason to have sexual thoughts toward this particular woman. Such a demonstration attempted to illustrate how human sexuality is an untamed force that actually leads to deceit and disruption in human relationships. Koresh stressed the ideal potential of the liberated person, free from lust, which even when legalized by marriage is a distraction from higher and ultimate purposes. He emphasized that the group, as part of the vanguard of the age to come, needed purity. Most went along with this teaching, and the men and women of the group began to live separately.

Based on an apocalyptic perspective, Davidian celibacy was situational, much like that of the apostle Paul, who justified his perspective "in view of the impending distress" (1 Cor. 7:26). It was a celibacy for the "new age," which the Davidians believed was imminent, but there was another, more significant justification. The apostle Paul had also told his followers that the purest and most undivided devotion to Christ, and the cause of his kingdom, could best be achieved during the "last days" by the celibate life (1 Cor. 7:32–33). By accepting celibacy, the Davidians viewed themselves as the privileged participants in a process in which "flesh and blood" mortality was being transformed into pure spirit. When asked by reporters about giving up his wife, Livingstone Fagan insisted: "You don't *understand*. You don't understand at all. We as Branch Davidians aren't *interested* in sex. Sex is so *assaultive,* so aggressive. David has shouldered that burden *for* us."[25]

Koresh further taught that the men of the group were actually "married" to him, as the Lamb, in a spiritual way. Every male, he explained, has a lost or hidden female spirit within, crying out for expression. Accordingly, that inner female spirit could be married to the male side of Koresh. Further, since the Christ Spirit, which the male Koresh had received, was actually female, the men as males would be attracted to this divine female Spirit (the Shekinah of God) and could form a powerful spiritual bond through Koresh. For the women, the process was somewhat different. By sexual union with Koresh they could unite their female side with his male side, and their hidden male nature could express itself through union with his female Christ Spirit. This idea underlies the references to the parted "he" and "she" birds in Koresh's poem "Eden to Eden."[26] Routinely opening his prayers with "Our Father and Mother in Heaven," Koresh often referred to his heavenly Father and Mother, whom he believed to be one God, manifested as masculine and feminine.

Koresh's own procreation of children with the Branch Davidian women, married or otherwise, was something entirely different, which he never attempted to explain to the outside world. Certainly one skeptical of Koresh's sincerity might view the imposition of celibacy upon the group as the most blatant form of social control. By denying sex to his followers he could exercise his power over their most intimate lives and at the same time reserve all the women of his choosing for himself. This may have been his motive, but it was certainly not how he explained things to the group, nor how its members justified their own behavior to themselves. The children fathered by David Koresh were valued as the most sacred aspect of their community life. During the first few days of the siege Koresh had allowed twenty-one children to exit Mount Carmel. On Friday, March 5, when the last of the other children came out, the FBI questioned Koresh about those remaining. He told them, "We're dealing with my children now, and my children . . . are different than the other children."[27] When on Sunday, March 7, the negotiators again pushed Koresh on this point, he told them, "You're dealing with my biological children now . . . that's what we've come to."[28] That same Sunday the Davidians made a videotape in which Koresh introduced each of his twelve biological children. Without really explaining, he tried to give the authorities some hint of how special the group considered these children: "We don't expect you to understand, but these children are serious business." Many of the mothers of the twenty-one children who were released during the siege expressed extreme displeasure over the way the authorities were treating the children: giving them candy and sodas, allowing them to eat junk food, letting them wildly run around the room, screaming and carrying on. Some had not wanted their children sent out at all, since from their perspective they were being thrust directly into the "Babylonian" society. However, Koresh had insisted that they leave. Generally, he did not feel he could take responsibility in that situation for any children but his own, since they were too young to speak for themselves. A very few, who were not his own, were allowed to stay, namely five of the older girls who said they did not want to leave and the children of Juliet Martinez. All the rest who stayed were his own, and all died in the fire.

According to Koresh's explanations, having children with the Davidian women, who were pure in body and spirit, had nothing to do with sexual lust or desire. The unions were for procreation only and of the most sacred nature. One of his wives who bore him two children recounts the following:

INTERVIEWER:	How did he choose who to "be with"?
WIFE:	I don't really know. Sometimes he told you that God told him to do this. He once apologized for lusting after me.
INTERVIEWER:	Even after you were his?
WIFE:	Yes.
INTERVIEWER:	Why?
WIFE:	I don't know, but I do remember early on, right around the time I became pregnant he actually apologized to me. He said, "I lusted after you. Just the sheer feeling of a man wanting a woman." He had sex with me that night and apologized afterwards.
INTERVIEWER:	So he actually felt that each time he had sex with one of his wives it was something that was God- directed, and not something out of his own desires?
WIFE:	Right. That was the feeling I got a lot of the times that he spent with me. It was that God made him do this.[29]

When asked whether she loved Koresh, this wife replied that she loved him as a person, as her teacher at first, and that over time feelings of a deeper love for him developed. Koresh believed that since the Christ Spirit had come upon him, transforming him, he had become a vehicle for the most awesome divine purposes. He not only had to teach the message of the Seven Seals, gather the "wave sheaf" group of the "firstfruits," seal the 144,000, and participate in the final scenario of events leading to the Day of Judgment but also was God's instrument for another mysterious task. As far as we know, this was never communicated to anyone outside the group.[30] In Revelation 4 its author, John, is taken up to heaven, where he sees the throne of God. After describing God himself sitting on an emerald throne, he writes: "And round about the throne were four and twenty seats: and upon the seats I saw twenty-four elders sitting, clothed in white raiment; and they had on their heads crowns of gold" (v. 4). In the next chapter this very group, the twenty-four "elders," sing a "new song" in praise to the Lamb who has opened the Seven Seals scroll. They cry out: "You have made us unto our God kings and priests: and we shall reign on the earth" (Rev. 5:10). Koresh thought that he had made an astounding discovery in this passage. According to this verse a select group of twenty-four "elders" who dwell in heaven before the throne of God must somehow end up reigning as kings and priests on earth. Based on the ideas of Victor Houteff, a crucial part of the Davidian teaching was that there was to be an actual kingdom established in Palestine just as Isaiah 2 and Micah 4 predicted. Koresh believed that the children he was fathering were in fact these twenty-four elders. Their destiny would be to rule in the very top positions with the Lamb in the coming Kingdom of God on earth. The women chosen were understood to be the most holy "vessels" of Yahweh, actually bearing his seed through Koresh, who as the final manifestation of Christ is part of the process of bringing these children to earth. Koresh developed this idea from a number of texts that we have quoted above. Isaiah's messianic servant figure is to see his "seed" and rejoice (Isa. 53:10). The messiah of Psalm 45 is to father children who will become the "princes" over the earth (v. 16). The select group of women, who eventually leave Babylon for Israel, are bearing God's vessels (Isa. 52:11–12). The "arm of Yahweh" will gently lead "those who are with young" (Isa. 40:11). Accordingly, those women chosen for this task considered it the highest honor, for which they needed to achieve the highest level of purity in both body and spirit. To this end, their diets, as well as those of his other followers, were restricted by Koresh. He felt that the entire group, but the women especially, were to attain a new condition of purity in keeping with their future role in the Kingdom of God. They would become examples for all the nations of the world that would be coming to Jerusalem to learn the ways of God (Isa. 2:2–4).

It should be noted that Koresh's understanding of this text absolutely depends on the King James Version translation, which itself is based on late Byzantine Greek manuscripts. All modern translations, which are based on earlier, more reliable Greek texts, render the verse as: "You have made *them* to our God kings and priests: and *they* shall reign on the earth" (emphasis added).[31] According to this more accurate textual reading, the elders are not referring to themselves as the kings and priests who will reign on earth but to human beings already on earth (Rev. 5:9). Koresh always insisted that his followers use only the King James Version, claiming that it was more accurate. This important example shows where a different English translation would have completely changed a major teaching.

THE BEGINNING OF THE END

By 1987 Koresh had an elaborately worked-out scenario of precisely what was to happen during the last few years of human history leading up to God's wrathful Judgment of humanity. He often said that Daniel 11 was the most important text to understand in the Bible, and he had woven together in the most intricate harmony the latter verses of that chapter, along with Matthew 24 and the central portions of the book of Revelation (chaps. 7–16). As we have mentioned, the Branch Davidians believed that their entire group, along with thousands of others whom they believed would eventually accept the message, would move to Israel. There in "Palestine," as Koresh often called it, the end-time drama would unfold. The climax, which is described in texts like Ezekiel 38 and Zechariah 14, Koresh understood to involve an attack on Israel from an American-led, United Nations multilateral force from the north, in which the Davidians would stand with the Israelis. In keeping with Psalm 89 and Isaiah 53, which talk of the death of the Davidic figure, Koresh expected to be killed in this confrontation. In another prophecy that supports this expectation (Rev. 5), the Lamb is pictured as "slain." He sometimes made the point that in the famous scene in the wilderness following the Jewish Exodus from Egypt, Moses strikes a rock twice to get water. Since the apostle Paul had argued that this "Rock" symbolizes Christ, Koresh concluded that the text indicated that *two* Christs would be "struck" (1 Cor. 10:4). In the same vein he pointed out that there were *two* goats, not one, in the Old Testament Day of

Atonement ceremony, again signaling two messiahs. Koresh often quoted Jesus regarding the gathering of God's chosen people immediately preceding the outbreak of the heavenly signs associated with the Sixth Seal: "For wherever the carcass is, there will the eagles be gathered together" (Matt. 24:28; Luke 17:24). Understanding the carcass, in this case, as his own, he taught that his body would be terribly marred and left to rot in the open field (Isa. 52:14). However, the fulfillment of these prophecies was expected in the distant future, not in Waco in 1993.

As we discussed in our first chapter, there were possible variables to this scenario. After the 1991 Gulf War the group even speculated that the earlier phases of the prophecy might play out at Mount Carmel in Texas and only the final climactic events in Jerusalem, Israel. Once the BATF raid took place and the Branch Davidians were thrust before the attention of the entire world, those at Mount Carmel began to look for clues as to what God was going to work out through those circumstances. They understood that they were possibly living "in the Fifth Seal," and if so, perhaps they would all be killed—not later in Israel, but now at Mount Carmel. Since they believed that humans were allowed to exercise a measure of free choice, they came to understand the whole Mount Carmel crisis as both a test and an opportunity for the world in general and for our society in particular. Now that there was a widespread awareness of Koresh's claim to bring the message of the Seven Seals, would anyone be interested? they wondered. Or would society destroy this Christ as the Roman and Jewish establishment of the first century had killed Jesus? Koresh felt he was to offer the world his manuscript on the Seven Seals, which, by the Davidian way of thinking, was ultimately a key to unlock the entire biblical revelation. What the world would do with this offer remained to be seen. He was never sure of either the absolute will of God, or of the choices those outside would make. The violent gas attack on the morning of April 19 answered that question for the Davidians. They saw the government's decision as a defamation and rejection of all that God was mercifully offering the world through his Christ, Koresh. Yet, as Koresh understood it, throughout the fifty-one days, the *potential* to hear and follow was continually held out to any and all who would heed. At one point in the March 7 videotape, after introducing his wives and children, Koresh said, "Hopefully God is granting us time." In his early radio messages that the FBI allowed to be broadcast in exchange for the release of some of the children, Koresh had urged everyone who could hear him to drop to their knees and pray: "Lord, we do not know this man, but we do not understand the Bible or the book of Revelation. We do not know how to open the Seven Seals. Please help us to understand who he is, why he has come, and what you would teach us." Presumably, few listeners were interested in the proposition. For the Branch Davidians, during the siege humanity was drawing precariously closer to the cataclysmic Sixth Seal: "And I beheld when he had opened the sixth seal, and, lo, there was a great earthquake, and the sun became black as sackcloth of hair, and the moon became as blood, and the stars of heaven fell to the earth. . . . And the kings of the earth, and the great men, and the rich men, and the chief captains, and the mighty men, and every bondman and every free man, hid themselves in the dens and in the rocks of the mountains, and said to the mountains and rocks, 'Fall on us, and hide us from the face of him who sits on the throne, and from the wrath of the Lamb. For the great day of his wrath is come, and who shall be able to stand?' " (Rev. 6:12–17). Although Koresh expected to come out of Mount Carmel with his followers, given his belief in the biblical prophecies, the potential for the world to reject and kill him was always present. He fully expected and often discussed his eventual death. According to his reading of the prophecies, it was an absolute. However, when, where, and precisely how it would come was not clearly indicated. In retrospect, Livingstone Fagan discusses the Davidian view: "Whilst it is true that we were aware of the fact they were coming even before they knew they were coming, it was not inevitable that events had to end the way they did. The final outcome was contingent on our adversaries' response to our efforts to communicate our position of faith [i.e., Koresh's offer to write the Seven Seals manuscript and give it to the world]. It will be clearly seen that all our efforts were ignored. Evidently the government wanted its deception, both for itself and its people."[32]

On that score the Branch Davidians maintain that the entire episode was completely unnecessary and that there could have been a peaceful resolution. However, given their biblical perspective, in hindsight the two dozen or so surviving Davidians believe that what happened on April 19 was nonetheless "meant to be" since humanity had once again rejected the manifestation of Christ. As they understand history, there is always a built-in variability to biblical prophecy based upon the response of humankind to God's initiatives. Since society did reject and kill Koresh and his community, as they now understand it, the next event in God's plan is Koresh's resurrection from the dead and the opening of the Sixth Seal, which ushers in the final Day of Judgment.

Those surviving Branch Davidians now view the events at Mount Carmel as a confirmation, rather than a disconfirmation, of their faith. "There isn't anybody in the group who has lost faith in David," said Janet Kendrick, a longtime Branch Davidian, one year after the fire.[33] Koresh had taught them for years that he would be killed; the uncertainty lay in when and where. Currently, they view themselves and their situation in the light of certain key texts that they believe address them directly, particularly Zechariah 13:7 and Daniel 12:7–12. In the former, God speaks of "my shepherd" being struck and the sheep scattered, which is precisely how the Davidians view things now. The text in Daniel is even more specific: it speaks of the "scattering of the power of the holy people" and of a period of 1,335 days until the end, beginning when the "daily" is taken away. They understand the daily as the morning and evening teaching that Koresh gave them when he was alive. From these biblical references the Davidians expect Koresh to be resurrected and return in glory and power sometime around December 13, 1996, which is 1,335 days after his death on April 19, 1993. They are waiting until then.

FOUR

The Sinful Messiah

KORESH'S CONVICTION that the Messiah would have to sin was based on his interpretation of the Scriptures. To his detractors, however, the idea of a sinful messiah came to mean something quite different. In their eyes, Koresh's obvious sins, particularly his multiple sexual partners and his liaisons with young girls, completely undermined his messianic claims. A "sinful messiah" was a contradiction and an indication of Koresh's unstable and menacing personality. The image of Koresh as a deluded and dangerous messianic pretender was first formulated for the public by investigative reporters Mark England and Darlene McCormick of the *Waco Tribune-Herald*, but its primary source was in the stories told by disaffected former members of the Mount Carmel community. The most powerfully damning testimony was furnished by Marc Breault.

INSIDE MOUNT CARMEL WITH MARC BREAULT

A computer expert and keyboard player, Breault was a candidate for the ministry in the Seventh-Day Adventist church when he first encountered the Branch Davidians. Perry Jones, Koresh's father-in-law, took advantage of a chance meeting in a southern California bookstore to spread the word about his son-in-law's teachings. Having provoked his interest, Jones made a startling proposition to Breault. He said, "I'd like to introduce you to a young man only a couple of years older than you. I think he has inspiration from God."[1] Breault recalls that his religious background actually prepared him to take such an unusual assertion seriously. He replied to Jones that "the Seventh-day Adventist Church was founded by a prophet. Who says God can't raise up another one. Sure, I'll talk to him."[2] After hearing a few of Koresh's Bible study sessions, Breault soon became an integral part of his circle of students, rising to the status of the prophet's trusted confidant and assistant. Only after Koresh promulgated his shocking New Light revelation, which had to do with his claim upon all the women of the group, did Breault waver and then break his commitment to the group. Subsequently, he became Koresh's relentless opponent.

With the Australian television reporter Martin King, Breault wrote a deliberately frightening account of his association with Koresh. Breault and King shaped their narrative as an inspiring account of one man's moral and spiritual awakening and of his heroic attempts to rescue his friends from a terrifying fate and to warn others about the evil lurking within cults. As King describes it in *Inside the Cult,* "Marc Breault decided to use the talents developed at Mount Carmel to save as many cult members as he could. He became a cultbuster. He committed his life to righting the wrongs of the past and, more importantly, to putting a stop to Vernon Howell before he could destroy too many more lives."[3] Their account can also be read in another way. It charts Breault's progress from curious seeker to faithful lieutenant to dissident to defector and finally to dedicated adversary. In the process, it offers a detailed account of the strategies he adopted in order to destroy his former mentor. Breault's personal odyssey also helps to illuminate how the once quiet and obscure life of a Seventh-Day Adventist splinter group suddenly exploded into the public consciousness with the BATF raid on Mount Carmel.

Breault's eventual quarrel with Koresh was directly based on his personal experience among the Branch Davidians. Whereas Breault reached a point at which he could no longer abide what he heard and saw among the Branch Davidians, even today he acknowledges Koresh's skill and insight as an interpreter of the Scriptures.[4] Most important, Breault couldn't square Koresh's scriptural justifications for his behavior with his own understanding of the Bible; and what precipitated Breault's final departure from the community was Koresh's controversial sexual appropriation of all Mount Carmel females, particularly the younger ones. As Breault recollects an important turning point, "I'm seriously beginning to doubt whether God has ever talked to this guy. That's a long way from where I was in the beginning. Little Aisha Gyarfas comes through the office door. She walks right past me and goes to the other door that opens up to a wooden stair case that leads directly up to Koresh's room. I hope she's not doing what I think she is. Ah, who am I kidding. This little 13-year-old is going up there to make love to David. I can't deny this stuff any more. But there's something inside me that says I have to make sure. I've followed Koresh for so many years. I have to know he's making out with a 13-year-old."[5] When Breault confirmed his suspicions to his own satisfaction, he decided to leave the group. Breault continues to insist, however, that his defection, along with his wife's, had a theological motivation. He argues that "many people believe we left Vernon solely because we couldn't stomach his behavior. This is incorrect. We vehemently opposed his biblical interpretation. We were able to convince many to leave because we showed flaws in Vernon's interpretation."[6] Breault's statement again shows how thoroughly the Mount Carmel community was steeped in the Scriptures. Few, if any, of those who left the group gave up the biblical, apocalyptic worldview that they shared with the remaining Branch Davidians. Their dispute focused solely on the prophetic authority of Koresh.

Breault and King portray Breault's resolution as fraught with danger: "You don't just leave a cult, you have to escape. But you don't just escape, either. You have to plan that escape, and plan it very, very carefully. In a cult like this one, one wrong move could mean a bullet through the brain."[7] Their hyperbolic description of the situation vividly expresses Breault's fears but fails to acknowledge that many others before Breault had left the group without being harmed and without being physically threatened by Koresh. Today, even after the destruction of the Mount Carmel center and the deaths of nearly all of its inhabitants, Breault still fears for his life.[8] Anonymous threats have made him understandably wary. It is important to note, however, how he and King have made his experience emblematic of "cults" in general. That form of exaggeration would only serve to exacerbate the hostility toward Koresh and the Branch Davidians that surfaced in the media and the general public.

After leaving Mount Carmel behind and joining his wife in Australia in late September 1989, Breault remained in virtual seclusion for three months. In King's words, "for twelve weeks he and Elizabeth purged themselves of Vernon's poison."[9] During that time Breault began to fashion a new identity for himself; no longer the chief recruiter for Koresh, he became his chief enemy instead. Not satisfied with changing his own life, Breault decided to make the world safe from Koresh, beginning with the Australian disciples. Breault and King describe how Breault decided to pose as a rival prophet in order to get the Branch Davidians' attention. Breault sent a letter to Lisa Gent, an Australian former member, in which he directly challenged Koresh's New Light theology of sexuality: "Since I am here in Australia at the Lord's direction[,] God has seen fit to reveal much new light so as to put to shame those who think they know the Scriptures because of all the 'wonderful new light' they are getting from the United States."[10] Some surviving Branch Davidians have claimed that Breault really did see himself as Koresh's rival for primacy in the group and that his bitter criticism of Koresh stemmed from his jealousy, but Breault insists that his claim of prophetic authority was only an attention-getting maneuver. At a subsequent meeting with the Australian Branch Davidians, Breault maintains that in an extended Bible study session, he succeeded in demonstrating that "Koresh was a pretender and a false prophet"[11] and thus weakened his former mentor's hold on the Australian contingent. Even a personal visit by Koresh himself failed to win back the disaffected Australians. Buoyed by his initial success, Breault redoubled his efforts to encourage defections from Mount Carmel.

A year after Breault's departure the conflict within the Branch Davidian group took a decisive turn, one that presaged the terrible conclusion of April 1993. King summarizes the momentous decision: "In September 1990 the breakaways from Australia, New Zealand, England and the United States, led by Marc Breault and his wife, Elizabeth Baranyai, conferred and decided that it was time to up the ante. Vernon was dangerous and needed to be stopped. What better way than to contact law enforcement authorities. They had the evidence; they had the numbers; and they also had the motive." [12] From that point on, Breault's battle against Koresh was fought in public. He joined with the Australian former members and their families to hire a private investigator, Geoffrey Hossack, to coordinate and supplement the information that he had uncovered about Koresh and the Branch Davidians. In addition, Breault reported his suspicions about the Mount Carmel community to United States authorities in Australia and urged them to conduct a formal investigation. Breault also turned to the media and, after eliciting little interest from those in the United States, found his champion in Martin King of National Nine Network's *A Current Affair*. King saw an important story in the defector's tale, and his interest gave Breault's cause a big boost, later helping to bring him into a fateful relationship with the BATF.

Leaving no doubt about either his perspective on events or the importance of his investigation, King describes his first visit to Mount Carmel: "We all felt it on that cold Texas morning, out there in the middle of nowhere. The fear, the alarm, and the panic we tried desperately not to show. Our predicament was this: Vernon believed we'd traveled half-way across the world on a public relations exercise so he could strike back at his disenchanted former followers. That was the only reason he had allowed us the world-first behind-the-scenes examination of the Branch Davidian cult. The truth was that we had come to Mount Carmel to expose him as a cruel, maniacal, child-molesting, pistol-packing religious zealot who brainwashed his devotees into believing he was the Messiah, the reincarnation of Jesus Christ, and who would eventually lead them into an all-out war with the United States government and, finally, to their deaths."[13] King refines Breault's postdefection understanding of Koresh and the Mount Carmel community into the virulent anticult sentiments that shape the entire book. All of the standard elements of the negative characterization of "cults" appear: the focus on the all-powerful leader, the representation of the followers as automatons completely under the leader's control, the intimations of abuse and violence, and the clinching comparison to Jonestown. Since Breault repeated his allegations in so many different forums, Breault and King's *Inside the Cult* is groundbreaking neither in its interpretive framework nor in its heralded glimpse inside Mount Carmel. However, *Inside the Cult* does provide a virtual step-by-step account of the career of a "cultbuster." Breault's attempt to put a stop to Koresh's excesses and to release what he saw as Koresh's unconscionable hold on the Mount Carmel community had an extraordinarily broad impact beyond the group itself. He succeeded in having his charges repeated in the media, acted upon in the courts, and investigated by BATF agents.

Breault's influence in the judicial system crystallized in the Michigan custody hearing concerning Kiri Jewell. After Breault's defection, Kiri was still living with her mother, Sherri, at Mount Carmel while her father had remarried and was living in Michigan. On October 31, 1991, David Jewell received a troubling phone call from Breault, who warned Jewell that "I've got something to tell you. And you're not going to like it. It's about your daughter, Kiri, and I have reason to believe she's in extreme danger."[14] David Jewell took seriously Breault's fears that his daughter was likely to be inducted into Koresh's harem of "brides" and enlisted in the final apocalyptic war against Babylon, especially after receiving a package of supporting evidence; and he soon began to plan with Breault to regain legal custody of his daughter. Breault even flew to Michigan to give supportive testimony in the custody hearing that David Jewell quickly arranged. Breault's accusations against Koresh, which are documented in his sworn testimony, were certainly shocking. He alleged that during his time at Mount Carmel, Koresh "became power hungry and abusive, bent on obtaining and exercising absolute power and authority over the group."[15] Breault described how Koresh saw himself as the unique recipient of a special divine revelation concerning the imminent end of the world and final judgment. The bulk of his testimony, however, concerned how Koresh saw his own prophetic role as including the propagation of a new family from his seed, and that as a result, he had arrogated to himself the sole right to engage in sexual relations with any woman in the community, including others' wives and those barely past the threshold of puberty. Breault testified that "on 5 August 1989, Vernon gave a Bible study in which he stated that he was the Lamb of God. As the Lamb of God he was entitled to have all the women and girls sexually. Only he had the right to procreate. Howell stated that he would give married couples time to adjust to this new 'revelation' as he called it. . . . Howell commanded that no one tell anyone of this 'new light' as he called it."[16] Though, in the context of the Jewell custody hearing, Breault focuses on allegations of sexual misconduct against Koresh, he also mentions what he saw as "the fundamental deprivation of human rights,"[17] including the injurious beating of children, deprivation of food and water, deteriorating sanitary conditions, and forced intensive physical exercise. In addition, Breault asserts that "Howell was increasingly obsessed with guns and the need to use them."[18] Breault also notes in his affidavit that his accusations were corroborated by the observations of many other former members. A damning document, his affidavit reinforces in detail the characterizations of the Mount Carmel community as a "destructive cult" and Koresh as a "dangerous" cult leader. It played a crucial role in persuading the court to grant David Jewell sole custody of his daughter, who was still a minor. Although Kiri Jewell's mother, Sherri, retained some visitation rights, she never exercised them. The court had stipulated that visits take place away from Mount Carmel and that Kiri not come in contact with Koresh or members of the Branch Davidian group. Sherri Jewell died in the fire on April 19, 1993. Eventually, Breault's accusations and those of the other defectors spurred not only a concerned parent into action but also the U.S. government.

The BATF contacted Breault some ten weeks before their ill-fated raid on the Mount Carmel center. In Breault and King's retelling of the BATF investigation, both Breault and his wife, Elizabeth Baran-yai, played essential parts. King states that the initial BATF phone call "was to be the first of many—almost daily—phone calls between Breault and senior officials of the United States Government, which included the [B]ATF, the FBI, Congress, the State Department, and the Texas Rangers. It was those dozens of highly confidential trans-Pacific telephone calls that helped authorities bring Vernon Howell's ten-year Reich to an end. A Reich in which child beatings, child sex, rape, violence, cruelty, mind control, food and water deprivation, enforced isolation, guns and terrorism were endemic."[19] In that view, Breault's own personal dissatisfaction with Koresh, and his un-tiring efforts to warn the world about what Koresh could do, played an important part in the events leading to the United States govern-ment's decision to storm the Mount Carmel center. Breault, how-ever, strongly disagreed with the methods that both the BATF and the FBI employed, once things were out of his hands. Over a year after the tragic ending, he offered his own analysis to James Tabor:

> When the [B]ATF approached me (I did not approach them) they told me that they believed Vernon had amassed a huge arsenal of weapons and that some of those were illegal. I am not a weapons expert and I can't say whether they did have illegal weapons or not. I wouldn't be surprised. . . . It was for this reason I strongly advised the [B]ATF that if they were going to arrest Vernon, they do so with no force, that they somehow lure Vernon away from Carmel. . . . I must say that it hurts both my wife and I when Branch Davidians accuse us of murder. We repeatedly advised the [B]ATF to use this tactic. . . . I am outraged that government mis-handling, along with Vernon's own delusions of grandeur, contrib-uted to the deaths of all those children I knew and loved, not to mention the adults. . . . The FBI mishandled a lot of things during the siege. They did not take sufficient note of Vernon's religion and its teaching. They assumed they were the experts. . . . The FBI and [B]ATF lied to the public numerous times.[20]

Nonetheless, Breault's brief but spectacular career as a "cultbuster" shows how anticult polemics, when repeated loudly and long enough and in the right places, can provoke not just disapproval but extremely consequential action as well. Even if Breault's centrality to the ongoing BATF investigation is discounted somewhat, as it is in the official government reports, the power of the anticult polemics to shape not only perceptions but also actions is vividly illustrated. Breault, in fact, has had the kind of impact that many within the anticult movement would aspire to imitate. Through his direct intervention, many severed their ties with Koresh. Moreover, his dogged persistence eventually brought this particular "cult problem" to the attention of sympathetic government officials who were inclined to act upon his allegations. Throughout the latter stages of his campaign against Koresh, Breault's efforts were immensely aided by the patronage of a supportive reporter, who used the impressive resources of a contemporary television program to promulgate Breault's cautionary tale.

While he was working with Martin King in Australia and the BATF in the United States, the tireless Breault was also serving as an informant for the *Waco Tribune-Herald*. Acting with the support of the *Waco Tribune-Herald* editor Bob Lott, who saw the Mount Carmel community as "a dangerous and sinister thing the public should know about," the reporters Mark England and Darlene McCormick began an extensive investigation of Koresh and the Branch Davidians. Lott committed significant resources from his relatively small daily paper because he perceived that "it was time to let the public know of this menace in our community." [21] He also decried the ineffectiveness of the local authorities who "knew about the situation and, as best we could tell, had done next to nothing." [22] England and McCormick carefully reviewed archival materials, legal records, and other documentary sources about the group, but the crucial material in their presentation comes from interviews with former members, particularly Breault.

Stories like Breault's have often played a central role in the contemporary controversy about new religious movements. Their immediacy, dramatic form, and wrenching emotional content virtually guarantee a broad audience. Their accuracy appears to be unimpeachable since their authors have been participants in the events described. Stories from former members, however, are actually a very complicated form of evidence. Defectors from new religious movements have typically experienced at least two extraordinary transitions. The initial transition is joining the group in the first place, often through a process of conversion. Affiliation frequently produces feelings of satisfaction and security, a reduction of previously felt tensions, and the conviction that one has made the right choice and embarked upon the appropriate or even divinely sanctioned course of life. For example, although she was living in California at the time of the destruction of the Mount Carmel center and lost a sister in the fire, one of Koresh's wives said, "I wish I could have been there. That's where the truth was." [23] All of those sentiments and perceptions, however, appear mistakes and illusions if a member later exits the group. Former adherents have to come to a conclusion about what went wrong and how and why they made such a terrible mistake. As Breault says ruefully of his first encounters with Koresh, "I decided to follow him. It was the biggest mistake of my life." [24] Most often, responsibility for such a mistake is assigned to someone else. Defectors see themselves as having initially been overwhelmed by forces beyond their control. In retrospect they view their membership as something that *happened to* them rather than as something that they freely and actively chose. So it was with many of the former members of the Mount Carmel community. England and McCormick tellingly summarize the common position of the Davidian defectors: "Former members also said Howell uses traditional mind control techniques to entrap listeners; putting Branch Davidians through rigorous daily Bible studies, some lasting more than 15 hours. . . . Lurking behind the Branch Davidians' blind faith in Vernon Howell was the acknowledgment that a ninth-grade dropout was keeping them spellbound. To these intelligent and, in some cases, highly educated devotees there was only one possible explanation: Howell was inspired." [25] In the words of Lisa Gent, "It's like he cooks women. He prepares them for the fire by the way he gives his studies. It's mind manipulation."[26] Whether cooked, entrapped, or inspired, former members portray themselves as having been virtually power-less in the face of Koresh's compelling personality; he was their teacher, their prophet, their friend, their leader, and, for many, their lover. The logic of many apostates' tales is simple and chilling: he lured them into the group, and expelled them at will. If in the begin-ning all credit belonged to Koresh, ultimately all blame did as well. The characterization of joining and leaving that predominates in the stories of defectors from the Mount Carmel community reinforces the image of the Branch Davidians as a "cult" and of Koresh as a "cult" leader. By concentrating virtually all of the power of attraction and repulsion in a single figure, the former adherents' stories magnify the leader to virtually superhuman proportions. He has only to beckon and they follow. The source of that power is explained as "traditional mind control techniques," which in the *Tribune-Herald* reports remain largely unspecified. The presence of a powerful char-ismatic leader who uses such techniques is then taken as confirming evidence that the group in question is a cult.

What the Breault-King account of Koresh's "power" seriously lacks is any attention to the biblical or theological dimension of the story. Breault has a master of arts degree in religion and is a serious student of the Bible. He admits that he was drawn to Koresh after listening to him teach the Bible. He later recruited Steve Schneider, who had also done graduate work in religion, on the same basis. All the Branch Davidians make this singular point when asked to relate their stories about how they were drawn into the group. Ironically, Breault's experience, as well as that of many other educated and in-telligent Branch Davidians, contradicts the standard "cult member" stereotype. Breault, Steve Schneider, and others were not robotic au-tomatons blindly led by some mysterious process of "brainwashing" to their doom. Rather, they were, first and foremost, serious students of the Bible. For them, the group's appeal lay in Koresh's ability to explain the Scriptures and their conviction that no one could possi-bly do what he was able to do, especially in "opening" the Seven Seals of the book of Revelation, without divine inspiration. Likewise, Koresh's justification for every aspect of his conduct and his very

identity as a second Christ were based primarily on textual arguments from the Bible. For the Branch Davidians, if Koresh was not
the messiah as he claimed, then the Bible itself was untrue. As
Schneider once put it, when he was tempted to leave Koresh on
personal grounds, "The book [Bible] compelled [me] to stay."[27] Unfortunately, Breault's account in *Inside the Cult* never allows the
reader to understand this aspect of Koresh's appeal, particularly as
his story has been shaped by King's journalistic flair. Without understanding the group's religious beliefs, the Branch Davidians seem
unfortunate dupes at best or unbalanced fanatics and lunatics at
worst. How else would they have been attracted to such a bizarre
phenomenon?

In retrospect Breault seems to recognize this point. In the course
of offering his valuable insights into Branch Davidian theology to
James Tabor, he expresses a surprising concern about this very book:

> You know as well as I do that Vernon's theology was reasonable—
> at least up to a point. For all his delusions of grandeur, even I
> admit that Vernon was profound in his thinking and way above
> the average Christian theologian. When people read your book,
> and many pro–Branch Davidian people will read it—they will see
> this, and become more incensed at us for our "lies" and our "con-
> tributions to their deaths." I believe I have helped you understand
> Vernon's theology, and in so doing, helped you understand its rea-
> sonableness. I am afraid that if people read your book, and are
> kept unaware of the contributions of Elizabeth and I, they will
> think us all the more "evil" and seek revenge even more than they
> have already. I'm not really worried about the Branch Davidians.
> It's the other crazies out there![28]

This is not to imply that Breault has reversed in any way his negative
evaluation of Koresh and the whole Mount Carmel experience. He
stoutly maintains that his book "accurately describes Vernon the
man, and it also accurately describes life in Mount Carmel. When
all is said and done about theology, Vernon was out of control and
he had to be stopped."[29] While Breault laments the degree to which

Koresh was able to "control" his followers, he nonetheless admits that the Branch Davidians *willingly* surrendered their autonomy to him. Again, he provides a fascinating observation:

> The Branch Davidians lived their faith to a degree most Christians would never dream of doing. For this I admire them greatly. They put to shame many who profess religion, but only do so verbally. Even Vernon falls into this category. I always said Vernon had courage and fortitude even though I opposed him. The problem is, as we see it, that these good sincere people surrendered their judgment, and their decision-making processes to one man, namely Vernon. They may have done so for sincere reasons, but they did so nonetheless. That, in itself, is not a crime and I do not mean to accuse the Branch Davidians of such a crime. *After all, weren't the disciples asked to do much the same thing to Jesus Christ?* Many of these people would do anything Vernon told them to do. Vernon said himself, and we have it on video, that these people would both kill and die for him.[30] (Emphasis added.)

Unfortunately, this more balanced assessment does not come through in the Breault-King account. The tone and tenor of the book, perhaps because of his coauthor's journalistic approach, is clearly otherwise. The details of the former members' stories in the *Waco Tribune-Herald*'s series on the Mount Carmel center and in Breault's own *Inside the Cult* replicate the portrait of the generic cult so frequently encountered in anticult pronouncements. Each element of that negative characterization reinforces the others, and the presence of one leads inexorably to the implied presence of the others. England and McCormick do note David Koresh's attempts to refute some of his opponents' accusations. But if the allotment of space, the distribution of emphasis throughout the articles, the interpretive sidebars that accompany the main story, and the very decisions to undertake the investigation and publish the series are any indications, the *Tribune-Herald* reporters were clearly persuaded by Breault and the other apostates.

The links between "cult" defectors, the news and entertainment media, the government, and the courts that run throughout Marc

Breault's story are also the paths along which the anticult activists' negative stereotype of cults travels. Defectors like Breault have dramatic stories to tell. Newspapers, newsmagazines, and television programs have a prodigious appetite for dramatic stories. Stories given wide currency in the popular media inevitably attract the gaze of government officials, often at the urging of their constituents. Constituents and media personalities frequently urge the government to "do something" about such issues. One way of "doing something" is to pursue litigation. Juries tend to be consumers of popular media accounts of sensational stories. The longer a standard account of any topic remains unchallenged in that tight and mutually reinforcing network of connections, the better its chance of being accepted as conventional wisdom. Opinions that achieve the status of conventional wisdom are rarely challenged. Thus, unchallenged opinions come to dominate public discourse about a subject and to shape decisively our perceptions, actions, and reactions. The treatment of Koresh and the Branch Davidians in Breault's book and in the *Waco Tribune-Herald*'s "Sinful Messiah" series indicates that the anticult activists' portrait of "dangerous cults." and manipulative, demented "cult leaders" has dominated the public discussion of the events at Waco. Breault's viewpoint gained even greater force because it conforms to the generic portrait of a "destructive cult" that has been vigorously promoted by a diverse group of amateur and professional "cult" opponents.

ON THE FRONT LINES WITH RICK ROSS

Whereas Breault's entanglement with Koresh and the Mount Carmel community resulted from his deep religious interests and personal curiosity about a man who might be a contemporary prophet, the self-styled "deprogrammer" Rick Ross became involved with the Branch Davidians because of his personal and professional preoccupation with "dangerous cults."[31] Long before Breault became Koresh's opponent, Ross had been active as a for-hire cultbuster specializing in "Bible-based cults." Breault's opposition to Koresh was founded on his deep personal disappointment that the man he had once accepted as a prophet turned out to be merely sinful and not a messiah. Ross's hostility to Koresh was part of his profession as an independent anticult contractor, but Ross also saw his work as part of a mission: he dedicated himself to protecting America from the destructive power of cults. In its own way, the cautionary story that Ross would develop about Mount Carmel was as arresting as Breault's. But whereas Breault's account depended on personal experience and intimate details for its persuasiveness, Ross's would depend on the simplifying power of generalizations. Although Breault came to conclusions about Koresh from the particulars of his own life with the Branch Davidians and, with the help of his coauthor, Martin King, about "cults" in general, Ross derived his judgment of Mount Carmel ("If there is a group that is going to go ballistic, it will be this group")[32] from his perception of a vast "cult problem" in American society. Moving from very different starting points, Breault and Ross arrived at a similar evaluation of the community. In the public discussion of Koresh and Mount Carmel, Ross did nearly as much as Breault to establish the image of Koresh as a dangerous and mentally unstable false messiah. For Ross, Koresh's "sins" were ethical, legal, and psychological, rather than religious, which, in his eyes, ruined his credibility just as effectively.

Ross presents himself as a battle-tested veteran of the cult wars. He claims that "for more than a decade, I have crisscrossed the country as a cult deprogrammer, confronting destructive cults and fanatical religious groups in every corner of the nation. In hundreds of cases, I have seen firsthand the suffering and broken lives they engender."[33] For Ross, however, all of those cases fit a single pattern. In his estimation, all "cult" leaders "are self-obsessed, egomaniacal, sociopathic and heartless individuals with no regard whatsoever for their followers. They seek only their personal aggrandizement, financial well-being and physical pleasure. Such leaders exercise total control over their followers. The personalities of those adherents have been dismantled by systematic brainwashing to the point where the leader's desires become their own. Cult victims and fanatical followers of radical sects are deceived, lied to, manipulated and ultimately exploited."[34] The Branch Davidians, led by Koresh, seemed to fit

Ross's paradigm of a destructive cult. Consequently, when he was contacted by the brother and sister of a Branch Davidian in 1992, Ross was eager to do battle against the "cult leader gone mad with a Bible."[35] The battlefield would be the conscience of a Branch Davidian named "Bill."[36] Alarmed by their brother's plans to quit his job and move permanently to Mount Carmel, his siblings had contacted Ross. Bill reluctantly agreed to a hurried phone conversation with Ross, who plied him with a litany of questions about Mount Carmel. Presenting the generic picture of a "dangerous cult," Ross asked: "Was there an absolute authority figure not accountable to anyone? Were members required to conform completely to the leader's dictates? Was outside information filtered through the leader? Was there an 'us against them' mentality? Were those outside the cult dismissed and berated? Lastly, . . . did the leader's claims from the Bible ultimately lead to his own aggrandizement, power and control?" Bill pondered those questions after his return to Mount Carmel and eventually agreed to meet with Ross. During four consecutive days of intensive discussions at a safe house set aside for their use, Ross eventually brought Bill to abandon his religious commitment to Koresh and the Branch Davidians.

Bill's deprogramming was in fact a relatively mild experience compared to that of others. Ross effectively used his broad familiarity with "cults" and a careful reading of the Bible outside of the compelling setting of Koresh's teaching sessions to raise doubts in Bill's mind. Just as Breault had claimed to unmask Koresh as a messianic pretender in a Bible study session with Australian Branch Davidians, Ross tried to discredit Koresh as a biblical interpreter. He maintains that he was able to show Bill that "the leader roamed freely from Revelation to Psalms with no rational means of connecting them. . . . It was all done on a whim."[37] More important to Ross's career as a cultbuster than effecting Bill's agreement to leave Mount Carmel was the way that Ross used Bill's change of heart to further his own designs against the Branch Davidians. Ross served as the conduit through which the reluctant defector's story reached the *Waco Tribune-Herald* and eventually the BATF. Trading on the familiarity with Mount Carmel that he gained through Bill's deprogramming,

Ross quickly became an eager informant for governmental agencies and journalists alike. In addition to providing crucial interpretations for *See No Evil,* where the author Tim Madigan asserts that "no one was more generous or shed more light into the dark mystery of David Koresh,"[38] Ross appeared on numerous television talk shows and news programs as a "cult expert."

Throughout his involvement with the Branch Davidians, Ross presented himself as a concerned citizen sounding the alarm about a pernicious danger. In his foreword to Madigan's *See No Evil,* Ross warns that "everyone must be aware of the dangers posed by these groups. But it is also time for government and law enforcement agencies, and child protection services to enforce the law. Destructive cults should not be allowed to hide behind the walls of separation of church and state."[39] Ross's deprogramming of Bill represents the most direct point of contact between dedicated amateur and professional opponents of all "destructive cults" and the Mount Carmel community. Ross was already relying on a fully formed generic picture of "cults" before Breault, Bill, or anyone else added any details from Mount Carmel. Ross's and Breault's contributions to the public discussion of the Branch Davidians flowed through the same channels that had already been deeply cut by the assiduous efforts of anticult activists during the preceding two decades.

The term "sinful messiah" meant very different things to different people. For the faithful Branch Davidians this epithet heralded their salvation. But beyond that tiny group it took on a sinister meaning. Koresh's closest religious critics, like Breault, beheld in him the failed promise of a false prophet. Others at greater remove saw the dangerous effects of distortion of the Scriptures and the power of sin. Koresh's secular critics were at once the most strident and the most confused. They saw in him nothing less than a threat to the stability of American society, a fear that they projected onto many other groups as well. That unspoken fear was the constant companion of the BATF agents who attempted to serve the search warrant on Koresh and to those who settled in for the fifty-one-day standoff.

FIVE

A Complex Hostage / Barricade Rescue Situation

THE CHASM BETWEEN THE government's perception of the Branch Davidians and Koresh's became evident within minutes of the initial February 28 raid. On the tapes of phone calls between Mount Carmel and the Waco Sheriff Department's 911 switchboard, Koresh states his understanding of the situation without equivocation. While he speaks with the Waco police lieutenant Larry Lynch, the officer tries desperately to make contact with the BATF forces on the property. Lynch clearly does his best, but he seems as baffled by Koresh's religious pronouncements as the BATF and FBI in subsequent negotiations:

911 DISPATCHER: Nine-one-one.

KORESH: Hello.

911 DISPATCHER: Yes.

KORESH: This is David Koresh. We're being—we're being—tough to call you guys.

911 DISPATCHER: This is who, sir?

KORESH: David Koresh, at Mount Carmel Center. We're being—shot all up out here.

LYNCH: Well, David, what—this—what I'm doing is, I'm trying to establish some communication links with you.

KORESH: No no. no. no. no. Let me tell you something.

LYNCH: Yes, sir.

KORESH: You see, you brought your bunch of guys out here and you killed some of my children. We told you we wanted to talk. No. How come you guys try to be [B]ATF agents? How come you try to be so big all the time?

LYNCH: Okay, David.

KORESH: Now there's a bunch of us dead and a bunch of you guys dead. Now—now, that's you're [*sic*] fault.

LYNCH: Okay, let's—let's try to resolve this now. Tell me this. Now, you have casualties. How many casualties? Do you want to try to work something out? [B]ATF is pulling back, we're trying to—

KORESH: Why didn't you do that first?

LYNCH: Okay, all I'm—all I'm doing is handling communications. I can't give you that answer, David.

KORESH: Okay.

LYNCH: Okay.

KORESH: The thing of it is this—is this. There is a God that sits on a throne. I know it sounds crazy to you, but you're going to find out sooner or later.

LYNCH: No, no. Sure, we all will. Sure.

KORESH: There are Seven Seals in the [unintelligible].

LYNCH: All right.

KORESH: The question that theology has overstepped, it never really opened that book, now that's what I've done.

LYNCH: Okay.

KORESH: It's your Bible, there are Seven Seals. Now, there—

LYNCH: Yes, sir.

KORESH: —are some things in that Bible that have been held as mysteries about Christ.

LYNCH: Yes, sir.

KORESH: Now, in the prophecies it says—

LYNCH: Let me—can I interrupt you for a minute?

KORESH: Sure.

LYNCH: All right. We can talk theology, but right now—

KORESH: Look, this is life, this is life and death.

LYNCH: Okay.

KORESH: —theology really is life and death.

LYNCH: Yes, sir, I agree with that.

KORESH: You see, you have come and stepped on my perimeter.

LYNCH: Okay.

KORESH: We will serve God first. Now, we will serve the God of the truth. Now, we were willing, and we've been willing all this time to sit down with anybody. You've sent law enforcement out here before.[1]

From those first moments of the raid through the entire fifty-one-day siege, Koresh's adamant conviction that "theology really is life and death" defined his approach to the government agents. What the FBI viewed as a complex Hostage/Barricade rescue situation drawn directly from their Crisis Management Program strategy manual, Koresh and the Branch Davidians saw as the beginning of the end of the world.[2] Although there was conversation back and forth between Mount Carmel and the government agents during the prolonged standoff, neither side proved willing or even capable of bridging the great gulf between those two very different understandings of the situation. The siege itself was marked by the same frustrating and fruitless clash of irreconcilable opinions that attended assessments of the character of Koresh. Whereas the faithful at Mount Carmel accepted him as a teacher, a prophet, and the Lamb of God, his opponents saw him as a con man, a poseur, and a madman. Whereas government officials considered the community members hostages, the Branch Davidians saw themselves as bound for salvation. The differences between those two worldviews were extremely consequential.

THE BATF RAID

The activities of Marc Breault and Rick Ross decisively shaped the original BATF investigation of the Mount Carmel community and influenced in turn the viewpoints of the FBI, Attorney General Reno, and President Clinton. The roots of their common outlook are clearly visible in the BATF agent Davy Aguilera's "Probable Cause Affidavit," which became part of the ill-fated search warrant signed on February 25, 1993, by Dennis Green, United States magistrate judge.[3] In his affidavit, Aguilera provides a chronological account of his investigation and reports that he began looking into possible firearms violations at Mount Carmel in the late spring of 1992. Much of his testimony is a technical discussion of the parts and procedures necessary for turning regular rifles into automatic weapons, the schedule of deliveries of parts and weapons to the group, and the circumstantial evidence that its members were indeed converting semiautomatic weapons to fully automatic without having paid the proper fees and followed the legal procedures for registration. What the public never understood was that the entire legal issue between the BATF and Koresh had to do with paperwork, fees, and registration, not possession of the alleged weapons and materials themselves. No matter how distasteful citizens might find such stockpiling of weapons, what the law forbids is clear: "[the] manufacture, possession, transfer, transport, or ship in interstate commerce [of] machine guns, machinegun conversion parts, or explosives which are classified, by Federal law, as machineguns, and/or destructive devices, including any combination of parts, designed and intended for use in converting any firearm into a machinegun, or into a destructive device as defined by Federal law, and from which a destructive device may be readily assembled, *without them being lawfully registered* in the National Firearms Registration and Transfer Record" (emphasis added).[4] Apparently Koresh had converted a certain number of weapons to a fully automatic capacity, which came out in the 1994 San Antonio trial of eleven Branch Davidians. However, even those weapons were not illegal; rather the violation was possession without proper registration.

Beyond these strictly legal matters, however, a broader and more subtly damning characterization of Koresh's "cult" is woven through Aguilera's account. The identification of the Mount Carmel community as a "cult" carries a self-evident force in Aguilera's testimony; he uses the term itself fourteen times in the affidavit, without any significant qualifications. More importantly, Aguilera, like many others, relied extensively on the reports of former members of the community. Aguilera states that he interviewed Robyn Bunds, Jeannine Bunds, Deborah Sue Bunds, Poia Vaega, Marc Breault, and David Block—all former members who had disapproved enough of Koresh and life at Mount Carmel to leave the group voluntarily. Their animus against Koresh decisively shaped Aguilera's expectations and opinions, and led him to discuss issues that were strictly outside his firearms investigation. Aguilera's affidavit covers several topics clearly not under the jurisdiction of the BATF. He includes stories of child abuse and reports of unconventional sexual practices within the community and also summarizes at some length efforts of the Texas Department of Human Services to investigate allegations of sexual abuse of young girls among the Branch Davidians. Though he fails to mention that the department did not find sufficient evidence to probe further, his introduction of the topic colors the rest of his statement; the taint of the child abuse allegations reinforces the suspicions of weapons violations. The same is true of the reports of the community's unconventional sexual arrangements from Robyn, Deborah Sue, and Jeannine Bunds, whose assertions also raise the specter of the power-mad, manipulative cult leader. Their primary function within the affidavit is to discredit Koresh so thoroughly that the circumstantial evidence concerning the fabrication of automatic weapons will seem much more compelling. Seemingly straining to collect damning evidence, Aguilera quotes an anonymous informant as saying that one Marshall Keith Butler, "a relative of the person who wishes to remain anonymous, is a machinist by trade, and is associated with Vernon Howell."[5] The apparent intent behind including this inconsequential fact is to establish that Koresh had access to people who could have fabricated the necessary parts for automatic weapons. However, the connection seems tenuous at best. Nevertheless, in the next paragraph Aguilera attempts to secure the link by dredging up Butler's criminal record: "The records of the Texas Department of Public Safety reflect that Butler has been arrested on seven (7) occasions since 1984 for unlawful possession of drugs. Two of the arrests resulted in convictions for possession of a controlled substance. Butler's latest arrest and conviction was in January 1992."[6] Aguilera's logic is clear: Butler was a convicted criminal; a criminal offense in one area implies criminal offenses in others; Koresh was "associated with" Butler; therefore, Butler helped Koresh fabricate automatic weapons. The implication that the Mount Carmel community was involved with illegal drugs, or at least drug users, is simply allowed to linger. In fact, the BATF later justified its requisitioning of U. S. military materiel for the initial raid by claiming that the Branch Davidian property housed a laboratory for manufacturing illegal drugs.[7] The effectiveness of Aguilera's strategy in the affidavit is indicated by comments of other law enforcement officials during the standoff and in the official Treasury and Justice departments' reports, which consistently intermingle accusations of firearms violations with allegations of child abuse and sexual improprieties.[8] He sets out with alarming clarity the expectation that the government forces will find themselves in conflict with a controlling, manipulative sexual deviate armed to the teeth. His report may well have strengthened the resolve of the BATF to move swiftly and surely against the group.

At no point does Aguilera include any interviews with current members of the Mount Carmel community, and he fails to mention that he refused to talk to Koresh by telephone on July 30, 1992, when gun dealer Henry McMahon had him on the phone in Aguilera's presence. Koresh told McMahon to tell the BATF agents to "come on out," and he would answer any questions.[9]

The BATF raid itself was code named Operation Showtime. Although BATF officials vehemently denied any connection, it is the case that the bureau was coming up for budget hearings on March 10, 1993, and allegations of sexual harassment made by female agents had been aired on the television program *60 Minutes* in January. Certainly, a well-executed raid against a dangerous "cult" of the type described in the *Waco Tribune-Herald* on February 27 would not hurt its image. It was unfortunate that such an array of factors was brought together in the first place: legitimate legal questions about weapons registration, charges of child abuse and polygamy, rumors of "brainwashing" and "mind control," and the BATF need to demonstrate its proper mission to enforce the law for the public good.

THE FIFTY-ONE-DAY SIEGE

The BATF requested the assistance of the FBI on February 28, a few hours after the shoot-out. Jeff Jamar, who became special agent-in-charge (SAC), was on the scene by 5:30 that afternoon as FBI negotiations and crisis management personnel were already arriving.[10] The FBI Hostage Rescue and SWAT teams had been called in, and by 5:00 P.M. on March 1, the very next day, at the request of the Treasury Department the FBI had taken full control of the situation and had set up a fully functioning command post.[11] It is important to bear in mind that the FBI agents called to the scene in these early hours had never heard of the Branch Davidians nor of David Koresh and had no idea of the unique situation they would face. FBI operating procedures included a Crisis Management Program, the goal of which is to preserve life and "minimize risks to all persons involved: hostages, bystanders, subjects, and law enforcement officers."[12] Accordingly, the Waco situation was officially defined as a complex Hostage/Barricade rescue situation, and a standard plan was implemented to coordinate the tactical (Hostage Rescue and SWAT) and negotiation components.

The problem with this definition, however, was that from the viewpoint of the Branch Davidians, there were no barricades or hostages, and no one needed rescuing. They understood themselves to be a religious community or *family* that had been brutally attacked, without provocation, by agents of the United States government. The FBI's entire emphasis was upon getting the Branch Davidians to "come out," to surrender to "proper authority," and thus to abandon and lose the only meaningful context for their lives—their home at Mount Carmel and their spiritual relationship with one another and with Koresh. They would not submit unless convinced that God had so willed it. One of the most insightful and honest paragraphs in the Department of Justice's own evaluation of the standoff, written by former Assistant Attorney General Edward Dennis, is his recognition of this very point, hidden in a footnote to his text: "Indeed, the "negotiations" are characterized as 'communicating' with Koresh or 'talking' to Koresh because the Davidian situation *lacked so many of the elements typically present in hostage barricade situations.* Koresh made no threats, set no deadlines and made no demands. Koresh and his followers were at Mount Carmel where they wanted to be and living under conditions that were only marginally more severe than they were accustomed to" (emphasis added).[13] The main volume of the Department of Justice report makes the same point in a somewhat different way. In discussing the March 8 videotape in which twenty-two Branch Davidian adults are interviewed inside Mount Carmel, it concludes: "Each person on the video—male and female, young and old—spoke in a calm, assured tone of their desire to remain inside, even after the experience of the [B]ATF raid only a few days earlier. Steve Schneider, who photographed the video and 'interviewed' the subjects, also speaks in a thoughtful, articulate manner on the video. The abiding impression is not a bunch of 'lunatics,' but rather of a group of people who, for whatever reason, believed so strongly in Koresh that the notion of leaving the squalid compound was unthinkable." [14] The FBI's initial strategy, according to the Department of Justice report, "focused on stabilizing the crisis situation, establishing a dialogue with Koresh and his followers, and gathering intelligence that might offer some insight into the motivations and intentions of Koresh and his sect." [15]

The question is, where would the FBI turn for this "intelligence"? How would they come to properly gain access to Koresh and his group? The two most readily available sources were the gossipy Aguilera affidavit of February 25 and the "Sinful Messiah" series that the *Waco Tribune-Herald* had begun to publish the Saturday before the BATF raid. Indeed, parts 3–7 of the story were rushed to print and published in a front-page story on Monday, March 1, just as the FBI were arriving in town. In one day the news had been flashed around the world with full details about this fanatical, dangerous, bizarre "cult" and its "wacko" leader, David Koresh. At the same time the FBI negotiators turned to its "experts." Dr. Park Dietz, professor of psychiatry and biobehavioral sciences at UCLA School of Medicine, arrived in Waco on Tuesday, March 2. The Department of Justice report reveals that upon his arrival he was handed "approximately 1000 pages of background material" about Koresh and the Branch Davidians. [16] Dietz was asked to develop a personality assessment of Koresh and to determine if he exhibited any possible mental disorders. From the conclusions Dietz reached, it appears that the FBI provided him with the unsubstantiated, negative, anticult propaganda assembled by the BATF, based exclusively on materials supplied by the Cult Awareness Network (CAN), the most prominent anticult group now active in the United States, and disaffected former members of the Branch Davidian group. Dietz returned to Waco on March 4 and the next day wrote a memorandum that unfortunately would dominate the perspectives of the FBI and other government agents for the duration of the siege. [17] He argued that Koresh was a psychopath and to appeal to the so-called rational aspects of his personality would lead to failure. He stated that Koresh had "antisocial and narcissistic personality traits that enabled him to become a master of manipulation." Dietz emphasized that Koresh would use "any ruse, pretext, trick, deception or force necessary to achieve his personal goals." He specifically made the point that "the experience of hearing the voice of God tell him to wait should be seen as a self-serving excuse for not keeping his promise." Dietz had had no contact whatsoever with Koresh, and these sweeping evaluations were based on his briefing papers provided by the FBI. It is also obvious to anyone trained in religious studies that Dietz's approach completely disallows the possibility of sincerely motivated religious behavior and is out of touch with the primary focus of the Davidian movement for the past fifty years, that of biblical prophetic interpretation. For the duration of the siege Dietz's essential perspective was echoed by the FBI spokespersons, particularly the agent Bob Ricks. Ricks's main responsibility was to handle the press briefings and to work with the negotiation teams. Ricks and his associates constantly portrayed Koresh as a lying, manipulating "punk" who thought he was God, abused children, had sex with minors, and "interpreted the Bible through the barrel of a gun." The official strategy of the FBI quickly become one of *manipulating the manipulator.* After all, they reasoned, if Koresh was first and foremost, a psychopathic "con man," then why not deal with him on that level? Dietz's wholly negative perspective was echoed by some of the other "experts" in their analyses. For example, Anthony Pinizotto, the forensic psychologist at FBI headquarters likewise concluded that "Koresh displayed psychopathic behavior, that he was a 'con artist' type, and that he had narcissistic tendencies."[18] In contrast, Dr. Di Giovanni, another psychiatrist consulted by the FBI, came to quite different conclusions. Apparently, he had been provided with better data from which to form an evaluation than Dietz. He visited Waco much later, March 27–29, and he was able to review the negotiation transcripts, as well as the videotapes, that the Branch Davidians had sent out of Mount Carmel the first week of the siege. Di Giovanni found no evidence that Koresh was actively psychotic, commenting that his speech patterns and logical expressions were quite normal. He also said he found no basis to conclude that Koresh's religious beliefs were "delusional," but that they appeared to be well grounded in his religious faith. This evaluation corresponds to that of the two seasoned attorneys, Dick DeGuerin and Jack Zimmerman, who are the only outsiders who spent extended time face-to-face with Koresh and Schneider during the siege. DeGuerin reported that Koresh was in touch with reality at all times, spoke in the most rational and normal way, and however "bizarre" his beliefs by conventional standards, he was certainly not a charlatan.[19]

The FBI constructed what they called a "coherent negotiation strategy," which had a number of interlocking and potentially contradictory components.[20] The negotiators hoped to drive a wedge between Koresh and his main assistant, Steve Schneider, as well as convince individual Davidians of the advantages of breaking from the group and coming out. Since all communications with Mount Carmel and the outside world had been severed, the twice-daily press briefings by the agent Ricks were primarily used to shape public opinion and manipulate the Branch Davidians inside, particularly to use psychology to get them to doubt Koresh's leadership. At the same time they tried to appeal to Koresh directly, arguing the advantages of exiting. They implied that his legal case was good, and that if he came out, he would be able to expand his message and gain many followers because of the wide publicity he had received. Finally, a "stress escalation" program was implemented to effect sleep deprivation, isolation, and group fragmentation. Electricity was cut off on March 12. Loud music, Tibetan chants, tapes of family members, and obnoxious sounds such as rabbits being slaughtered were played continuously during the night.[21] Floodlights were focused on the building while helicopters constantly flew over at low altitudes. The personal vehicles and other property of the Branch Davidians outside the compound were either moved or destroyed. The FBI later admitted that the negotiators felt that these tactical components of the FBI's strategy often conflicted with their own efforts. The Department of Justice report notes that "the negotiators' goal was to establish a rapport with the Branch Davidians in order to win their trust. As part of this effort, negotiators emphasized to Branch Davidians the 'dignity' and fair treatment the group would receive upon its exit from the compound. By contrast, the negotiators felt that the efforts of the tactical personnel were directed toward intimidation and harassment. In the negotiators' judgment, those aggressive tactics undermined their own attempts to gain Koresh's trust as a prelude to a peaceful surrender. . . . all of these actions were viewed by the negotiators as counter-productive to their efforts."[22] Agent Jamar was in charge of coordination of the tactical and negotiating efforts. Although he considered these factors, he ultimately decided to continue and even increase the pressure tactics as the days passed. He felt it was imperative to show the Branch Davidians that the government, not Koresh, was in control.[23] The FBI log shows that both Koresh and Schneider became increasingly combative, particularly around the middle of March when as a result of a decision to step up the harassment tactics, Jamar told the FBI negotiators to "get tough" and not allow any more "Bible babble" from Koresh.

In fact, this "Bible babble," as the FBI characterized it, was what both Koresh and Steve Schneider were most interested in. Dialogue was no problem from Koresh's point of view. In the 911 call, while the shooting was still going on, he said to Lieutenant Lynch, "We told you we wanted to talk" and proceeded to interpret the opening of the Seven Seals. For the entire fifty-one days, Koresh expounded on the Bible at length to negotiators, trying to convince them of his prophetic gifts of interpretation. The negotiation transcripts show that much of the time the FBI either talked down to Koresh or failed to seriously listen or fully grasp what he was trying to communicate. They were understandably unprepared to deal with someone who used the Scriptures on such a highly technical level. One of the FBI negotiators admitted to Phillip Arnold that some of them initially thought the Seven Seals of the book of Revelation, about which Koresh talked incessantly, were animals. In the transcript of the March 2 tape, the following conversation takes place between the negotiator "Henry" and Koresh:

HENRY: We can't let you die within the compound. If you're going to die, that's fine. That's God's will. But you need to come out so that the people can believe.

KORESH: Okay. Is that it?

HENRY: There are many, many people, millions of people, that heard you [the fifty-eight-minute taped sermon that had been played over radio that day]. You promised that you would come out immediately. Okay, you didn't come out immediately because you had to, to listen to God. He needed to talk to you. That's fine. Do not let this date go by because some of the people will fall by the wayside. You started something very big. We need to see this through.

KORESH: Do you have your Bible with you now, Henry?

HENRY: Yes.

KORESH: Can you turn to Psalm 18?

Koresh subsequently launches into a long and complicated explanation of the situation from his biblical perspective. It is clear in the transcript that negotiator "Henry" is not really following; he periodically answers only, "Um-hum," to Koresh's monologue. Finally, after more than an hour of Koresh's most intense efforts to impart his message, Henry interrupts him as he is quoting the book of Nahum from memory. On the second day of the siege, Henry is obviously already highly frustrated.

HENRY: Let's not talk in those terms, please.

KORESH: No. Then you don't understand my doctrine. You don't want to hear the word of my God.

HENRY: I have listened to you and listened to you, and I believe in what you say, as do a lot of other people, but the, but the bottom line is everybody now considers you David who is going to either run away from the giant or is going to come out and try to slay the giant. For God's sake, you know, give me an answer, David. I need to have an answer. Are you going to come out?

KORESH: Right now listen.

HENRY: Right now you're coming . . .

KORESH: "He that dasheth in pieces is come up before thy face: keep the munition." What's the munition? "Watch the way."

HENRY: One of the things, one of the things is I don't understand the scriptures like you, honestly, I just don't.

KORESH: Okay, if you would listen, then I would show you. It says here—it says here, "The chariots shall be with flaming torches." That's what you've got out there [referring to the tanks].[24]

This conversation reveals a clear case of miscommunication. Highly intelligent, Koresh is obviously not fooled by Henry's flattery or disingenuous statements that he "believes" what Koresh is saying and wants to see it spread to the world. On the other hand, from his perspective, Koresh is discussing matters of substance, particularly how the Branch Davidians view what is happening as the fulfillment of certain biblical prophecies. Although this dialogue offered the FBI a chance for fruitful communication, Koresh's interpretations went completely over the heads of the FBI negotiators, who were understandably put off by this approach. Koresh seemed naive in these matters. Unless he was speaking with someone from a Seventh-Day Adventist background, or one who otherwise had a technical interest in the complexities of biblical prophecy, most of what he said appeared nonsensical. Throughout the siege both Schneider and Koresh asked to talk to biblical scholars, specifically Phillip Arnold, whom they had heard speak on the radio. A survivor of the fire who was inside Mount Carmel during the entire siege, David Thibodeau reported that when Koresh received the Arnold-Tabor tapes discussing the book of Revelation on a technical level with him, he was elated, thinking that this might be the beginning of a fruitful dialogue with biblical scholars who would give his views a fair evaluation.

Even the four cryptic letters Koresh sent out a few days before the fire, which mostly consisted of a complicated web of biblical quotations, were coded messages reflecting the Branch Davidian perspective. To one trained in these texts, they are quite comprehensible. Unfortunately, in making their final assessment of the situation in the week before April 19, the FBI turned the letters over to anticult activist Murray Miron, professor of psycholinguistics at Syracuse University. Miron concluded the letters reflected "rampant, morbidly virulent paranoia," which is an interesting observation about the Bible itself since the letters are almost entirely quotations from the Old Testament prophets. As late as April 17, just two days before the CS gas attack on the property, the FBI asked Dr. Park Dietz for another evaluation. He concluded that "continuing to negotiate in good faith would not resolve the situation, because Koresh would not come out" and that "Koresh would continue to make sexual use of any children who remain inside."[25] This final memorandum, prepared by Dietz and given to Attorney General Reno, was apparently decisive in its impact.

From start to finish, with a few minor exceptions reflected in the sympathetic approach of some negotiators, the FBI played the role of the "adversary," the quintessential "outsider," and thus, in the Branch Davidian view, the prophetic "Babylonian" opposition to the people of God. The Davidians were trying to understand their situation in the light of biblical prophecies and according to God's will. The FBI's behavior served to confirm to them that this was indeed a war between the "sons of light and the sons of darkness." On the other hand, to the FBI, Koresh was a manipulating "con man" who, out of self-interest, would only respond to a "get tough" policy. Even if they were right in their estimation, the results were a disaster. Perhaps the dominant theme running through the Department of Justice evaluation of the entire episode is that no other course of action taken by the government would have substantially changed the outcome.[26] Edward Dennis, who was charged with the final assessment of the way things were handled, went so far as to say that speculation regarding the possibility that Koresh might have surrendered is "irresponsible" since further negotiations would have been fruitless. He asserted that there is no place for blame and that no gross errors in judgment were made by the government. In the final analysis, he said, the government simply had no way to deal with a man "who held himself to be God" and a group of "seemingly intelligent people who pursued a course of insanity and mass murder." [27]

Eleven surviving Branch Davidians were tried in federal court in San Antonio in early 1994 on charges of conspiracy to murder federal agents and on a number of lesser charges. Throughout the trial the representatives of the government evinced an unwillingness to take the beliefs of the Mount Carmel community seriously. Early in his remarks the prosecutor W. Ray Jahn asserts that "this is not a trial about religion." [28] But what he appears to mean is that their religion is illegitimate at best and, most likely, not religion at all. Concerning the defendants Jahn argues that "these were people who were followers of a man named Vernon Howell. They went to Mount Carmel, men, women and children, to follow this person." [29] Jahn appears to endorse the anticult stereotype of the enormously compelling and dangerously powerful "cult leader." However, in contrast Jahn does not also characterize the Davidians as cult members completely under Koresh's control and thus not responsible for their actions. During the trial both the prosecution and the defense freely scramble the purported inexorable logic of the anticult position when it suits their argumentative purposes. To admit that the defendants were thoroughly under their leader's power, of course, would have seriously weakened Jahn's case against them. Instead, Jahn contends that "the evidence is clear that everyone was there—was there because they chose to be. They weren't there because they were being held. They were there because they wanted to be." [30] Thus, whereas the cultbusters' stereotype served Jahn well in his description of Koresh as a monstrous force of evil, Jahn had to reject a related part of that generic portrait in order to make his case against the defendants. In so doing, he moved toward what we see as a much more accurate understanding of what Jahn himself called "the symbiotic relationship" between leader and followers, acknowledging that "if he doesn't have the followers he has no power." Jahn rejoins company with the anticult forces, however, by denying any religious legitimacy to the Mount Carmel community. He ignores both the Branch Davidians' deep roots in the Adventist tradition and the central place that Bible study had within the group. When he does address their theology, it is only to raise implicitly the specter of Jonestown. Jahn asserts in his opening argument that the evidence will show that "Koresh told these people his name was 'Death.' And, so, it's going to be a story about a group of men and women and, unfortunately, children, who traveled to a location named Mount Carmel to follow a man by the name of 'Death.' "[31] In his closing arguments, Jahn makes polemical comparisons between the fate of those who died at Mount Carmel and the mass death perpetrated by Hitler and Stalin, elevating Koresh to a level of evil far beyond that of Jim Jones. Furthermore, Jahn repeatedly sets Koresh in a nonreligious context. For example, he downplays the role that apocalyptic expectations played in the community's understanding of the February 28 raid. He promises the jury that "we will put a firearm in everyone's hands that's charged today. We will show that they were not mere biblical students there, but instead, that they took an active role in connection with this particular conspiracy."[32] The government's strategy in the trial displays a heavy reliance on the negative stereotype of "dangerous cults." The prosecution clearly endorses both the notion that the "cult leader" exerts an enormous and troubling power over the followers and the expectation that cults are prone to violence and murder. Only in its characterization of the followers does the government's case differ from the anticult portrait. If the government had embraced the conception that cult members are victims of some variation of brainwashing or coercive persuasion, it would of course have been difficult to convict them of conspiracy to commit murder. All responsibility would have remained with Koresh. Instead, the government prosecutors chose to emphasize that the defendants were acting on their own free will. That departure from the anticult stereotype indicates two very important things. First, it again calls into question the descriptive accuracy of the anticult position. Second, it clearly shows that to explain the behavior of cult members as the result of brainwashing or coercive persuasion is an *interpretive* option, rather than a description. As such, it tells us more about the particular commitments and values of the person interpreting than it does about the inherent nature of cult life. Thus, the government's prosecution of the surviving Branch Davidians, which was welcomed by anticult activists, has had the unintended effect of exposing once more the fatal weaknesses in the anticult position.

In representing their clients, the defense attorneys had to wrestle with a similar dilemma. It was tempting in many ways to lay all the blame on Koresh, especially since he was not there to speak for himself. Joseph Turner, who represented Ruth Riddle, went the farthest in that direction. Turner attempts to dissociate his client from any negative connotations associated with cult membership. He argues that "the evidence will show that the Government doesn't know Ruth Riddle. They know her only as another Branch Davidian in their indictment, another Branch Davidian to blame. But to the people who really know Ruth, she's a loving and caring woman. She's quiet and shy, naive but not violent. She is generous and giving, deeply devoted to God, obedient. She doesn't smoke, she doesn't use profane language. You wouldn't see her out here dancing at the country and western dance halls, but she's the perfect daughter that every mother and father would like their daughter to be like. This is not the rebellious daughter who runs off to join some ridiculous cult." [33]

In contrast to that portrait of pedestrian normalcy Turner juxtaposes Koresh, who was paradoxically at once "charismatic and persuasive" *and* "paranoid and delusional." [34] Ultimately, Turner concludes "It was David Koresh who should be held accountable." [35] Such a strategy, however, risks admitting doubts about the religious seriousness and sound judgment of the defendants. If the man whom they accepted as their teacher and prophet, in whom they put their faith and trust, could be established as paranoid and delusional, then doubts about their own judgment would logically follow. In an interesting turnabout, Turner verges on accepting more of the anticult argument than does the prosecution. By placing responsibility for whatever wrongs or evils occurred at Mount Carmel onto Koresh himself, Turner magnifies the power that Koresh exercised while he simultaneously exonerates his own deeply religious client. But like the prosecutor, Turner rejects an important part of the anticult position, denying any direct link between cult membership and violent acts, at least in the case of his own client.

Turner's statements illustrate both the polemical character and the malleability of the anticult activists' portrait of cults. Both defense attorneys and prosecutors felt free to pick and choose from among the defining characteristics of a "cult." Their choices were determined by their goals, specifically either the exoneration or the conviction of the defendants in the conspiracy trial. Since a portrait of the defendants as the passive victims of brainwashing or coercive persuasion would undermine the prosecution's case, the prosecutors emphasized instead that "they were there because they wanted to be." Conversely, when it served their purposes, the defense attorneys were willing to concentrate virtually all responsibility and blame for what went wrong in Koresh himself. Such different uses of crucial elements of the stereotypical "dangerous cult" suggest a much more malleable interpretive model than the anticult forces represent in their own publications and statements. In turn, its flexibility points attention away from questions about descriptive accuracy and allows its use by those with opposing goals. In the specific case of the trial, major elements of the anticult paradigm were employed by the prosecution to magnify the evil perpetrated by Koresh, increase the perception that the defendants were prone to violence, and secure their conviction on all charges. In the hands of the defense, components of the same paradigm were used to displace culpability from the defendants to their deceased prophet and teacher. The specific investigation of the Mount Carmel community by concerned citizens, the news media, and the government, both before and after the April 19 tragedy, reveals at least as much about the particular values, commitments, and concerns of the outside observers as it does about the group's religious beliefs and practices.

On February 26, 1994, following a seven-week trial, the jury rejected murder and conspiracy charges against all eleven Branch Davidians for their role in the bloody shoot-out. Two Davidians were acquitted of all charges and freed; two others were similarly acquitted but held for immigration violations; five were convicted of aiding voluntary manslaughter; another of possessing a grenade; and one of unlawful (that is, unregistered) possession of machine guns.[36] Attorney General Reno was obviously disappointed but characterized the jury's decision as "thoughtful," arguing that the verdicts contradict the attorneys' claims that the Davidians had acted in self-defense. "This clearly indicates that the killing of these four agents was not justified," she said.[37] On June 18, 1994, ignoring pleas for leniency from the defendants and even the foreman of the jury that convicted them, Federal Judge Walter Smith sentenced five of the Branch Davidians to forty years in prison for their roles in the shoot-out, fined them amounts ranging from $2,000 to $10,000, and ordered them to pay restitution of $1,131,687.[38] The others were sentenced to prison terms ranging from five to fifteen years and ordered to pay fines as well.[39] Some have said they would appeal; however, Livingstone Fagan rejects the entire judicial process as hopelessly unjust. In the opening lines of his recently completed manifesto, "Mt. Carmel: The Unseen Reality," he says, "In writing this book, I bypass the judicial process of appeal, and appeal directly to the good citizens of this nation."

SIX

The Wacko from Waco

As WITH NEARLY ALL NEW or unconventional religious groups, most people learned about David Koresh and the Branch Davidians from secondhand sources, particularly the popular news and entertainment media. The portraits of the Mount Carmel community in those sources quickly took on a remarkable uniformity, both because of the widespread influence of the series of investigative articles that appeared in the *Waco Tribune-Herald* at the time of the BATF raid and because of the media's broad sympathy for depicting the group as a strange and dangerous "cult."

THE "SINFUL MESSIAH" SERIES

The *Tribune-Herald*'s "Sinful Messiah" series is an influential example of how the Mount Carmel community and its teacher were widely interpreted. It also shows how most descriptions of the group in the popular media implicitly promoted the agenda of the anticult activists while at the same time discounting or denying outright the seriousness and even religiousness of the Branch Davidians. Because few people actually have any firsthand acquaintance with new religious movements, the electronic and print media played a crucial role in the dissemination of the dominant characterization of "cult" leader David Koresh and the Branch Davidian "cultists." The dramatic tales of former members fed the public's taste, and the media's corresponding need, for simple morality plays. By providing the public with a convenient interpretive shorthand, the characterization of the community as a "cult" unfortunately made it all too easy and attractive to deny Koresh and the other students of the Seven Seals of biblical prophecy their full and complex humanity. Koresh almost instantly became "the wacko from Waco" and an apparently inexhaustible subject for macabre humor; the Branch Davidians joined a long procession of vaguely amusing and slightly irritating American weirdos.[1] Unfortunately, sorting out the assertions and claims of former adherents of religious groups is much like trying to understand the breakup of a marriage by listening to the impassioned account of either former spouse.

The popular caricature of Koresh and the Branch Davidians might have remained only a minor annoyance to the group had it not contributed directly to the disastrous consequences of both the BATF raid and the final FBI assault. The widespread failure to take the religious convictions of Koresh and the other Davidians seriously, signaled by the facile adoption of the term "cult," contributed directly to their deaths. Since "cults" purportedly represent intellectual, moral, and spiritual aberrations, for many it is unnecessary, and even counterproductive, to delve too deeply into their teachings. Accordingly, the FBI brusquely dismissed the Branch Davidians' religious discourse as "Bible babble." Since "cults" represent a dangerous threat to the social order, it is necessary to oppose them with all the resources that the state can muster, including tear gas, SWAT teams, and tanks. Since "cult leaders" are power-mad megalomaniacs, no one should lament their passing and they alone should bear the blame for the deaths of their followers.

As soon as the BATF raid occurred, the "Sinful Messiah" series, the first installment of which had been published the day before, became the central source of information about Mount Carmel. For example, the *San Francisco Chronicle* reprinted the initial installment of the *Waco Tribune-Herald* series on March 1; the main *New York Times* story of the same day relies heavily on the *Tribune-Herald* account; and an edited version of the entire series was reprinted by the *Fort Worth Star Telegram* on March 3. The *Washington Post* and the *Chicago Tribune* were also indebted to the investigative work of Mark England and Darlene McCormick. Though the factual information presented in the *Tribune-Herald* series is important, its interpretation is of greater significance.

Several prominent aspects of the commonly used evaluative "cult" model are displayed in a March 2 article in the *Washington Post*. Its central concern is the possibility of mass suicide, and the specter of the nine hundred deaths at Jonestown is raised in the third paragraph. The events in the Guyanese jungle in November 1978 had confirmed the most acute fears of anticult activists, and Jonestown was used to maximum polemical effect. Since Jonestown, even to raise the question of mass suicide, as the *Post* article does twice, is to suggest that the community in question is a self-destructive "cult." The article reinforces its portrait of a violence-prone "cult" led by a dangerous madman by invoking the example of Charles Manson in its final two paragraphs. The comparisons in the *Post* deny religious legitimacy to the Branch Davidians and especially to Koresh by assimilating them to the anticult activists' generic image of a destructive "cult." Other elements of the anticult stereotype reinforce that stance. For example, the *Post* describes the process of affiliation with the Branch Davidians by relying on former member Robyn Bunds's March 1 press conference. Like many quoted in the "Sinful Messiah" series, Bunds presented herself as a passive victim of the "cult" and its leader: "Describing herself as once 'brainwashed' by the sect, she said, 'You are not exposed to the outside world.' "[2] Former members of the community, antagonistic Seventh-Day Adventists, suspicious psychologists, and wary academics are well represented in the *Post*'s article, but Koresh and the Branch Davidians are conspicuously absent. Because they do not have the opportunity to represent themselves in the *Post* article, others' hostile interpretations of their beliefs, practices, and motives become the only readily available "facts" about the group. As a result, the agenda of the anticult activists is implicitly advanced by both the tone and substance of the reporting.

The dominance of the anticult stereotype is most clearly revealed in the discussion of Waco on television programs, particularly on the talk shows that invite audience and listener participation. For example, the March 10 *Donahue* show united many of the major figures in the public discussion of the Mount Carmel community. The program initially focuses on the testimony of Kiri Jewell about her life with them. The host clearly sets the tenor of the discussion in his opening remarks. Addressing Kiri Jewell, Phil Donahue notes that "you lived in this compound from age six till about a year and a half ago. You're no longer in the cult because your father successfully sued your mother for custody and you made your way to freedom, we might say, a year and a half ago."[3] In addition to depicting life at Mount Carmel as a form of incarceration, Donahue progressively teases out other prominent elements of a "destructive cult." Concerning Koresh's marathon Bible study sessions, he observes, "So the pressure was enormous, wasn't it? He was a very controlling person."[4] As the program proceeds, Kiri Jewell, her father, and her aunt are joined by Marc Breault. About Breault's own involvement with Koresh, Donahue invokes the anticult activists' dictum that no one is immune to the attraction of cults. Donahue asks, "As you look back on it now, Marc, just give us a read, how a bright young guy like you could get sucked in on this. We have to understand this. Apparently, most of us are at least seducible. I don't—I don't know. How'd it happen, Marc?"[5] Donahue's question, of course, includes the premise of the passive, easily seducible self. Comments from audience members and callers reinforce the general trend of the discussion. Their remarks presume that all "cults" are the same and that the worst is to be expected of them, including something "like Jim Jones did to his followers."[6] Or, as another audience member vividly admits, "Usually when I hear about cults, I hear about sacrificing animals and babies."[7] Rick Ross, identified simply as a "cult expert," completes the picture by drawing the various elements together. Ross paints a sharply contrasting portrait of the good people at Mount Carmel and what happened to them at the hands of their evil leader: "Many of the people in this compound are highly-educated, very intelligent people, many very idealistic, very loving, very kind. And the fact is that it's sad to say, but we're all vulnerable to the kind of mental manipulation that this man pulled on these people and he has exploited them, dominated them and taken control of their lives."[8] Reprising the sentiments of many other anticult activists, Ross characterizes Koresh's power in the community in this way: "The group's got an absolute leader. Everything the leader says is right, is right. Whatever he says is wrong, is wrong. And if you think for yourself, you're rebellious, you're evil and your family is, too."[9]

The same polemic surfaced on the March 25 *Oprah Winfrey Show*. The guests on that program were Jeannine and Robyn Bunds, a contingent of defectors from Australia including Peter and Lisa Gent and Michelle and James Thom, and Balenda Ganem, the mother of David Thibodeaux (Thibodeaux was living at Mount Carmel during the entire siege and escaped from the fire on April 19). Tellingly, the program also featured Timothy Stoen, the former attorney for the Reverend Jim Jones and the Peoples Temple. Of Stoen, Winfrey claims that "if anyone understands the cult mentality, it's my next guest who was Jim Jones' right hand man."[10] Her comments show again that well before the final cataclysm at Mount Carmel the events at Jonestown were being used as an interpretive model for Koresh and the Branch Davidians. Despite the prescient comment of Balenda Ganem "that using images of Koresh and Mount Carmel side by side with Jones sets up a very negative expectation,"[11] Winfrey and most of the other guests endorse Stoen's assertion that there are "definite similarities" between the two situations. In Winfrey's presentation, the parallel to Jonestown is but one of the prominent marks of a "cult." Throughout the program she introduces most of the other hallmarks of a "destructive cult." For example, her purpose in doing a show titled "Inside Waco and Other Cults" "was to—if we in any way could influence anybody else from becoming involved in something like this we would like to, you know, encourage people not to give over your power, especially your mind, to somebody else." [12] As that comment suggests, the interpretation of affiliation as brainwashing is a cornerstone of Winfrey's understanding of the danger posed by "cults." Winfrey also elicits from Ronald Enroth, a prolific Christian anticult writer, another central tenet of the anticult position, that "the people who are in cults don't realize that they're being manipulated." [13] All blame, therefore, belongs to the authoritarian "cult leader."

Even when a guest declines to accept her interpretation of events, Winfrey refuses to abandon the negative stereotype. This exchange with Jeannine and Robyn Bunds is revealing:

WINFREY:	So one of the questions, I—I think, we all want to know, is—we all see this as a cult. We all see this as somebody who's taken over your mind.
MS. JEANNINE BUNDS:	We didn't.
WINFREY:	Did you, at the time, recognize that—that it was indeed a cult and that you were being brainwashed?
MS. JEANNINE BUNDS:	No. I didn't feel that way.
WINFREY:	You just believed him.
MS. JEANNINE BUNDS:	I didn't feel that way at all.
WINFREY:	Do you believe he's evil?
MS. ROBYN BUNDS:	I believe he's lost his mind.
WINFREY:	Mm-hmm.
MS. ROBYN BUNDS:	I don't believe that he's evil.
(APPLAUSE)	
WINFREY:	So what kinds of things would you have to go through there within the—the cult compound?
MS. ROBYN BUNDS:	Well, life is pretty normal, I mean—to me, anyway, when I was there.
WINFREY:	As cults go.

MS. ROBYN BUNDS: Yeah, as cults go.

WINFREY: Yeah.[14]

Faced with testimony that does not support her preconceptions, Winfrey simply ignores it and plows ahead. Even though Robyn Bunds's comments are more to her liking, Winfrey also imposes on them a construction not initially intended. It is obvious that Winfrey thinks she knows precisely what a cult is, precisely how individuals come to join a cult, precisely what life is like within a cult, and precisely what the dire consequences are likely to be. The guests are there simply to illustrate the host's beliefs. Her convictions are apparently so strong that any evidence that challenges them is simply brushed aside. As with the *Waco Tribune-Herald* series and most other coverage of the Branch Davidians in the popular media, Winfrey's program implicitly depends upon and reinforces the image of "cults" promoted by the anticult activists.

The anticult viewpoint completely pervades the relatively democratic medium of the televised talk show. Host, guests, studio audience, and viewing public alike share a common perception. Neither the host nor the audiences subject the guests' claims to skeptical scrutiny. If anything, the comments from both the studio and home audiences are even more alarmist and less attentive to differences than those of the host. In the world of the television talk show all "cults" are the same, all "cultists" are under the control of manipulative madmen, and all are very dangerous. Even when dissident voices do emerge, as in Larry King's May 11 interview with Stan Sylvia, a former resident of Mount Carmel who retained his conviction in Koresh's teachings even after the fire, they receive a hostile reception from the audience. Concerning Sylvia's claim that he had no evidence whatsoever that his daughter had been violated by Koresh, the show's first caller initiates this exchange:

IST CALLER: My question is, this gentleman, I believe, has blinders on to believe that his daughter was not violated. What proof does he have that she was not?

MR. SYLVIA: Well, what makes people— What proof does anybody have that she was?

1ST CALLER: You don't think that Mr. Koresh, in his sick, demented mind, could have—

MR. SYLVIA: He wasn't sick and demented, sir.

1ST CALLER: That's an opinion, sir.[15]

The next caller is equally suspicious of Sylvia's positive account of life with Koresh:

2ND CALLER: Yes, how do you think that you have any grounds—
that being the guest and his ambulance-chaser friend
[Sylvia's attorney, also on the show]—to be suing the
government for—I mean—you're suing the wrong individual. This was—[16]

Though the calls lessen in their animosity after the first two, they are uniformly suspicious that anything good could have happened at Mount Carmel. While the callers do not make any startling new contribution to our understanding of the events at Waco, they do testify to a pervasive, deep-seated, and not fully articulated suspicion and fear of "cults" among the viewing public.

Talk-show callers are far from the only ones to express that fear and suspicion. In an April 20 ABC News special, "Waco: The Deci-sion to Die," Peter Jennings opines that "certainly there is a determi-nation in many quarters to know more about cults and the power which cult leaders exercise on the vulnerable."[17] Reflecting on the previous day's deaths at Mount Carmel, Jennings asserts that "there are other cults in the United States. This tragedy upon tragedy may be a lesson, in part, for the future."[18] The program makes extensive use of footage filmed by an Australian crew for Martin King's report on *A Current Affair* and provides its own voice-over. In a few short sentences, the correspondent Tom Jarriel clearly states his evaluation: "The power of this madman, as told by three who broke away from the cult, were his skills at manipulation and mind control, powerful skills, frightening skills."[19] To support that characterization Jarriel cites the Melbourne musician James Thom's recollection of his first meeting with Koresh: "When I first saw him, I thought, 'This guy is the spitting image of Charles Manson.' This guy manipulates minds the same way that Charles Manson did."[20] The comments of Jennings, Jarriel, and Thom are designed to identify cults in general and Koresh in particular as problematic, suspicious, and menacing to both individuals and society. In a revealing decision that mimics the way that the "cult problem" is treated throughout the popular news media, toward the end of his broadcast Jennings turns to "experts" for help: "We said at the beginning of the program that we were going to try to understand cults a little better, and we're joined this evening by two people who can give those of us in the country who know so little a better insight into what is going on. . . . Cynthia Kisser, who's the executive director of the Cult Awareness Network . . . [and] Vicki Fallabel, who is a former member of the Branch Davidians."[21] Once more, a self-professed opponent of all "destructive cults" and a critical former member are presented as experts without even a cursory examination of their motivations or qualifications. Apparently, none of the surviving members of the Mount Carmel community were deemed capable of providing testimony about their own beliefs and practices. From the outset, the choice of experts stacks the deck against Koresh and the Branch Davidians. Kisser's and Fallabel's comments only confirm the predetermined interpretation. Kisser appeals to the hallmarks of a "destructive cult" that she has frequently described in other settings. Using both therapeutic and legal models, she asserts that at Mount Carmel, "you did not have people actually understanding and making decisions about what was in their best interest. You had people who were under control. You had people, in a sense, who were ill, who had a mental illness, and who made decisions not fully thinking. They basically have had their human rights violated, whether the public understands that or not."[22] Kisser's final comment echoes Ronald Enroth's judgment that "cult" members are being manipulated whether they realize it or not. In both instances, opponents of "cults" claim a special, superior insight into the dynamics of those religious movements; those who disagree are simply deluded or have been manipulated into ignorance. Even more distressing than the specific events at Mount Carmel, in Kisser's view, is that "this cult is not that different from a lot of cults that are out there. It just happened to have collided with law enforcement, and I think that's the real tragedy here."[23] Explicitly making a keystone connection of the anticult position, Kisser also offers a preview of what the anticultists' arguments will look like after Waco. Addressing Jennings, she notes that "you yourself recalled Jonestown in '78. Now we're in '93 with Waco."[24] Fallabel's analysis is much more succinct. In response to Jennings's query about whether there might be a lesson "for all of us" in the horrific demise of the Mount Carmel community, she cautions, "Think for yourself. Don't let someone else take over your mind."[25]

Although ABC's "Waco: The Decision to Die" doesn't have the lively inclusiveness of shows like *Donahue, Oprah,* and *Larry King Live,* it nevertheless reaffirms the interpretive framework that dominates the discussion of "cults" on those programs. For Peter Jennings, his fellow correspondents, and the experts on whom they rely, "cults" conform to a single pattern developed and aggressively promoted by cultbusters and by the aggrieved former members who provide them with so much polemical ammunition. As in most newspaper and newsmagazine accounts, on television voices from within new or unconventional religious movements are only faintly heard. When they do break through, the voices of faithful and committed participants in "cults" are greeted with overwhelming hostility. Something about the intensity of their commitment, even more than the purportedly strange forms that it may take, seems to unsettle the American public.

Perhaps the television production that had the single greatest impact on the American public perception of Koresh and the Branch Davidians was the ABC made-for-television movie, *In the Line of Duty: Ambush in Waco,* which was aired on Sunday evening, May 23, 1993.[26] The film had been scripted and was well into production while the Waco siege was still in progress. An exact replica of the Mount Carmel complex had been hastily constructed south of Tulsa,

Oklahoma. By any measure it was a sensationally dramatized hybrid of fact and fiction, essentially the King-Breault book and the *Waco Tribune-Herald* series, with a strong pro-law enforcement BATF message thrown in for good measure, presented at prime time. The *Dallas Morning News* called it "an effective and engrossing tale with a vivid performance by Tim Daly as David Koresh."[27] The Davidians come across as cowering zombies, powerless under the control of their charismatic leader. At no point is any aspect of their biblical or theological motivation portrayed, nor a more natural and human side of their personalities. The filmmakers tried to make a strong case for the necessity of the BATF raid, which contradicts in many places the Department of Treasury's own official evaluation of its actions. This television movie, airing as it did barely one month after the April 19 fire, powerfully cast in stone the images, for millions of Americans, associated with the names Waco or Koresh. The movie was aired a second time, also at prime time, in June 1994, the very week that stiff sentences were meted out to the Branch Davidians convicted in the San Antonio trial.

POPULAR BOOKS ABOUT WACO

In public discussion the dominance of a single representation of "cult" activities testifies not only to the success of the anticult activists but also to most people's deep-seated fears about the loss of personal autonomy, profound unwillingness to question fundamental personal and social values, and suspicions about intensely held and acted upon religious convictions. Those attitudes are evident as well in the first wave of popular books about the events at Mount Carmel. Many who served as important sources for newspapers, newsmagazines, and television programs, particularly Marc Breault and Rick Ross, again contribute crucial "information" and shape the perspectives of the first popular books about Waco.

The titles of those books, and particularly their extensive subtitles, are sufficiently evocative of their authors' viewpoints. Tim Madigan of the *Fort Worth Star-Telegram* wrote *See No Evil: Blind Devotion and Bloodshed in David Koresh's Holy War.* Clifford L. Lindecker, a former reporter and the author of several "true crime" books, titled his account *Massacre at Waco, Texas: The Shocking True Story of Cult Leader David Koresh and the Branch Davidians.* The former police reporter Brad Bailey and the Texas journalist Bob Darden borrowed the title *Mad Man in Waco: The Complete Story of the Davidian Cult, David Koresh and the Waco Massacre* from a rock-and-roll song that Koresh had actually written about George Roden, his onetime rival for leadership at Mount Carmel. Marc Breault and Martin King's *Inside the Cult: A Member's Chilling, Exclusive Account of Madness and Depravity in David Koresh's Compound* should be included with the other three. As the titles suggest, these books evince great sympathy for, and sometimes the direct influence of, the anticult movement. Striking departures appear only on occasion.

Mad Man in Waco is the most distinctive of the four books, if only for its often flippant tone. Discussing Koresh's biblical interpretation, Bailey and Darden paraphrase Carly Simon: "Vern's so vain, he probably thinks this book [the Bible] is about him."[28] They are suspicious of all certitude, particularly any pronouncements that claim to be religiously grounded. In their eyes, "Stumbling around down here as humans is always dangerous. But the biggest danger of all may lie in *thinking* that you know. *Thinking* that you are not blind; *thinking* that you *can* see."[29] The lesson that they draw from Waco "is the danger of allowing yourself to be deceived."[30] No one, in Bailey and Darden's estimation, was more deceived about his own character and abilities or more deceptive in his promises than Koresh himself: "He had managed through the magic of words to invert, subvert, and pervert the concept of God, twisting it into something that pushed down rather than pulled up. Yes, David Koresh had a secret, and it wasn't the Seven Seals. The secret was that he was a child molester, pure and simple. A vampire of the innocent, the sucker of virgin blood. David Koresh was a thing of darkness. David Koresh was a cockroach, albeit a big one, waiting for the lights to go out so he could paddle his feet in our butter and scuttle his claws on our bread. David Koresh was a cockroach that ran over children's faces while they slept, to deposit his filth in their dreams."[31]

Unlike Breault and King or Lindecker or Madigan, Bailey and Darden extend their skepticism to the negative stereotype of the cult leader. They find no evidence of a keen manipulating intelligence in Koresh. Instead, they maintain that "David Koresh personified the deepest, darkest, dreariest, and smuggest narcissism-induced stupidity."[32] Bailey and Darden are even harder on those who embrace the image of the omnipotent "cult leader," and they make some sharp observations about the motivations behind such decisions and their connections to the news and entertainment media's thirst for simplified drama: "We like to imagine our antagonist, the Man in the Dark Tower, as a 'malevolent *genius*' or a 'mastermind,' because this is more televisable, more watchable—than the truth. The FBI and the [B]ATF also played to this mythic stereotype, for even more obvious reasons. He is a master manipulator, they said. That's why we can't get him out. He is a sociopath who is capable of the direst of deeds. He is a mastermind, a shrewd, calculating adversary who will stop at nothing. In short the FBI wanted to say: Who else would have held us at bay for nearly two months? But this is not how Vernon Howell *was:* It was how he *wanted* to be."[33] Bailey and Darden's equal-opportunity skepticism maintains the familiar negative evaluation of Koresh, but it also recognizes more complexity in events. In their view no one is without blame. They gleefully disclose how the FBI manipulated the "news" to serve its own purposes, unmasking its press conferences as "rigged events with three major agendas: Controlling the media; controlling public perceptions of David Koresh; and further inflaming the already beleaguered cult leader."[34]

In *Mad Man in Waco* all are subject to Bailey and Darden's criticism. Their relatively evenhanded scrutiny of the motives of Koresh, the Davidians, the press, and the government agencies avoids the simplistic play of good versus evil that marks the anticult stereotype. They make an important move toward acknowledging the complex interplay of values, commitments, self-justifications, and legitimations that marks any "cult" controversy. Their overriding psychological interpretation, however, is much less satisfying, just as their sarcasm is eventually annoying. For Bailey and Darden, Koresh was self-evidently a narcissist, which explains virtually everything. Bailey and Darden never make a sustained case for their diagnosis, and they never attempt to explain why Koresh's "narcissism" was expressed in the particular religious idiom that he chose. Their book is less an explanation than a caricature of a complicated personality. Though they do not invest Koresh with overwhelming power, his character and role as leader are the unvarying focus of their analysis. Description of Koresh's personality is presumed sufficient explanation for the motives and actions of all the other members of the Mount Carmel community. As a result, the other members remain ciphers. Thus, although Bailey and Darden are suspicious of certain elements of the anticultists' position, their interpretation reinforces such a view.

CRITIQUES OF THE DOMINANT IMAGE OF "CULTS"

In the coverage of the events at Waco, the unrelievedly negative treatment of "cults" by daily newspapers was echoed by weekly news magazines, the electronic media, and popular books. Even specialty publications like *Soldier of Fortune* magazine, which bitterly criticizes the BATF and stalwartly defends the Davidians' right to arm themselves, describes the Branch Davidians as "a bizarre doomsday religious cult."[35] Furthermore, the few exceptions underscore the dominance of the negative evaluation of "cults" in public discussion. In *The Christian Century*, Michael Barkun observes that "both the authorities and the media referred endlessly to the Branch Davidians as a 'cult' and Koresh as a 'cult leader.' The term 'cult' is virtually meaningless. It tells us far more about those who use it than about those to whom it is applied. It has become little more than a label slapped on religious groups regarded as too exotic, marginal or dangerous. As soon as a group achieves respectability by numbers or longevity, the label drops away."[36] Similarly, the *New York Times* ran an editorial piece by Karl Meyer that surveys the prominence of sectarian movements in American history and cautions that "if a 'cult' is a group of believers devoutly attached to a leader claiming divine inspiration, then the most respectable religions share the same cradle. And more than anywhere else, America was a magnet for 'cults.' "[37] That position, however, seems largely to have been ignored in the *Times*'s reporting about the continuing standoff at Mount Carmel.

The issue of the media's largely uncritical adoption of anticult stereotypes was raised in a 1985 article on "The 'Cult Beat' " in the *Columbia Journalism Review*. Leslie Brown notes how the term is heavily value laden, how it is of limited descriptive usefulness, and how it might also expose a reporter to charges of libel. Brown also endorses the recommendation made by several "cult beat" reporters that the term be avoided entirely. That suggestion, however, seems not to have found broad favor. Indeed, the media's largely unreflective advancement of the anticult activists' position helped to create a climate in which the actions of both the BATF and the FBI were viewed as not only defensible but also necessary. When the term "cult" is used to describe any religious group, it becomes easier to view that group as religiously illegitimate, psychologically and physically harmful to its members, and dangerous to society.

While publications such as *Soldier of Fortune, American Hunter,* and *Guns & Ammo* spent little time considering the fine points of Koresh's teaching, they did review the original warrant for the search of Mount Carmel with extraordinary care. This statement from *Soldier of Fortune* combines an easy acceptance of the Branch Davidians as a "cult" and an excoriation of the BATF: "The fuse on the Waco disaster was lit by the knuckle-dragging pariah of pistol-packing feds, the Bureau of Alcohol, Tobacco & Firearms ([B]ATF). The [B]ATF alleges a laundry list of legal violations by cult members, some over which the [B]ATF even has jurisdiction. The main allegations involve illegal machine gun conversions. But nothing—*nothing*—anyone in the cult might have done comes even close to justifying what the government did to them."[38]

The incident at Mount Carmel also drew criticism from a number of "patriots" who saw the siege as the illegitimate intrusion of the government into the private lives of its citizens. Many communicated through flyers and other broadsides, through computer networks, and through the American Patriot Fax Network (APFN).

This last group produced some of the most detailed reporting about the 1994 San Antonio trial of eleven surviving Branch Davidians on charges of conspiracy to commit murder. Participants in the fax network were also instrumental in circulating audio- and videotapes, which included the original 911 call from Mount Carmel on February 28, Koresh's fifty-eight-minute statement delivered on tape to the FBI on March 2 and broadcast on KRLD radio that day, and interviews and statements by surviving Branch Davidians. Similarly, extensive discussion of Koresh and Mount Carmel has taken place on the Internet, the most macabre artifact an exhaustive file of Waco jokes and parodies.

Equally critical of the government role at Waco was Linda Thompson, an Indianapolis attorney. Thompson has produced two videotapes in which she claims to present hitherto-suppressed evidence about the government's actions at Mount Carmel on April 19. One videotape, "Waco: The Big Lie," is based on raw news footage downloaded from satellite transmissions. It attempts to show how the tanks used to gouge holes in the wooden structure of the Mount Carmel center actually were equipped with flamethrowers that started the conflagration. Thompson's videotapes have generated a considerable amount of discussion, much of it negative, but they have provoked more careful scrutiny of the official government accounts of the causes of the April 19 fire.[39]

The Committee on Waco Justice, an ad hoc citizens group based in Washington, D.C., also kept alive through a variety of means both a skeptical inquiry into what transpired at Mount Carmel and the memory of those who died there. The committee conducted extensive personal investigations, letter-writing campaigns, and memorial vigils, and it produced an exhaustive report, *The Massacre of the Branch Davidians: A Study of Government Violations of Rights, Excessive Force and Cover Up,* written by Carol Moore. However, the cumulative effect on public opinion of critical and skeptical examinations of the siege at Mount Carmel has been slight.

Some of the most effective criticism of the negative view of "cults" came from the eleven surviving Branch Davidians charged with conspiracy to commit murder, among other things. From the beginning of the trial, the defendants were keenly aware that the prosecution's characterization of their religious commitments could have a very damaging effect on their defense. In a pretrial motion, the defendant Paul Fatta petitioned to have use of the word "cult" prohibited in court. The *Waco Tribune-Herald* reported that "Paul Gordon Fatta had objected to the word, saying it carried a 'negative and dangerous' connotation, according to papers on file in federal court. Fatta's lawyer, Mike DeGeurin of Houston, said the government should 'not be allowed to use derogatory terms to describe the defendants or the faith it is alleged they shared.'"[40] Fatta's petition was part of a broader, and ultimately unsuccessful, defense effort to purge the court proceedings of a series of terms that expressed negative evaluations of the Mount Carmel community, in part by conforming it to the generic anticult characterization of a "dangerous cult." That strategy met with only limited success. The *Tribune-Herald* recorded the presiding judge's decision:

> After jury selection, Smith ruled on whether terms like "cult," "compound," "Ranch Apocalypse," "Mighty Men," and "Branch Davidians" could be barred from testimony. Smith denied the motions except for the term "Ranch Apocalypse." Smith agreed it has a negative impact. The term will only be allowed if the prosecution can prove the defendants ever used it. Smith had already denied a December motion to bar the word "cult" from proceedings. Defense attorneys argued that the terms have negative connotations and were never used by the defendants to identity themselves or their Mount Carmel home. "When you add this together, and keep throwing it in front of the jury, it tarnishes us," Rosen [the attorney for Kevin Whitecliff and Livingstone Fagan] said. . . . Smith said words like "compound" are neutral. He remarked that even the Kennedy family's home has been called a compound. He also noted that the term has been used to describe Mount Carmel "one zillion times by the media." . . . Attorney Joseph Turner, who represents Ruth Ottman Riddle, said the defense wanted to ensure that the jury isn't swayed by such terms. "They don't want the jury to make up their minds based on some semantic distinctions and labels," he said.[41]

Such pretrial maneuvering directly reflects some central issues in the broader discussion of "cults" in American society. The defendants and their attorneys clearly felt the sting of the negative characterizations of the beliefs and practices of the Branch Davidians. The defendants feared that such negative images would impede their ability to represent themselves effectively in court, because a jury willing to see their religion as a "cult" and their home as a "compound" might be more inclined to believe that they conspired to commit murder. Judge Smith did display some sensitivity to their dilemma by limiting the admissibility of "Ranch Apocalypse" as a name for the Mount Carmel center. By admitting "compound" on the grounds that it had been used so frequently by the media, however, Judge Smith did not take full account of how the description of Mount Carmel as a "compound" was associated with the negative depiction of a "cult." Despite the judge's comparison, the repeated use of the term "compound" in the press hardly conjured up images of the Kennedy family's palatial seaside estates. Instead, the dominant image of Mount Carmel was that of an armed camp.[42] Thus, the term was directly linked to the anticult assertion that any cult was a potential Jonestown, dangerous and prone to violence. Ruth Riddle's attorney, Joseph Turner, was correct to assert that the choice of a descriptive vocabulary for Mount Carmel also implied a specific interpretive framework and that a particular term could well sway the jury in its deliberations.

Though the defense was unsuccessful in its pretrial motions, several of the attorneys returned to the issue of negative stereotyping in their concluding remarks at the trial. For example, Paul Fatta's representative, Mike DeGeurin, asserts that "the government has said and the touchstone to their entire case is, that David Koresh taught these people and they, like zombies, were following him, that, 'The [B]ATF are going to come and raid us, and we need to kill them, or we need to kill federal agents in order to go to heaven.' That's the kind of idea they want somehow for y'all to pick up, calling us a 'cult,' calling us everything they can think of to dehumanize. Remember, these people are the survivors. These people gave up everything for their faith. They were sin free or trying to be.

To them judgment day is near."[43] Rocket Rosen, representing Kevin Whitecliff and Livingstone Fagan, sounds a similar note: "That's what this case is about. It's about people who lived in that home who the [B]ATF and now the prosecutor thinks are weird, weird because they had the guts enough to follow their convictions and travel and leave their friends and their schooling and their home and their jobs, because they wanted to better themselves. No, the government wants you to believe that they are the enemy."[44] Throughout the pretrial arguments and the trial itself, the defendants and their attorneys displayed a keen sense of the implications of the characterization of the defendants as "cult" members. Their arguments kept before the jury and the court the difficult task of evaluating the actions of the defendants on the basis of the specific evidence, rather than through the invocation of the stereotypical image of a "cult."

CHALLENGING THE STEREOTYPE

The influential picture of a "cult" as under the control of an omnipotent leader who determines every move of its members, even provoking them to violence against both others and themselves, is fundamentally flawed. Among other things, it rests on a misunderstanding of charismatic leadership, a misconception of the process of conversion, and a distortion of the similarities between the Peoples Temple and other new religious movements.

Anticult activists have every right to speak their minds, and they typically do espouse generally accepted values, such as the importance of the nuclear family and of personal autonomy. But other voices need to be heard. Disgruntled former members and professional anticult workers offer distinctive perspectives on new religious movements on the basis of their personal experiences, but up to the present their interpretations of "cults" have overwhelmed all other viewpoints. A prime case remains the decision of England and McCormick of the *Waco Tribune-Herald* not to base their conclusions on the less critical observations made by Barbara Slawson and

Jeannine Bunds about their own encounters with Koresh. England and McCormick's reliance on the testimony of antagonistic defectors from Mount Carmel was the earliest indication of how such testimony would come to color the judgments about the Mount Carmel community in the popular media, the BATF, and the FBI.

England and McCormick's espousal of the anticult position represents a choice of perspective, rather than a simple description of the facts, as two remarks from their own articles demonstrate. Barbara Slawson had two granddaughters in the Branch Davidians and had herself been a member when the group was under the leadership of Ben and Lois Roden. When Lois Roden invited her to the Mount Carmel center in 1984 to hear the teaching of her protégé, then known as Vernon Howell, Slawson was singularly unmoved. She tartly recalled her reaction, "At one time I wondered if he put something in the water. Why do they think God gave them brains if they're going to listen to someone and let him make all their decisions?"[45] If Howell was indeed using "traditional mind control techniques" at that time, they were obviously not universally successful. Slawson's comments show that resistance and rejection were real possibilities. The testimony of Jeannine Bunds is even more pointed and refers to a later period in Koresh's career. She and her husband, Donald, were early supporters of Koresh in California. Donald was living at Mount Carmel on the day of the BATF raid but had left the grounds early that day and remained outside for the entire siege. In California, the Bunds family purchased a van for Koresh's use and eventually purchased a home where he and other members of the community could stay while they were in the state. Robyn, their daughter, was initially much less taken with him than were her parents, and she even left home for a time to escape the religiously charged atmosphere. Eventually, Robyn experienced a significant change of heart and became a member of the Texas community and subsequently one of the leader's wives in the "House of David," the term Koresh used to refer to his collective family. Later, her parents also took up residence in Texas, and Jeannine herself ultimately joined the wives. This development was sufficient to shake Robyn's faith and to hasten her departure from Mount Carmel. Her mother, however, provided a poignant and complicated account of her own feelings in an interview that she gave England and McCormick:

> Even now I don't hate him. Even after all he's done to my family. It's hard for me. I've seen both sides of him. He can be nice. He cares about people, or at least he seems to . . . I do have feelings for Vernon. Sometimes they overwhelm me. But all my life, this has been my daughter, my baby, my doll. . . . Because of this, I really lost my husband [who stayed in the group]. So what did I accomplish? I just sit back sometimes and it feels like I've been hit by a bomb. I think I should have done this; I should have done that. But it's too late for me. It's too late for my family. It's been blown to smithereens. . . . I'm over 21, intelligent. I could have walked at any time. I chose to stay. He doesn't keep you. You can leave. What you have to understand, though is he keeps you by emotion. When you're down there, it's all so exciting. You don't know what he'll come up with next. I guess everyone is looking for Utopia, Shangri-La. You don't want any problems. It wasn't all bad times, you know. The people in this are great. They'll give you the shirt off their back. They're nice, like everyone else in the world. Except they believe this.[46]

Despite ample opportunity, Jeannine Bunds didn't place the responsibility for the dissolution of her family, the strain of her relationship with her daughter, the radical change in her material circumstances, and the evaporation of her fondest hopes at the feet of Koresh. Whereas she admitted that some of his actions were manipulative, she acknowledged that she was a willing participant. Although she had a vivid appreciation of the unfortunate things that befell her and her family, Jeannine Bunds still saw much to admire in the kindness and generosity of her former coreligionists. Though she might have been tempted to absolve herself of any responsibility for what transpired, she was able to assert that she "chose to stay."

Implicit in Bunds's comments is a very different model of the processes of joining and leaving new or unconventional religious movements. Its outlines and presuppositions become clear in contrast to the model presumed by anticult activists and by most former members. The stories of cultbusters like Rick Ross and of former Davidians like Marc Breault have at their core an image of a passive self at the mercy of virtually irresistible forces. Bunds and Slawson, however, envision an active self that makes its own choices and decisions.

Had England and McCormick considered the possibility that many Branch Davidians had actively, consciously, and intelligently chosen to join the group, or if they had balanced the reports of defectors with serious analysis of the beliefs of continuing members of the community, their investigative report would have looked rather different. They may, for example, have trained a more skeptical eye on the testimony of former members and asked more pointed questions about their motivations. Convincing the authorities and the public of the threat to society posed by Koresh played as powerful a legitimating role for the apostate Marc Breault as convincing people of Koresh's prophetic status when Breault was still a member of the group. Breault's opposition to Koresh became an essential element of his postdefection identity; it enabled him to forge close personal relationships and to create through them a semblance of the intense community life that he had once enjoyed at Mount Carmel. His opposition to David Koresh gave Breault's new life direction and meaning, just as his acceptance of him as an inspired prophet once did. Breault was not simply a disinterested observer. His rejection of Koresh was carefully considered and firmly founded on his own understanding of the Bible, and his concern for the welfare of the friends he left behind was heartfelt. But the more powerful Breault could make Koresh seem, the more courageous and necessary Breault's campaign would appear. The same holds true for the other former Branch Davidians whose stories figure less prominently in the *Tribune-Herald* articles. Apostates tend to be keenly aware of the social processes that shaped their identity and beliefs while they were members of the group and strikingly oblivious to the similar processes that shape their postmembership identity and beliefs. Even when their opposition to their former community is principled, as Breault's clearly is, the reports of former members need to be carefully scrutinized. Similarly, the statements about the group from professional anticult workers like Rick Ross may be evaluated in light of the financial and ideological stakes that they have in cultbusting.

If England and McCormick had taken their interpretive cue from Jeannine Bunds instead of Marc Breault, their series would likely have focused on the difficult and complicated choices that both members and former members of the Mount Carmel community had made. They might have produced a thorough inventory of reasons both for joining and for leaving the community and a reasoned assessment of the dangers it may have posed for its members, for Waco, and for the world. They might also have explored in much greater detail what could have led married members to sanction Koresh's sexual liaisons with their wives, because, as one member put it, of "what they were going to accomplish in the kingdom."[47] They might, in sum, have taken the reasoning, explanations, and self-justifications of the remaining Branch Davidians just as seriously as those of the defectors. Indeed, one of the most pernicious effects of branding the Branch Davidians a "cult" is that it effectively silenced those within the community. Since the nature and dynamics of a "cult" are purportedly well known, patient accumulation and sifting of the evidence appear scarcely necessary. Labeling takes the place of analysis. The term "cult" brings with it a ready-made interpretive framework, fully constructed out of past experience with other such groups.

Challenging the widely accepted position of the anticult activists is not likely to be either an enjoyable or immediately rewarding task. If the experience of the Branch Davidian Stan Sylvia on *Larry King Live* is any indication, those who profess to see rationality, moral character, and spiritual insight in someone identified as a "cult leader" will be exposed to harsh criticism. So will those who see adult "cult" members in most instances as independent decision makers who have consciously determined to join particular groups as a result of their own spiritual interests, idealism, and deep commitment to seeking the truth. Similarly, those who fail to see any "cult" as a potential Jonestown run the risk of being accused of blindness to the numerous dangers posed by such groups. For example, Cynthia Kisser of CAN argued that "the belief that the tragedy was an isolated incident" was a common misconception about the events at Mount Carmel.[48] Academics who challenge the monolithic view of a "dangerous cult" or who reject the blanket explanation of conversion to "cults" as a result of brainwashing or mind control will be accused of being "misguided," "erroneous," or even of "condon[ing] human rights abuses,"[49] as Nancy Ammerman of Emory University, one of the Justice Department's consultants, has been. But the stakes are high in the contemporary discussion of "cults." At times, as at both Mount Carmel and Jonestown, lives may hang in the balance. If the anticult activists are right, "cults" constitute a pernicious threat to American society on the same scale as the contemporary plagues of drug use, AIDS, and gang violence. If participants in "cults" and their defenders are right, not only personal freedom but also ultimate salvation are at stake.

The superficial strangeness of many "cults" and their sometimes striking difference from what most Americans recognize as religion provides all the more reason for treating them carefully and respectfully. In our view that attitude is best served by the painstaking effort to capture the compelling logic of a particular group's self-understanding and religious view of the world, the powerful attraction it exerts upon certain people, and the abiding sense of peace or satisfaction that many members claim to experience as a result of their affiliation. We have tried to exhibit the logic of Koresh's religious system in chapter 3 and to explain some of its allure for those who joined the Mount Carmel community in chapter 2. But for an outsider to take another's religious commitment seriously does not necessarily mean either that the outsider will approve or agree with it or view it as "just as good as" any other. Tolerance and relativism are not the same thing. One can and, we believe, should be tolerant and respectful of differences while still making judgments according to one's own perspective and commitments. It should be possible to take the religion of Koresh and the Branch Davidians seriously while still withholding the right to make judgments about that religion. The widespread adoption of the stereotype of a "destructive cult" makes it very difficult to accept any "cult" as a religion and as a result makes it very difficult for "cults" to be treated as religions in American public discourse. The consequences of that general attitude have often been disastrous for both individuals and religious groups.

THE "CULT" LEADER

The popular coverage of the Mount Carmel community focused narrowly and consistently on Koresh himself and repeatedly made him out to be "the wacko from Waco." That was due not simply to Koresh's status as teacher and prophet. Opponents of "cults" often attribute virtually superhuman powers to the leaders of such groups. A recent CAN brochure lists seven "marks of a destructive cult": mind control, charismatic leadership, deception, exclusivity, alienation, exploitation, and a totalitarian worldview.[50] CAN sees the "cult" leader as deceiving followers and controlling their minds so that they become alienated from all others outside the group and can be exploited for the totalitarian leader's personal gain. What is missing in that picture is any sustained consideration of precisely how such leaders acquire their extensive power. It is most often portrayed as simply an inherent personal characteristic, though some religious opponents of "cults" suspect demonic influence.[51] Typically, however, the leader's power to influence and control is presented as a given. That attribution implies a strategy of exoneration designed to relieve all "cult" members of any personal responsibility for their actions. Since "cult" members are victims of mind control, the leader, who is actually controlling them, is responsible for what they have done. Blame, power, and responsibility are concentrated in the leader in equal and impressive amounts.

That concentration on the leader, however, represents a naive misunderstanding of the social dynamics of charismatic leadership. In both popular and scholarly discussion, the use of the term "charisma" to refer to a quality of certain leaders has its roots in the work of the influential German sociologist Max Weber, who identified three "ideal types" of legitimate authority. The first, legal authority, rests "on a belief in the 'legality' of patterns of normative rules and the right of those elevated to authority under such rules to issue commands."[52] During the seige at Mount Carmel, legal authority was asserted and exercised by the BATF, FBI, and other law enforcement agencies. Weber's second type is traditional authority, which depends "on an established belief in the sanctity of immemorial traditions and the legitimacy of the status of those exercising authority under them."[53] The claims of Lois Roden to succeed her husband, Ben, and of George Roden to succeed his mother as the leader of the Branch Davidians expressed the conviction that authority was located solely within the Roden family and was to be conveyed traditionally from one member to the next. Weber's third type is charismatic authority. Unlike the previous two, it is founded "on devotion to the specific and exceptional sanctity, heroism or exemplary character of an individual person, and of the normative patterns or order revealed or ordained by him."[54] Koresh, who asserted his unique ability to decipher the message of the entire Bible hidden in the Seven Seals in the book of Revelation, claimed charismatic authority. His conflict with George Roden represented, among other things, a clash between charismatic and traditional authority.

Despite misunderstandings of Weber's intentions, it is clear that he saw charisma as embedded in a social relationship. The dilemma is simply put. An individual may feel or claim to be charismatic, but unless that charisma is recognized and acted upon by others, it can have no meaningful social consequences. As Weber writes, "It is recognition on the part of those subject to authority which is decisive for the validity of charisma."[55] In accurate usage, "charisma" is always a relational term. The anticult image of the virtually omnipotent leader completely ignores that relational character. Only by disregarding the extent to which a would-be charismatic leader is evaluated by potential followers can the anticult characterization of the dangerous "cult" leader be maintained. In a Weberian perspective, the story of Waco cannot be the story of Koresh alone. It is not the story of how his magnetic, mesmerizing, and deranged personality exerted a powerful and virtually inexplicable hold on the minds and hearts of a uniform group of followers. It is instead the story of the gradual elevation of Vernon Howell into a position of preeminence in the Mount Carmel community through an extensive series of interactions that in many cases confirmed and enhanced his charismatic authority. Vernon Howell only gradually became the David Koresh that the world encountered after the BATF raid. Along the way, he lost as well as gained followers. The most telling example of that process was Koresh's controversial New Light revelation. It strengthened the bonds between Koresh and those able to accept the difficult new religious message, but it simultaneously proved to be the breaking point for those who could not approve what they saw as a self-serving innovation or worse. The defection of people like Marc Breault in itself undermines the image of Koresh as an all-powerful leader. In fact, the very existence of numerous former members of "cults," especially those who have not been deprogrammed, represents a powerful counterargument to those who would exaggerate the power of the "cult" leader.

The standard anticult argument not only misconstrues the source, nature, and extent of the leader's power and authority, it also reduces the other members of the group to anonymity. As one observer pointedly commented about the great majority of presentations of the events at Mount Carmel, "The major actors were Federal officials and David Koresh. The people in the compound were forgotten, erased."[56] A more accurate understanding of the charismatic leadership Koresh exercised among the Branch Davidians would also have the salutary complicating effect of restoring the diverse individual members of the community and their idiosyncratic motivations to the discussion. Followers play a crucial role in constructing and maintaining any leader's charisma. To a significant degree the followers actually make the leader.

The Seventh-Day Adventists who made up most of the population of the Mount Carmel center had long been prepared by both tradition and personal experience to expect a living prophet among them. Moreover, Branch Davidians were familiar with the prophetic careers of the Rodens, Victor Houteff, and Ellen G. White. Nearly all community members were of course quite familiar with biblical prophecies concerning the end of time and particularly with the enigmatic symbolic imagery of the book of Revelation; for them the Bible was to be studied for the direct messages that it contained about their current situation and what awaited them in the near future. People who encountered him evaluated Koresh's claims to leadership in light of their specific experiences, traditions, and commitments. Some people who shared many of his religious ideas and practices remained unmoved by his personality. Others who wouldn't have been able to distinguish a Branch Davidian from a Texas Ranger were beguiled by the man and his message, and in some cases by his music, and eventually joined the group. Even among those with very similar backgrounds Koresh did not have a uniform effect. The anticultists' picture of the omnipotent "cult" leader posits in advance that only those personal testimonies that fit a preconceived notion of "cult" dynamics will be accepted at face value whereas all others will be dismissed as evidence of brainwashing or coercive persuasion.

The image of an all-powerful "cult" leader does everyone a disservice. When it is used as the basis for anticult activity, the "cult" problem is oversimplified, distorted, and ultimately trivialized. Individuals may indeed suffer harm in new religious movements, just as they do in mainstream religions and in many other social groups. To identify the leader as the sole source of that harm robs the other participants of their integrity, seriousness, individuality, and responsibility. Focusing all blame on the leader is an undeniably effective strategy of absolution for the followers, particularly when the deceased leader cannot reply to accusations. But it raises serious and complicated questions about the nature of human volition that cannot be solved by invoking the simplistic explanation of either "brainwashing" or the marginally more sophisticated "coercive persuasion." If there is a "cult" problem in our society, and if anticult groups are to address it effectively, they need to develop a more accurate understanding of how authority is gained and used in new religious movements.

When the image of the irresistible "cult" leader is used as the basis for "news," the public is misinformed. By extracting individual leaders from their specific networks of social relationships, news reports can magnify the leader's power, exaggerate the influence over the other members of the group, and create concern and fear within segments of the populace that are highly unlikely to come into contact with the leader in question, let alone find either the message or the messenger attractive. The discussion of Koresh and the Mount Carmel community in newspapers, newsmagazines, and on television typically presented them as evidence of a social problem. But if the anticult stereotype of leaders is substantially flawed, the conclusion that "cults" constitute a social menace needs reexamination. Careful investigators may well find abuses of power, threats to personal autonomy, and needless suffering experienced by some people in some religious groups outside the mainstream. But it is a large, and as yet unjustified, jump from that evidence to the conclusion that "cults" as such constitute a dire threat to American society.

When the anticultist's characterization of "cults'" serves as the basis for legislative attempts to control or outlaw such groups, as in a recent initiative in Illinois, it makes for unjust law (see chapter 8). Legislators end up attempting to maintain untenable distinctions between acceptable and unacceptable forms of religion in order to appease a vocal minority and without clearly perceiving the potential effects of such legislation on all of their religious constituents. Moreover, such legislative efforts are based on a questionable interpretation of the First Amendment of the Constitution. According to the Yale law professor Stephen Carter, "The metaphorical separation of church and state originated in an effort to protect religion from the state, not the state from religion. The religion clauses of the First Amendment were crafted to permit maximum freedom to the religious."[57] That reading of the First Amendment also suggests that the anticult activists' call for early government intervention in the affairs of "cults" directly contradicts both the spirit and letter of the Constitution.

SEVEN

The Cult Controversy

THE TREATMENT OF THE siege at Mount Carmel in the electronic and print media revealed the pervasive influence of those who see "cults" as dangerous and troubling movements in America today. Many anticult workers, like Marc Breault, speak out of deep personal concern for loved ones who have, in their eyes, involved themselves in harmful situations, and their opposition is principled. Others lack such direct personal experience and focus on the existence of "cults" as a sign of serious ills in American society. For many years, anticult activists have been very successful in bringing their concerns before the general public. They had, in effect, constructed an interpretive framework for Koresh and the Branch Davidians well before the final events at Mount Carmel took place.

THE ANTICULT MOVEMENT AND WACO

Since the mid-1980s, led by the efforts of CAN, various loosely related groups and individuals have worked hard to stigmatize many new or alternative religious movements. Those groups branded "cults" are portrayed as pervasively negative influences in American society, particularly on unsuspecting adolescents and young adults,

The Mount Carmel buildings before the BATF raid on February 28, 1993. Approximately 130 people lived on the property at the time, including 43 children. By April 19, 1993, 80 Branch Davidians were dead, among them 21 children.
© Bobby Sanchez/Waco Tribune Herald/SYGMA

David Koresh (*left*) with Branch Davidian Clive Doyle, late 1980s. This photo was taken on one of Koresh's trips to Australia.
© Elizabeth Baranyai/SYGMA

Steve Schneider, Marc Breault, Elizabeth
Baranyai, and Sherri Jewell, Waco, 1989. This
photo was taken shortly before Breault and
Baranyai, his wife, broke with the group.
Schneider functioned as Koresh's chief confidant
during the siege. He and Jewell died in the April
19 fire.
© Elizabeth Baranyai/SYGMA

Cyrus Koresh, oldest son of David and Rachel
Koresh. Cyrus and his two sisters, Star and
Bobbie Lane, died in the fire with their parents.
© Elizabeth Baranyai/SYGMA

Floracita Sonobe with her daughter Angelica. Sonobe and her husband, Scott, died in the fire. Angelica and her sister, Crystal, were sent out by Koresh during the siege and survived.
© Ian Manning/SYGMA

Anita, Sheila, Lisa, and Wayne Martin, Jr., in 1988. Their father, Wayne, a graduate of Harvard Law School, was a leader in the Branch Davidian community. He made the 911 call on February 28, just after the BATF assault, pleading for the shooting to stop. He and the four of his children pictured here died in the April 19 fire. His wife, Sheila, and three younger children exited during the siege and survived.
© Ian Manning/SYGMA

The initial BATF raid on the Mount Carmel
Branch Davidian community, February 28, 1993.
Just after 9:00 AM, 76 armed agents stormed the
property in what was called a "dynamic entry."
Gunfire broke out on both sides. Four BATF
agents and six Branch Davidians died; many
more were wounded.
© Rod Aydelotte/Waco Herald Tribune/SYGMA

A wounded BATF agent being transported from
Mount Carmel during the initial February
BATF assault.
© Rod Aydelotte/Waco Herald Tribune/SYGMA

The stills on this and the following page are taken from two videotapes made inside Mount Carmel by the Davidians in February 1993, a week after the initial BATF raid. These tapes were intended for public viewing but were never released by the FBI. On the tapes about two dozen Branch Davidians speak about their lives, their current situation, and their beliefs. A wounded Koresh also appears, introducing his children and wives. Everyone pictured here died in the April 19 fire: (*top*) David Koresh and his two-year-old daughter, Bobbie Lane; (*middle*) Alison Monbelly, British citizen; (*bottom*) Scott Sonobe.

Everyone pictured here died in the April 19 fire: (*top*) Rosemary Morrison and her daughter Melissa, age 6, British citizens; (*middle*) Judy Schneider holding daughter Mayanah, age 2, and showing her right index finger, which was wounded in the February 28 raid; (*bottom*) Audry Martinez, age 13.

The final day of the siege, April 19, 1993. At 6:00
AM the FBI used M-60 tanks to insert CS gas into
the Mount Carmel building. Around noon a fire
broke out, which quickly consumed the building.
74 Branch Davidians died; nine escaped.
© Rod Aydelotte/Waco Herald Tribune/SYGMA

Aerial view of the ruins of the Mount Carmel
property a few days after the fire.
© Steve Reece/Waco Herald Tribune/SYGMA

Clive Doyle, who was acquitted of all charges in
the 1994 trial, now provides leadership for the surviving Branch Davidians in Waco, Texas. Here he
is seen with his mother, Edna Doyle, on the day of
his release from custody. His daughter, Shari, age
18, died in the fire.
© Morris Goen/SYGMA

Livingstone Fagan being taken into custody. He
and 10 other Branch Davidians were charged with
conspiracy to commit murder and other related
crimes. All 11 were found not guilty of the conspiracy charge. However, five, including Fagan, were
sentenced to 40 years for aiding voluntary
manslaughter. Fagan still maintains his innocence.
© Rod Aydelotte/Waco Herald Tribune/SYGMA

and, more recently, on senior citizens.[1] As a CAN brochure puts it, "A serious problem exists in our society as a result of the emergence of groups, popularly called 'cults,' using mind control (undue influence) and unethical means to recruit and retain followers. Association with these groups can be harmful to followers and disruptive to families, friends and society."[2] Participants in the anticult movement typically see themselves as proponents of critical thinking, defenders of personal autonomy, supporters of the traditional nuclear family, public-spirited citizens, and guardians of fundamental human rights. Organizations like CAN, the American Family Foundation (AFF), the Council on Mind Abuse (COMA), and others see their mission as raising public consciousness about "destructive cults." In an early flyer CAN presented itself as "a national, non-profit corporation founded to educate the public about the harmful effects of mind control as used by destructive cults."[3] Similarly, COMA provides the following self-description:

> COMA informs people about the deceptive recruitment and indoctrination techniques used by the cults.
>
> COMA holds lectures and classes for corporations, schools, and universities, as well as community and religious groups.
>
> COMA promotes the study of mind control techniques.
>
> COMA produces radio and television programs on the subject of mind control.
>
> COMA publishes literature about cults and cult techniques for public circulation.
>
> COMA counsels families who have lost members to the cults.
>
> COMA provides an information service for people to check an organization's possible cult affiliation.[4]

Anticult groups often have overlapping membership and rely on the same small group of psychologists, lawyers, and journalists for their intellectual legitimation. For example, psychiatrist Robert J. Lifton's *Thought Reform and the Psychology of Totalism* has become a canonical text for "cult" opponents. Its discussion of brainwashing in China has provided a keystone in their argument that certain religious groups exercise undue influence over their members through a process of "mind control."

In their literature and public statements cultbusters rely on a generic portrait of a dangerous "cult" that simultaneously blurs the characteristics of different groups and tars all of them with the worst attributes of any one. The effect of that homogenization is to exaggerate greatly the power and influence of any specific group and to overstate wildly the vulnerability of individual citizens. COMA warns that "everyone is susceptible" and that "most new recruits are totally unaware of the manipulation being employed even at the first meeting they attend."[5] The way in which Koresh and his followers were consistently portrayed in the popular media is one measure of the extent to which the anticult activists have succeeded in their mission.

The viewpoint of the anticult movement has gradually come to dominate discussions of new and alternative religious groups not only in the popular media but also in law enforcement organizations,[6] and even in many primary and secondary schools. For example, another anticult group, the Citizens' Freedom Foundation, alerts "educators, students, and parents" that "cult abuse" constitutes a problem as threatening as alcohol, drugs, and sex. The group counsels concerned citizens to

1. Inform local school boards of this problem.
2. Advocate for "cult awareness" programs in your curriculum at middle and high school levels.
3. Encourage school authorities to mandate workshops for guidance personnel and "family life" instructors to include skills needed by students to avoid destructive cult involvement.
4. Promote any community awareness programs *anywhere* that can expose the deceitful, illegal recruitment techniques used by destructive cults.[7]

Much of the information disseminated about "cults" by their critics, however, comes not from personal experience but from various secondhand sources, which have been accepted unquestioningly by cult opponents eager to buttress their own position. Concerning the dramatic accounts often featured by the popular media, David Bromley and Anson Shupe observe that "despite the fact that many of the new religions maintained a high profile in their witnessing/fund-raising activities, few Americans had knowingly encountered their members in any other context. Most of what the average citizen 'knew' about 'cults,' therefore, was obtained by stories reported by the media."[8] The dominance of a single perspective in most public discourse has almost completely excluded those of neutral or sympathetic outside observers and, most important, of members of new religious groups themselves. Since "cult" leaders are psychologically unstable, motivated by greed or lust or both, and power crazed, what citizens in their right minds would look to them for legitimate religious insight? Since members are passive dupes brainwashed by their manipulative teachers, what sensible people would look to their lives for examples of commitment, idealism, and spiritual honesty? Since the "cults" themselves constitute pernicious attacks on all that we value and hold sacred, what else should we do but oppose them at every turn and eradicate them when necessary?

A few examples of what anticult activists said about the events at Mount Carmel illustrate their typical form of argument. A week after the BATF raid, Cynthia Kisser of CAN asserted that "cults" constitute a deadly social problem. Summoning up parallel images of addictive and toxic substances, fatal diseases, and virulently antisocial behavior, she revealingly argued that "if we can educate about the dangers of drugs, AIDS and gangs, we can provide important information about cults."[9] She claimed that far from being an isolated aberration, "groups such as Koresh's Branch Davidians are certainly not a new phenomenon. And the real story is not that this violence has occurred, but that there are many other groups in our society that could turn to such dangerous behavior."[10] That danger is proportional to the degree of control that such leaders exercise over their followers. In Kisser's view, "Many cults were formed by leaders with a lust for power, a willingness to cross the bounds of ethical and moral behavior to satisfy that lust, and a knowledge of how to use influence techniques (some call them mind-control techniques) to control others in a bid to satisfy that lust."[11] Kisser's position was echoed by her colleague Patricia Ryan on the day of the destruction of Mount Carmel. Ryan is the daughter of Representative Leo Ryan, who was murdered by members of Jim Jones's Peoples Temple during a fact-finding mission in Guyana in November 1978. She is one of the founders of CAN and served as its president at the time of the Waco siege. Taking the events at Jonestown as a model for all cults, Ryan asserted that "it's all in the hands of the leader. The people are under his control. Whatever the leader asks you to do, you do it. Including suicide, including murder."[12]

Opponents ascribe other ills to "cults" as well. In addition to their tendency toward violence and their destruction of personal autonomy by placing unchecked power and authority in the hands of the leader, Kisser argued that "cults" also compete unfairly against legitimate businesses by employing what amounts to slave labor and that they also "undermine the democratic process by voting in solid blocs."[13] In keeping with CAN's self-definition, Kisser's solution is education. She stated that "we can teach individuals how to think critically and how to ask the right questions so that they know what they're truly joining." The issue, for her, is one of human rights. Through their deceitful practices "cults" deprive potential members of their right to know the truth; "cults violate constitutional rights, destroy the family and exploit the weak," and thus threaten the integrity of American society itself.[14]

Immediately after the destruction of the Mount Carmel center, Kisser observed that "these situations keep coming up over and over and we never seem to learn that we have a serious cult problem. What happened in Waco isn't surprising, but it's very tragic."[15] Kisser's lack of surprise is connected to her espousal of a uniform image of a "cult" that includes a megalomaniacal leader, brainwashed victims, and an inherent propensity for violence directed both against those within and outside the group. If the Branch Davidians had fit this description of a "cult," then the outcome would not have been surprising. During the early days of the standoff, Kisser had argued that a massive campaign of public education was urgently needed. After Waco, however, Kisser envisaged an expanded role for the government as well. In the *Waco Tribune-Herald*'s February 27, 1994, retrospective on Mount Carmel, Kisser promoted the concept of early governmental intervention in cult affairs: "To not do that now is to ignore the rights of people who get wrapped up in cults and those affected by cults as well, including communities like Waco. . . . It's something that wasn't done after Jonestown, and if we don't do something now, something like the tragedy in Waco will, no doubt, happen again sometime in the future."[16] Kisser lamented, however, that despite all the publicity given to Koresh and the Branch Davidians, the anticult cause is scarcely more prominent in the public consciousness one year after the BATF raid on Mount Carmel than it was before February 28, 1993. She observed that "Mount Carmel didn't do a whole lot to help us deal with this problem in terms of advancing awareness of the mental health, human rights and public safety issues for the long term."[17] Despite her lament, it seems clear that Waco has become a model to the public of the destructive nature of such "cults."

Kisser's comments in particular show a sophisticated self-understanding among anticult activists that testifies both to their growing skill in presenting their argument to the public and to the impact of the legal and public relations setbacks that their cause has suffered at the hands of new religious movements themselves. Kisser professed deep concern about human rights and the public good, not just the fate of an unfortunate few who "get wrapped up in cults." She presented the "cult" problem as having profound implications for the social, political, and economic life of the nation. She carefully steered away from such controversial topics as deprogramming, which many in her camp now style "exit counseling" and whose direct relevance is restricted to relatively few citizens, and instead associated "cults" with problems that are widely acknowledged to plague American society. If the country needs, she implied, a War on Drugs, a War on AIDS, or a War on Gang-related Violence, then it surely needs a War on Cults. Kisser and the other cultbusters occupy the front lines in that war, and she contended that only by increasing dramatically the number of recruits can the war be won. The alternatives, in her view, are terrible to contemplate. There will be more Wacos, more Jonestowns, because "these situations keep coming up over and over." Only intensive action by individuals and the government offers any hope of avoiding such tragedies in the future.

In addition to associations like CAN and COMA, there is another highly influential wing of the anticult movement, the evangelical Christians. Two of the major organizations are the Christian Research Institute (CRI) and Watchman Fellowship. Although they lack the direct political and social influence in mainstream establishment circles of a group like CAN, their grassroots efforts are quite effective. The most conservative groups define "cultism" as "any deviation from orthodox Christianity relative to the cardinal doctrines of the Christian faith," which includes all forms of Judaism, Hinduism, Islam, and just about anything else.[18] Both CRI and Watchman Fellowship appear much more sophisticated in their analysis. For example, Watchman Fellowship states that it "endorses freedom of religion in both thought and expression . . . [but] is compelled to exercise its freedoms to expose questionable doctrines and abusive or manipulative practices and to offer spiritual alternatives in the form of traditional Christian faith."[19] Their resource guide shows that they attempt to expose such groups as the Mormons, the Jehovah's Witnesses, Christian Scientists, the Unification Church, the Family, the Worldwide Church of God, and the New Age movement. Their agenda is a strong mix of standard conservative Christian apologetics with the typical concerns about brainwashing and manipulation associated with the popular notion of "cults." Still, a clear definition to identify which group deserves the label "cult" seems a problem. Kenneth Samples of the CRI asks, "How dangerous are these groups? Quite often we don't find out how dangerous they are until after an event like Jonestown or Waco draws our attention to the seriousness of extremist groups. It is difficult to determine how dangerous an extremist group is until former members make it known. A key to finding out is to examine the doctrines, practices, and how the group views its leader. Countercult groups such as the Christian Research

Institute can be helpful in determining the threat of a particular group."[20] Samples then lists six characteristics that might be considered "dangerous" in a group and if found, would alert those concerned that it required monitoring:

1. Total commitment to the leader's interpretation of the Bible
2. Belief that the leader can do no wrong
3. Belief in continued revelation that can contradict previous revelation
4. Strong belief that we are in the times prior to the end of the world
5. A "we-they" mentality
6. Pressure to conform to the dictates of the group[21]

The great irony is that these six sentences describe Jesus and his early followers so precisely. From this commitment to "Christian tradition," it seems acceptable to claim to be God and to have the ultimate and only truth, to break up families, and to be an "extremist" if, in fact, you *are* the true Messiah. However, groups like CRI and Watchman do make genuine efforts to be evenhanded and factual in their analysis of the teachings of nontraditional groups. For example, the special issue of the *Watchman Expositor* that Watchman Fellowship published on Waco contains some of the most accurate analysis of the biblical teachings of the Branch Davidians that has appeared in print. However, the theological agenda of such conservative Christian groups presents them with a genuine problem. Since their own doctrinal convictions compel them to believe that anyone who denies the fundamentals of the Christian faith is by definition working on the side of Satan and is deceived, it is hard for them to be tolerant in the name of religious freedom. Exposing error as they perceive it, doctrinal and otherwise, is their reason for existence, and the stakes are high: eternal salvation or punishment in hell.

The anticult forces, however, do not have a monopoly on discussion of human and civil rights. Several groups branded "cults" have responded with a vigorous defense. The Family, a "Fellowship of Independent Missionary Communities" that grew out of the

Children of God movement, has issued a comprehensive response to charges that it exerts "undue influence" over its members. Their report asserts that

> all members of The Family are free moral agents, able to make and abide by their own decisions, and free to leave our communities at any time they so desire. No member is in any way coerced or hindered from leaving our fellowship at any time if they wish to depart. Nor are they forced to accept beliefs or practices against their own will. They are in fact encouraged to make their own choices and to think for themselves, according to the Scriptural injunction, "Let every man be fully persuaded in his *own* mind" (Romans 14:5). The Family categorically denies all accusations, allegations and insinuations which suggest that our membership are not free-willed and mentally responsible individuals. We reject, as does much of the scientific community, the attempts by anti-cult advocates to foist fanciful and mythical "robot" brainwashing theories on the public. . . . Anti-cult religionists and anti-cult organisations, particularly in the USA, cultivate and sponsor "experts" in mind control for the purpose of attacking the membership of various churches and religious organisations. These "experts" help them cloak religious bigotry under a wrap of scientific and medical-sounding terms to gain respectability for their unscientific deeds and claims. Organisations that are opposed to freedom of religion, freedom of membership, or freedom of association are collectively referred to as the anti-cult movement (ACM) or anti-cult network (ACN).[22]

The argument that opponents of "cults" actually represent the forces of bigotry and repression has been made by many other new religious movements as well.

Both sides of the contemporary "cult" controversy depict themselves as the defenders of individual freedoms. Neither has been especially temperate in its rhetoric. Evoking Hitler, Martin King describes Koresh's tenure as leader of the Mount Carmel community as a "ten-year Reich." Similarly, in his summary argument at the trial of the surviving Branch Davidians, prosecutor W. Ray Jahn argues that "people like David Koresh need followers even more than the people like the Defendants need a leader. The monsters that have walked this particular Earth have always had to have followers, whether it's Adolph Hitler, whether it was Joseph Stalin, whoever it is. When the monster walks the Earth, he has to have the follower, because if he doesn't have the followers he has no power." [23] The comparisons proposed by both King and Jahn reach as far as possible for damning parallels. Implicitly, they deny all moral and religious legitimacy to Koresh and the Branch Davidians. They are designed to trouble the consciences of any who defend them or explain them. The terrifying possibility of another Hitler or Stalin is meant to silence debate and instigate action. Groups accused of being "cults" are themselves well aware of the power of such imagery. In his foreword to a broadside against CAN produced by the Church of Scientology, the Reverend George Robertson contends that "the hatred fomented by this small group is not unlike that generated in the 1920s and 1930s in Germany by the Nazis." [24] Such extreme language can hardly claim to be descriptive; it is instead primarily polemical and evaluative. The comparisons used by King, Jahn, and Robertson are intended to arouse our passions, enrage our moral sensibilities, and move us to action. Even if such exaggeration is sometimes an effective motivational tool, it is employed at the price of fairness, clarity, and accuracy. Since cultbusters frequently argue that "cult" leaders demonstrate their extraordinary power by coercing conversions, it is worth examining that process in greater detail.

AFFILIATION AND CONVERSION

Though the cultbusters' understanding of religious conversion may appear to have advanced in sophistication beyond the audacious claim by Ted Patrick (an originator of the deprogramming process) that "cult" recruiters practice "on-the-spot hypnosis," [25] the hallmark of their position remains the universal vulnerability to "cults." To the question "Who is vulnerable?" a CAN flyer answers, "Everyone—often those who believe they are too intelligent or strongwilled to be recruited."[26] Another piece from CAN asserts that "anyone— *even you*—can be deceived."[27] If true, those assertions would seem to doom CAN's efforts at public education since apparently no amount of education or self-awareness is sufficient to immunize anyone against the lure of "cults." But even if CAN's statements are taken as argumentative hyperbole, they still can be called into question. The underlying image of conversion as the result of an irresistible attraction exerted by surpassingly powerful "cult" leaders has no empirical basis. Statistical data simply do not indicate that a significant percentage of Americans have succumbed to the enticements of new and unconventional religions. In fact, simple observation shows that the number of American citizens actually involved in new or unconventional religious groups is quite small. (It is simply impossible to canvas those who may, at some time, have entertained or actually held an unconventional religious idea.) If, as the anticultists assert, anyone can be deceived, relatively few actually have been. The large-scale effects of the "cult" problem have simply not materialized. After all, at the height of its popularity the residents of the Mount Carmel center numbered barely over a hundred, and many of them were foreign nationals. Similarly, the population of the Peoples Temple Agricultural Mission in Jonestown, Guyana, was around a thousand. In the light of those numbers, the alarm expressed by the anticult activists seems out of proportion to the number of people involved. Also, social-scientific research on conversion to new religious movements has shown that the vast majority of those who encounter such groups are eminently capable of resisting their attraction.

For the anticult activists everyone is a potential convert. One reason for that universal susceptibility is the great power attributed to "cult" leaders, who serve as powerful magnets. Anyone coming within its field of attraction will inexorably be pulled into the tightest possible relationship with the wily and alluring leader and will be converted. The convert's own intentions, convictions, or commitments have little or no role to play in such a scenario; whether the initial contact is intentional or accidental, the outcome is the same. Such a view of a passive self at the mercy of vastly superior forces has much in common with both theological and demonological images of the conversion process;[28] the only difference lies in the nature of the superior forces in question. Most often in contemporary anticult arguments, the external forces are identified as psychological; the overwhelming personality of the leader through a process of brainwashing, mind control, or coercive persuasion generates the power that produces conversion. Whatever these forces, the explanations share a common structure. In each case, the convert is taken over by a power outside the individual's control, which essentially replaces his or her will and directs all subsequent activity. It is difficult to square such a portrait of conversion with the tiny number of people who actually become members of new or unconventional religious groups. Few authors have made that point as effectively as Eileen Barker in her seminal study *The Making of a Moonie: Choice or Brainwashing?* Barker's is one of the few examinations of the process of conversion to new or unconventional religious groups to incorporate trustworthy statistical evidence. In her quest to determine the validity of the brainwashing hypothesis to explain membership in the Unification Church in Great Britain, Barker conducted an extensive survey of people whose contact with the church included at least a visit to one of its centers. Barker's research offers no support whatsoever to the notion that "cult" leaders exercise an irresistible magnetism on potential converts. She summarizes her findings in this way: "If we start our calculations from the number of those who get as far as visiting an Unification centre, a generous estimate suggests that no more than 0.5 per cent will be associated with the movement two years later, and by no means all of these will be full-time members. In other words, it is just not true that anyone can be brainwashed by Unification techniques."[29] The anticult activists' contention that all "cults" are alike gives Barker's conclusions even more force than she herself claims. But even if important differences between the Unification Church and the Mount Carmel community are granted, Barker's finding that only one person in two hundred who come into direct contact with the "Moonies" proves susceptible to their blandishments raises serious doubts about the magnetic theory of conversion to "cults."

As with their characterization of "cult" leaders, the anticult activists' depiction of the process of conversion turns out to be a flagrant oversimplification of a complicated social process. It vastly overestimates the power of leaders as it simultaneously reduces all participants in "cults" to interchangeable, faceless nobodies. Such reduction can be an effective polemical tool because it brushes aside any potential complications by making diverse evidence about individuals' contact with "cults" appear homogeneous. But it does not stand up to extended scrutiny. There are significant constraints on the power that any leader can successfully wield, and that which they do exercise is in many ways bestowed on them by their followers; similarly, their adherents are able to influence their own situations. Those who come into contact with "cult" leaders frequently have, can, and will reject both the messenger and the message.

WACO AND JONESTOWN

Opponents of "cults" assert that powerful leaders can get their followers to do virtually anything. They often use Jonestown as a case in point. The tragic deaths of nearly all the residents at the Peoples Temple in the Guyanese jungle in November 1978 were quickly incorporated by anticult activists into their alarming scenario of "cult" life, and Jonestown gave the anticult forces graphic and terrifying evidence that they had previously lacked. David Bromley and Anson Shupe observe that "Jonestown incorporated all of the ACM's [anticult movement's] worst fears and most dire predictions. Whereas the public previously had been confronted with individuals joining a plethora of religious groups characterized by varied ideologies and organizations and about which there was only speculation as to their 'destructive potential,' Jonestown seemed to provide dramatic confirming evidence for their claims in an undeniable, horrible event. Further, events at Jonestown made accessible once again to the ACM both the media and political institutions."[30] Fifteen years later Waco had a similar effect. Indeed, among anticult activists the events at Mount Carmel only confirmed their analysis of what had happened in Guyana and underscored the need for renewed vigilance and even stronger measures against "cults." Anticult proponents and other observers rarely ventured beyond the obvious parallels. The proof of the similarities between the Peoples Temple and the Mount Carmel community was directly afforded by the great equalizer, death. In that view, the bottom line with "cults" is death; leaders become murderers, and followers, and others as well, their victims. Accordingly, the cultbusters assert, any morally sensitive citizen should be outraged.

The effectiveness of the anticult position in determining a public interpretive framework for Waco can be traced in the early and pervasive expressions of concern that the residents of Mount Carmel would commit suicide. Although the government's own reports emphasize that Koresh insisted repeatedly that suicide was not an option for him or for the other community members, the topic nonetheless remained at the forefront of the media coverage throughout the prolonged siege.[31] Though survivors continue to maintain that the community members did not set the all-consuming fire, the public perception was succinctly summed up by President Clinton in his April 20 press conference. Clinton asserted that he was surprised to hear "that anyone would suggest that the attorney general should resign because some religious fanatics murdered themselves."[32] The anticult activists' characterization of "dangerous cults" both encourages and is fed by such thinking. Similar events are held to have similar causes, and a blanket explanation can then be applied to all cases, regardless of their differences. If Waco is similar to Jonestown, the anticult argument gains force; if it isn't, the argument is seriously weakened. It is therefore worth looking more closely at the two cases.

The central point of comparison that was repeatedly made between Waco and Jonestown concerned first the possibility and eventually the actuality of mass suicide. But in the logic of opponents of "cults" those outcomes were also linked because they were directly caused by megalomaniacal leaders. Before April 19 the common reasoning was that since Koresh was a charismatic "cult" leader like Jim

Jones, the community he led could reasonably be expected to suffer the fate of Jonestown. For many, the events of April 19 only confirmed that expectation. But the processes by which Koresh gained, held, and expanded his power and authority within the Mount Carmel community were specific to that situation and not a replication of what had transpired between Jones and the members of the Peoples Temple. There are intriguing similarities between Koresh and Jones, but there are striking differences as well. We will focus on three interrelated topics: the self-conception articulated by each leader, the understanding of religion and particularly of the Bible that each espoused, and the relative openness of each community to interaction with the world outside its boundaries.

Neither Koresh nor Jones saw himself as inconsequential. Koresh was convinced that he alone had unlocked the mystery of the entire Bible by deciphering the message of the sealed heavenly book in Revelation 4 and 5. He saw himself as a Christ, as one of God's anointed who throughout history have been charged with revealing God's will to an often-heedless humanity. Through intricate biblical reasoning Koresh also came to believe that he was the Lamb of God, who had received the awesome responsibility of preaching the heretofore hidden message of the Bible to humankind. That message, as Koresh's poem "Eden to Eden" describes it, concerns "the pending judgment of the King who rules the universe."[33] Koresh's role, however, was not restricted to preaching. As he disclosed in his New Light revelation, his was also to begin to father a new family of "God's grandchildren," in anticipation of the coming kingdom. Koresh's sexual claim upon all the women of the community was depicted as his response to a divine call. It was his duty, not his whim.

Jones also came to see himself as *a,* if not *the,* Christ. He once proclaimed, "That's what I am, . . . the word, the spoken word! Say, 'you blasphemer!' I am doing what Jesus got nailed to the cross for doing."[34] Similarly, in what could be construed as an indirect response to the negative stereotype, Jones asserted that "you can call me an egomaniac, megalomaniac, or whatever you wish, with a messianic complex. . . . I don't have a complex, honey, I happen to know I'm the Messiah."[35] But in the latter stages of his leadership of the

Peoples Temple, Jones added a dimension to that assertion that clearly set him apart from Koresh. In Jones's fully developed understanding what made him the Messiah was his embodiment of the principle of "Divine Socialism." In Jones's discourse, Christian messianism and Marxian revolution joined in a distinctive ideology with himself as the focal point. Mixing biblical allusions with revolutionary rhetoric, he claimed, "I'm everywhere. Self has died. I'm crucified with Christ, nevertheless I live. I've been crucified with the revolution. . . . The life that I now live, I live through this great Principle, the Christ, the socialist Principle that was on the day of Pentecost when it said, 'God is love, and love means they have everything in common.' "[36] Also like Koresh, Jones employed metaphors drawn from family life to describe his preeminent place within his religious group. To the members of the Peoples Temple, Jones became their father; he encouraged them to address him as "Dad" or even "Daddy-O." Like Koresh, Jones claimed the right to indulge himself sexually with the members of his community, in his case both women and men. There is no indication, however, that Jones saw his mission as being the biological father of new family fit for the kingdom of heaven. Jones's own "rainbow family" relied more on the mechanisms of both figurative and literal adoption than on strictly biological paternity.

Opponents of "cults" would hold that the differences between the self-conceptions of Koresh and Jones are much less significant than the overwhelming similarities. However, the links in a chain of differences cumulatively contribute to the distinctive identities of each individual and the group that he led. Jones's peculiar mix of Marxian and Christian rhetoric, for example, signals a major difference between himself and Koresh and between the Peoples Temple, especially in its latter phases, and the Mount Carmel community. As Jones's self-understanding changed over time, he came more and more to express his message *in opposition to* the Bible. In fact, he developed a gnostic myth that identified the God of the Bible and particularly the creator God of Genesis as "an evil, egomaniacal, and grotesque parody of a cosmic creator."[37] In periodic sermons dedicated to that theme, Jones made a crucial distinction. "I'm not talking about the *true* God," he would declare. "I'm talking about the God of the old King James Bible."[38] That venerable translation of the Bible, central to Koresh's life and crucial to some of his interpretations, came in for particular criticism in Jones's religious view because it sanctioned a system that oppressed Blacks, women, and the poor. In a vivid claim to charismatic authority over and against the traditional authority embodied in the Biblical text, Jones proclaimed that "the Bible has taught you to be content, . . . that you were not to speak up to a white man. Well I'm telling you to speak up to anyone that oppresses you."[39] Ultimately, Jones claimed an authority that had a source outside of, and far superior to, the Bible itself. Throughout his adult life Jones moved further and further from any form of orthodox Christianity. In its final stages, what he preached to the Peoples Temple was truly a new religion, an idiosyncratic blend of his own experiences, insights, fancies, and, probably, delusions. Jones derived his authority not from his ability to interpret a preexisting sacred text but from his ability to supplant it. In place of the Biblical text Jones presented himself to the Peoples Temple as the living embodiment of a new and superior God.

Despite a fairly widespread misunderstanding that he claimed to be Jesus Christ, Koresh never took as radical a step as Jones. Far from wanting to supersede the authority of the Biblical text, Koresh consistently endeavored to demonstrate his authority precisely through his ability to interpret the Bible. Koresh's sole claim to authority was that he could do what no one before him had been able to do: unlock the secrets of the Seven Seals in the New Testament book of Revelation. Koresh clearly saw himself in a position of supreme importance but one within the Biblical apocalyptic worldview. Koresh saw his interpretive work as confirming and clarifying the message of the Bible and not in any way as supplanting it. As he wrote in his unfinished exegetical treatise that survived the fire, "Every book of the Bible meets and ends in the book of Revelation."[40] In his self-understanding, Koresh remained a servant of the text. He needed no other sources because "John's record contains the past, present, and future events that revolve around the Revelation of Jesus Christ."[41] Whereas Jones came to see the Bible as a tool of oppression and as an obstacle to personal salvation, social transformation, and historical progress, Koresh held fast to the Bible as the sole repository of saving truth.

Those differences between Jones and Koresh are the key to what went wrong at the Mount Carmel center. For Koresh and the other members of the community there was no higher authority than the text. The Bible provided the script for their lives. Even Koresh's own pronouncements about its meaning were always at least theoretically subject to independent verification, precisely because the biblical text was the common property of the entire community and had long been cherished by the broad Adventist tradition in which the Branch Davidians were steeped. In that context, Koresh's marathon Bible study sessions appear less as indoctrination and more as a testing and confirming of the persuasiveness and validity of his interpretations. In fact, some members of the community did reject Koresh's interpretations of the Bible, particularly his New Light revelation; their defections only highlight the primacy of the authority located within the biblical text. However, an understanding of the specific characteristics of Koresh's charismatic leadership—including its location within a biblical apocalyptic worldview, its interpretive nature, and its acceptance of the authority of the text as primary—is possible only if the anticult activists' homogenized picture of a generic "cult" leader is abandoned.

Though Mount Carmel was a tightly knit community, it was markedly more open to the world outside than Jonestown. Because its central source of authority was shared with so many in American society, serious and productive conversation between the members of the community and those outside was an ever-present possibility. Indeed, such a dialogue seems to have been the goal of Koresh's initial contacts with the authorities, beginning with his first harried conversations with Lieutenant Larry Lynch. In contrast, Jones's denigration of the King James Bible, his development of a gnostic myth of redemption, and his espousal of Divine Socialism produced such an idiosyncratic worldview that it virtually precluded the possibility of any serious exchange with outsiders on the basis of shared assumptions and values. Also, in more practical terms Mount Carmel was a more open community than Jonestown. It did not have the geographical or social isolation of the community in the Guyanese jungle. Several Branch Davidians worked daily in the world outside; for a time the children of Mount Carmel attended local schools; Koresh himself could often be found in local music clubs, restaurants, or other places of business. Mount Carmel was surely a place apart—ideologically, socially, and geographically—but its isolation was never total. Such connections between those inside and outside the center could have been used to turn the negotiations in a more positive direction; however, the FBI negotiators never took advantage of those possibilities during their conversations with Koresh and other Mount Carmel residents. They dismissed Koresh's religious convictions as "Bible babble," failed to learn how frequently Koresh and other community members interacted with outsiders, and heightened the isolation of Mount Carmel by rigidly controlling access to the center during the standoff. The siege itself did as much to make the center a "total institution" as anything that Koresh did.

In contrast, the transfer of the Peoples Temple from California to Guyana signaled an explicit desire to be completely self-sufficient, an effort to create from scratch an earthly utopia. The ideological, social, and geographical isolation of the people at Jonestown was much greater than of those at Mount Carmel. Even before Representative Leo Ryan's visit to Jonestown, the residents' contact with the world outside was very carefully monitored. Jonathan Z. Smith has proposed that while in California, the Peoples Temple still occupied "subversive space"; that is, "it participated in civil activities and won major forms of public recognition for these efforts. But, hidden from public view, it was also a parallel mode of government. Internally, it was a counterpolis. It had its own modes of leadership, its own criteria for citizenship, its own mores and laws, its own system of discipline and punishment."[42] After disgruntled defectors and external critics promulgated damaging stories about the internal workings of the California Peoples Temple, Jones made the momentous decision to move the entire operation to Guyana. He abandoned the subversive situation of his community within American society for what he envisaged as the less troubled "utopian space" of the Guyanese jungle, where he could build without external interference the perfect society. At Jonestown, Jones claimed, "We enjoy every type of organized sport and recreational games. Musical talents and arts are flourishing. We share every joy and every need. Our lives are secure and rich with variety and growth and expanding knowledge. . . . Now there is peace. . . . There is freedom from the loneliness and the agony of racism. . . . We have found security and freedom in collectivism and we can help build a peaceful agricultural nation."[43] Even if the Mount Carmel community aimed at similar self-sufficiency, it never forsook its "subversive" situation within American society. Like any "cult," the Branch Davidians intended to subvert the dominant American way of life by offering at least a compelling alternative, in this case based on an apocalyptic understanding of the biblical message. But the community never accomplished, or even contemplated, such a complete withdrawal from American society as Jonestown represented. Individual items as disparate as the Mount Carmelites' participation in gun shows throughout Texas, Koresh's attempt to form a Christian rock-and-roll band, and his missionary journeys to California, England, and Australia show how thoroughly the community was engaged with the world outside. To be sure, its stance was fundamentally critical; its fond hope was to transform the world before the coming end, but unlike the Peoples Temple the group did not wholly retreat from American society in order to pursue that goal of transformation in isolation. Because the community always wanted to maintain communication with the wider world, the possibility of a peaceful negotiated ending to the standoff was always there. In that sense, too, Waco was not Jonestown.

Like their understandings of charismatic leadership and the process of conversion, the anticult activists' assimilation of Waco to Jonestown obscures more than it clarifies. Its sole value is polemical; it enables opponents of certain religious groups to compound the negative attributes of one "cult" by transferring them to another, and by extension, to all others. This is not just a matter of abstractions. The comparison of Waco to Jonestown contributed directly to the tragic consequences. Virtually from the beginning, it thrust the issue of mass suicide directly to the fore and shaped both governmental and public expectations of what the residents of Mount Carmel might do under pressure. In the absence of compelling evidence and against the specific findings of the Texas Department of Human Services, it nonetheless lent credence to accusations of child abuse, which, in turn, served as initial justifications for the FBI's actions. Finally, it continues to influence how people portray, respond to, and act against new and unconventional religious groups, promulgating ideas that can lead to dangerous consequences.

PERSISTENCE OF THE NEGATIVE IMAGE OF "CULTS"

The influence of the negative stereotype of "cults" has continued well after the end of Mount Carmel. Postmortem reports have cited the same anticult experts that the initial articles did. Though an interpretive essay in the May 3, 1993, issue of *Newsweek* nonetheless repeats without examination many elements of the anticultists' definition of a dangerous "cult," it is critical of the FBI's religious illiteracy and acknowledges the difference between "a criminal mind-set" and "an apocalyptic mind-set." The essay cites Rick Ross: "The cults to worry about, according to Rick Ross, an expert who advised the FBI during the confrontation in Waco, can be identified by the character of their leadership. The Branch Davidians, he says, were 'totally dependent' on Koresh, who, like Jim Jones in Guyana, systematically brainwashed his followers and cut them off psychologically from the outside world. That's a danger signal in itself—a clear sign that in any confrontation with the law, the group will resist all forms of psychological pressure and close ranks around its leader. And if the group sees government as corrupt, as many religious extremists do, pressure tactics of the sort the FBI used in Waco are a big mistake."[44] By letting the attribution of total dependency and the comparison between Koresh and Jones stand unquestioned, the authors tacitly accept, but do not explicitly endorse, the position of the cultbusters. Neither Koresh's "total control" of his followers nor the process of brainwashing is demonstrated in the essay; the only appeal is emotional: the haunting image of more than a thousand dead at Jonestown and Mount Carmel.

A May 17, 1993, *Newsweek* article on posttraumatic stress disorders in children, including those released from Mount Carmel, reveals a similar pattern. It begins with this characterization of the deceased Koresh: "Suppose he was right. Suppose, after all, David Koresh was not just the half-crazed leader of a fringe religious sect but a genuine, board-certified Redeemer, come to prep the world for the Apocalypse."[45] As for Koresh's teaching about biblical prophecy, the article opines that "loony as that gospel may have sounded to outsiders, scores of seemingly rational, intelligent adults on the inside believed it faithfully enough to follow its prophet into the fire." Despite ironic concessions to the religious seriousness of the Mount Carmel community—Koresh was only "half-crazed" and the Branch Davidians were "seemingly rational"—the article perpetuates the negative stereotypes of both "cult" leaders and "cults." It makes a feint toward investigating why rational people might embrace a decidedly unpopular minority viewpoint and the disturbing and challenging practices that go with it but quickly retreats to the common wisdom about "cults." Not surprisingly, anticult activists again figure as prominent sources for the article's views.[46]

If anything, Waco has tightened the cultbusters' hold on the American imagination. That is unfortunate because the exaggerated rhetoric of the anticult forces has obscured, not clarified, discussion of new and unconventional religious groups in American society. The consequences have been damaging to those groups stigmatized as "destructive cults" and, ironically, to the cause of the cultbusters.

CRITICIZING "CULTS"

Framing the discussion of "cults" in terms of civil and human rights has produced a stalemate rather than a widely accepted resolution. Where cultbusters see people exposed to "mind control," members of new religious movements see "free moral agents." There is no uniformly acknowledged index of coercion. One's evaluation of another's behavior instead seems to depend entirely on the standards of judgments that one adopts. There is no purely objective standpoint from which all religions can be judged. Although that doesn't preclude judgment, it does make it a much more complicated proposition. In his brief comments on the Branch Davidians in *The Culture of Disbelief,* Stephen Carter provides some intriguing suggestions about how such judgments might be formulated. He suggests that "perhaps the Davidians were indeed as crazy as the news media has chosen to paint them. Certainly they broke secular laws, were violent people, and may have abused children. The secular state had no choice but to try to punish them, especially after they murdered four law enforcement agents. In short, much about their theology and their practices seems to represent moral evil. As a Christian, I might call it sin; and as a secular citizen, I would agree that their actions, if proved, merited punishment under criminal laws. But even if we judge them harshly, we must not make the mistake of confusing their sinfulness with their religiosity."[47] In this passage Carter identifies three standards against which the Mount Carmel community might be judged: psychological, legal, and religious. There may be others, but these can serve as effective examples.

Carter correctly identifies the popular psychological evaluation of Koresh and the Branch Davidians, and he correctly views that judgment as remaining unproven. Practiced at a distance, instant psychoanalysis can be especially dangerous. In an April 21 opinion piece in the *Los Angeles Times,* Mary Zeiss Stange bluntly argues that "what we don't like or understand, we call crazy. We make it a subject of jokes. Sometimes, we kill it." Though she also asserts that she was "in no way defending Koresh or his views" and that "what he practiced and preached is repellant to me,"[48] she nonetheless expresses profound concern that the slapdash labeling of Koresh as "crazy" had fatal consequences.

The psychiatrists and other behavioral scientists who provided information to the FBI during the standoff made somewhat more finely tuned evaluations of Koresh's mental health without direct and extended access to their subject. While generally agreeing that Koresh was to some extent "delusional," the psychiatrists differed on the specific ramifications of that diagnosis. One FBI consultant, Park Dietz from the UCLA School of Medicine, attributed to Koresh "an elaborate system of grandiose delusions," along with undesirable personality traits.[49] Another consultant, Murray Miron of Syracuse University, found his delusions to be "narrowly focused and limited to the 'self-aggrandizements of his chosen status as God's hand.'"[50] Despite his anticult sentiments, Miron carefully distinguished Koresh from another notorious "cult" leader, concluding that "Koresh's communication does not resemble the suicidal sermon made by Jim Jones in the last hours of Jonestown. His is not the language of those at Masada or Jonestown."[51] One other consultant offered the sobering and largely unheeded caution that "absent a personal examination of Koresh [my] opinions [can] only be regarded as speculative."[52] The suppositions about the mental health of Koresh and his associates point to a set of psychological standards by which the Mount Carmel community could be evaluated. However, the successful completion of such an evaluation was hindered by lack of direct access to the subjects. In too many instances, careless and superficial labeling took the place of careful psychological analysis. A solidly grounded and persuasive psychological evaluation of any of the people at Mount Carmel thus remains an unfulfilled possibility. Similar psychological analysis of other cult leaders would likely encounter the same difficulties. Accordingly, any diagnosis of the mental health of cult leaders or members should be rigorously scrutinized.

A legal evaluation of the actions of members of the Mount Carmel community seems on firmer ground. Carter, among others, is certain that community members broke secular laws. But from the beginning of the BATF investigation strictly legal questions about weapons at Mount Carmel were inextricably interwoven with suspicions about unconventional sexual practices and child abuse. Those allegations, along with the vague charge that the group was a "cult," both obscured specifically legal questions and helped create a predisposition to expect the worst of the community. In view of Koresh's previous cooperation with McLennan County law enforcement officers, it is hard to understand the BATF's assault on Mount Carmel as an appropriate response to the charge that some residents were converting semiautomatic weapons to fully automatic without registration. In the case of Mount Carmel, legal issues have been almost always clouded by moral and religious ones, and keeping the charges separate has proved difficult. The results of the trial of the surviving Branch Davidians, hailed as a decisive victory by both prosecutors and defendants, again demonstrate the confusion. Nonetheless, illegal acts committed by members of new or unconventional religious groups should be punished, just as illegal acts committed by nonreligious people or by people who are members of mainstream religions should be. But whereas committing certain illegal actions may say something about the character of the perpetrator, it says nothing about the nature or quality of that person's religion or the entire group to which that person belongs. Possession of unregistered automatic weapons does not necessarily indicate that someone's religion is either unorthodox or spurious; nor, for that matter, does it indicate that someone's religion is good or true. In itself, such an illegal action indicates nothing specific about the religious group to which the perpetrator belongs. It is, and should remain, a very long jump from the identification of specific illegal acts committed by members of a religious group to the condemnation of that group as a whole.

In fact, the legal and psychological discussion of "cults" masks a more fundamental conflict over values. The British sociologist of religion James A. Beckford has observed that " 'cult controversies' are very revealing about taken-for-granted notions of normality."[53] Images of what is "normal" derive their power to shape human activity from being embedded in a more comprehensive view of the world, such as the biblical apocalyptic worldview of the Branch Davidians or the secular, scientific, psychological worldview that pervades CAN and other anticult groups. The frequency with which "cults" are purported to involve "excessive" devotion to a leader who exerts "excessive" control over members is a good indication of how "cults" are located outside the norm by their opponents. For example, a CAN brochure describing methods of recruitment warns against "a person who is *too* interested in what you like to do."[54] COMA's warning against the mind-control technique of "confusing doctrine" depends on an assumption that there is a taken-for-granted understanding of religious truth. According to COMA, confusing doctrine "encourag[es] blind acceptance and rejection of logic through complex lectures on an incomprehensible doctrine," but the specific measures of logic, comprehensibility, and complexity are not spelled out. An implicit worldview gives such value judgments their power and self-evident accuracy. Bringing that worldview to light is as crucial to unraveling the contemporary "cult" controversy as is uncovering the logic of Koresh's biblical apocalypticism is to understanding Waco.

Some anticult activists, such as conservative evangelical Christians, make their religious commitments quite explicit. For them, the defining characteristics of a "cult" usually include specific doctrinal errors, such as a reliance on extrabiblical revelation or a misunderstanding of the doctrine of salvation by faith. Their literature is studded with references to scriptural passages that expose the perceived errors of "cult" doctrine. Their dispute with "the cults" has the merits of particularity and clarity. Larger umbrella organizations, such as CAN, adopt a different approach. Eschewing a religious argument, they base their opposition to "cults" on explicit concern for personal integrity and civic order. CAN expresses its opposition to "the practices of any organization which clearly violates our laws, our ethics, and our morals" and strives to defend "every individual's right to believe in whatever he FREELY chooses."[55] In the process CAN intends to "pass no judgment on which doctrine is 'right.'" CAN thus claims that its campaign against cults is founded on widely shared legal and moral grounds. Perhaps the most interesting question raised by CAN's self-definition, however, concerns the specific community for which it intends to speak. "Our laws" would seem to have a precise reference to the legal statutes of the United States and its constituent political entities. "Our ethics" and "our morals" have less precise referents. The standard of judgment in such statements is less clear than it is when, for example, conservative evangelical Christian groups mount a critique of cults based on their understanding of the Bible. At times, CAN seems to appeal to fundamental values that it presumes all Americans share, but the very existence of "dangerous cults" undermines such a presupposition. CAN exists precisely because at least some Americans do not share what CAN sees as "our ethics" and "our morals" and because some Americans have started or joined religious groups that offer distinct alternatives to widely held civic, moral, or religious presuppositions.

The secular anticult position encounters insuperable logical difficulties. In an endeavor to convince Americans that "cults" embody a serious threat to personal autonomy and social order, broadly based anticult organizations like CAN have created a uniform profile of a "destructive cult." In their polemical literature and statements, that image is opposed to a vaguely defined civic and moral community whose fundamental values are transgressed by "cults." The confrontation is pitched at such a high level of generality, however, that it saps the ability of the cultbusters to offer effective opposition. The generic formulation of the "cult" problem by organizations like CAN contains the seeds of its own undoing. On one hand, it leads to careless, misleading, and inaccurate assertions about the similarities purportedly shared by all "cults." On the other, by attempting to unite all opponents under a single banner, it founders on its own vagueness. It fails to represent forcefully enough the considered judgment of a distinctive social or religious community and the specific values that it endorses. In many ways, the conservative evangelical Christian critique of "cults" is much more effective, though for a smaller audience, because it identifies more fully and precisely both the fundamental values being defended and the definite errors being opposed.

There are much more fruitful avenues for a critical discussion of cults in American society, one of them signaled by Stephen Carter. His broader argument seeks to restore explicitly religious discourse to the center of American public life. Though he does not take the time to develop them at length, Carter measures both the theology and practice of the Mount Carmel community against explicitly Christian standards. Using that standard, we might find the Branch Davidians in error on religious grounds on several issues, that is, sinful. With that approach, description of Koresh as the "sinful Messiah" has a precise religious meaning, a definite background, and a specific audience. It identifies precisely what is at stake in this specific "cult" controversy, and for whom, providing a firm grounding on principle, which is lacking in most contemporary discussions of "cults."

EIGHT

Waco and Religious Freedom in America

THE EVENTS AT THE MOUNT Carmel center in early 1993 brought before a large public a set of issues that do not normally receive such prominence. Despite recent public surveys that indicate a majority of Americans expect the actual return of Jesus Christ to earth, Koresh's immersion in biblical prophecy and his determined focus on the imminent apocalypse offered a glimpse into an unfamiliar exemplar of such beliefs.[1] Similarly, opponents of "destructive cults" enjoyed an access to the general public unrivaled since the mass suicide at Jonestown in November 1978. Issues such as the right to bear arms, religious freedom, sexuality, and childrearing—all had a broad, if brief, currency. Many troubling matters need careful and sustained scrutiny in the aftermath of Waco, and very few of these were adequately addressed by either the Treasury Department's or the Justice Department's official reports. One of the most disquieting is the threat to religious freedom posed by the contemporary war on so-called cults.

PROPOSED ANTICULT LEGISLATION IN ILLINOIS

A case in point is the public hearing about "cult" activities on college campuses held by the Illinois Senate Education Committee on December 7, 1993. It shows that after Waco, cultbusters tried to add force to their argument by appealing to the example of Mount Carmel. The hearing was the direct result of State Senator Frank C. Watson's encounter with a friend whose daughter had gotten involved with a so-called cult while at college. Senate Resolution 448 begins its authorization of the hearing with a clause that refers to "the recent activities of David Koresh and his Branch Davidian sect in Waco, Texas [which] have increased national awareness of the destructive nature of cult activities."[2] The resolution purports to identify the negative effects that generic "cults" can have upon college students. Clearly echoing the position of opponents of "cults," it asserts that "college students who become involved with cults undergo personality changes, suffer academically, are alienated from their families, and are robbed of the very things universities were designed to encourage; freedom of thought, intellectual growth, and personal development."[3] Ironically, it is precisely the values of "freedom of thought, intellectual growth, and personal development" that lead students to explore the alternatives offered by such groups. Further, to attempt to legislate against a system of religious belief and conduct, however unconventional, undercuts the very purposes of a university education as described in this resolution. The legislators who sponsored it obviously did not perceive any positive effects from involvement with a "cult." Like many others, the sponsors of the resolution portray new and unconventional religious groups as a social problem and a threat to individuals. There is no effort made to define a "cult" with any precision or to distinguish it from a new or unfamiliar religious movement that might be seen in a positive light. The assumption is that everyone knows what a "cult" is and that no one would want his or her children to be involved in one. That impression is confirmed by the list of witnesses to be called. The resolution directs the committee to "solicit testimony from cult awareness organizations, former cult members, college administrators, campus security personnel, campus ministers, families of cult members, and other interested witnesses on the recruitment and organizational practices of cults, the extent of cult activities on Illinois campuses, the response of college administrators in Illinois and around the nation to cult activities, the debilitating effect of cult involvement on students, and suggestions for State or campus level policies on such activities."[4] Current members of so-called cults are conspicuously missing as they are in most media or government portrayals of the Mount Carmel community. In a familiar circular procedure, the charge to the Illinois Senate Education Committee effectively determines what the committee's findings should be.

Fortunately, the committee's final recommendations, issued in February 1994 after two public hearings and assorted other inquiries, piously nod to the constitutional separation of church and state and the importance of the free exercise of religion, and do not propose any new legislative initiatives against "cults." But the investigating committee nonetheless felt that an extensive campaign of "cult awareness" was called for on college campuses throughout the state. The report consistently portrays unspecified "cults" as potential problems for individuals, their families, and the state. State Senator Watson promised continuing vigilance, saying, "This is a first step to protect students and their families. We will continue to monitor the situation and how our colleges and universities respond."[5]

Despite its weaknesses, this polemical characterization of a "dangerous cult," now fortified by the indelible image of Mount Carmel in flames, continues to be used to incite public opinion and government action against new and unconventional religious groups, provoking deep suspicion and even hatred. Such strong emotions cannot be explained on the basis of direct personal contact with cults since even the most generous estimates of cult membership represent only a tiny fraction of the population. Something else is going on.

The intensity of commitment demanded by some religious groups, particularly when it results in purportedly strange forms of behavior, disturbs many Americans. We suspect that the common understanding of "cults" as dangerous to both individuals and society is indeed accurate but not for the reasons usually given. The crucial issue is not the enormous power of a leader who exercises total control over passive followers. Such groups are threatening because they offer, sometimes with relentless aggressiveness, another way of seeing and being. Their very existence calls into question, as it is meant to do, what we hold most important and what our society values above anything else. Serious belief in the imminent end of the world, for example, challenges the prevailing secular view of time as stretching into an indefinite future and drastically foreshortens the period in which we may forge an identity, make our place in the world, and shape our lives in conformity with a hoped-for future. Committed adoption of unconventional living arrangements similarly challenges our broad acceptance of the nuclear family as the most important and appropriate social institution for inculcating and preserving our central social values. Insistence that families are formed by affiliation and commitment, rather than by biology, introduces a disruptive and disturbing new set of connections and priorities that casts doubt on what many see as the eternal verities of the relationships between parents and children. Participation in unorthodox sexual relationships seriously tests our notions of intimacy, carnality, and passion. Accepting that a human prophet's communication represents an irresistible divine command supplants cherished notions of free will by a disturbing call to a higher obedience.

Cults are "dangerous" in American society, not merely for what they might do to an unfortunate few, but for what they actually do to an uneasy many. Cults offer alternatives, not on matters of superficial importance, but on what most intimately and ultimately concerns us. Cults explicitly endeavor to get us to examine what we care most about and to consider unsparingly whether we are satisfied with our own beliefs and commitments and with the state of the world. All the statistical evidence about membership in new and unconventional religious movements shows that they are rarely successful in inspiring many dramatic conversions. The widespread fear of cults and the diligent opposition to them, however, suggest that they are amazingly successful in raising fundamental questions about human life. Few want to confront directly any challenges to the status quo. It is easier to condemn the messenger than to take the implications of the message seriously, either on a personal or societal level. Thus the eagerness to condemn "cults" masks an unwillingness to confront ourselves and to question our society.

"CULTS" AND THE SELF

Opponents of "cults" spend much of their time keeping tabs on suspicious groups, answering queries from anxious relatives or friends, producing and disseminating literature in support of their position, and holding and attending meetings. But their efforts impinge most directly and intimately on the groups they oppose in the process of deprogramming, as in Rick Ross's encounter with a Branch Davidian described in chapter 4. That practice has long been passionately contested, and even when it is euphemistically labeled "exit counseling," the "cult" member is seen as under the control of external forces.[6] According to its proponents, only intervention by skilled diagnosticians can return the victim to normality. Such attempts depend on a series of revealing assumptions that are crucial to the general anticult position. The fundamental premise is expressed most directly by David J. Bardin, the Washington counsel for both the American Family Foundation and CAN, in a pamphlet produced by the latter organization to mark the first anniversary of the fire at Mount Carmel and to answer critics of the anticult position. He voices an unshakable conviction that "mind control exists."[7] Everything follows from that assertion. From that perspective, people are drawn into "cults" by mysterious powers that they cannot effectively resist. Their perceptions are manipulated and their actions controlled by an overwhelmingly powerful leader. They are, in effect, programmed, just as a computer is, to perform certain tasks. The only way to get them out of the group is to erase the program. Only then, proponents of deprogramming claim, will former members be able to think and act for themselves. However, its advocates consistently refuse to follow the logic of their position to its conclusion and to acknowledge that former members of "cults" will need to be *re*programmed with a different and more acceptable program in order to function successfully after leaving their group. In the anticultists' view "cults" rigorously control the formation of their members' identities at the explicit direction of the leader. But outside the group, they imagine, former members are remarkably free to fashion themselves in any way they wish. Programming is limited to the activity of "cults," and the pressures to conform that typify life within the "cult" are apparently inoperative outside it. Clearly, this approach is naive and simplistic about the controls and pressures that exist outside the "cult." None of us is completely independent; no one is free from powerful forces of influence and persuasion, whether parental, conventionally religious, or political.

As we have shown, opponents of "cults," and especially advocates of deprogramming, base their understanding of affiliation on an image of the *passive self* acted upon by others and manipulated according to their will. Things *happen to* the passive self, which is at the mercy of irresistibly superior forces. Such a model functions to pardon former "cult" members of any wrongdoing since they have been powerless to withstand the enticements of the wily charismatic leader. The recruits' vulnerability and the leader's power intensify one another. In this view, former "cultists" can regain the capacity to act for themselves only when they leave the group and escape the leader's control. In contrast, many members of new or unconventional religious groups, and many outside observers, presume an alternative and more complicated model. Their alternative understanding is founded on an image of the *active self* that considers options, weighs consequences, and makes choices. The active self *makes things happen.* While not omnipotent, the active self retains certain powers of self-determination. In this model, current and former cult members take primary responsibility for their own actions. As we have described, although many defectors believe that they have been victims of deception, they see, in retrospect at least, how they have willingly cooperated in the process. In this model, the powers of the leader may be great, but they are limited. The focus on the self in explaining conversion extends to each member of the community. The process of affiliation is characterized as a give-and-take relationship; potential members consider what a particular group or leader might offer and decide whether to pursue matters further.

Their affiliation is neither compelled nor a foregone conclusion, but an open question. Similarly, members may exit the cult sadder and wiser, but their departure is prompted by their exercising the same intellectual capabilities and moral and spiritual discernment that led them into the group in the first place. Whereas the model of conversion or affiliation founded on the passive self paints all events in dramatically opposed blacks and whites, the model based on the active self uses primarily shades of gray. Whereas the passive model tends to dehumanize or infantilize converts, the active model acknowledges their complex maturity.[8]

The models implied by different characterizations of the conversion process are not solely descriptive. The choice of one rather than the other often serves polemical purposes; it is guided by and expresses some of the observer's fundamental values and assumptions about normality. Those, like deprogrammers and other opponents of "cults," who choose to see conversion to new religious movements as involving the deception and manipulation of passive victims convey their own view of human nature. While remaining immune to self-doubt, they see most others as weak, uncertain in their commitments, and endlessly prone to self-deception. As a result, as CAN, COMA, and other anticult organizations constantly advise, anyone might fall prey to the lure of a "cult." They also see some individuals as having a boundless capacity for evil and the exploitation of others. These become "cult" leaders, and Hitler and Stalin are invoked as standards for comparison. Ultimately, those who use the model of the passive self to explain conversion to new religious groups subscribe to a simplistic and negative view of human nature: all people are weak, but the strongest will invariably take advantage of the others. Anticult workers are apparently the only exceptions. In contrast, the cultbusters continue to claim that deprogramming, or exit counseling, is an effective and positive technique. Restored to "freedom," former "cult" members somehow regain their ability to act for themselves, to maintain commitments, and to lead productive and satisfying lives although they remain vulnerable to deception.

In the end, cultbusters send confusing messages about the dimensions of the "cult" problem, the power of the "cult" leader, and the nature of the audience for "cults." The anticult position is founded on a logical contradiction. Either the attraction of "cults" is significantly weaker than their opponents would have the American public believe, or the willpower, commitment, and purpose of the general populace is significantly stronger. The opponents of "cults" bring to their discussion of the process of affiliation a short-circuited logic that signals something else is going on just out of sight. The hyperbole and exaggeration, which are the hallmarks of their argumentative style, lend an edge of desperation to their pleadings. "Cults" come to represent fundamental challenges to their adversaries' view of the world and way of life, mirroring the cultbusters' anxieties about loss of control and acceptance.

"CULTS" AND SOCIETY

Anticult activists see themselves as involved in a battle for the heart and soul of America. Ironically, the groups they oppose often see themselves in the same way though they are more likely to focus on a chosen few, such as the 144,000 whom Koresh believed would be initially saved. The anticultists ruefully observe a society in which beliefs are quickly abandoned in favor of a new or exotic message presented with sufficient guile and flair. In that view, whatever success "cults" achieve testifies to the inherent weaknesses of contemporary American society, rather than to the personal situations of those who are attracted to such groups. On that point as well, cultbusters and cult members agree. Cults strive to provoke us to an unsparing examination of both self and society; they anticipate that we will find both wanting; and they claim to offer remedies for our individual and social problems. Cults offer a vision of an alternative society and a plan for implementing it. The anticult activists see a nation in which the necessary social support for traditional values no longer exists, and they see new and unconventional religions capitalizing on that weakness. In this view, "cults" appear a symptom, not a cause, a lamentable indication of the deterioration of a valued way of life.

Many new and unconventional religious movements offer a similar diagnosis of life in America today. They see inattention to spiritual matters, moral laxity, a weakening of communal ties, a failure to uphold biblical standards, and any number of other problems, and they offer their own solutions. Their innovative remedies often derive from their perception that they enjoy the privilege of divine revelation; and they typically demand a strong and uncompromising response.

Under the surface of the anticult position there is a pervasive dissatisfaction with the prevailing ethos of contemporary American society, which has made the supposed proliferation of "cults" possible. The anticultists' vigorous defense of traditional religion, the nuclear family, personal autonomy, and other core values against the challenge of the "cults" allows them to locate the vexing problems of Americans and American society outside themselves in a dangerous and alien "other." Cults *are* alien in many ways. In some cases, they introduce foreign beliefs and practices into American society; but in others, such as the Branch Davidians, they give distinctively different interpretations to common religious elements such as the biblical book of Revelation. However, cultbusters see "cults" as alien whatever their place of origin because they manifest psychological instability, moral evil, religious error, or any combination of the three. By portraying "cults" as the "other," cultbusters absolve themselves of any complicity in the problems they discuss.

Since "cults" represent an invasive presence, rather than an acceptable variation from the norm, anyone who rejects the cultbusters' values by participating in a "cult" is asserted to have acted under external compulsion, rather than as a result of a careful, rational choice. Such a view contrasts markedly to the democratic ideal of our society as an arena for competing and conflicting ideas, thriving on debate, differences, and diversity. In such a society, persuasiveness is valued, and minority views are welcomed, often proving their enduring value to the majority. To admit that one may join a new or unconventional religious group for "good" reasons leaves one's own choices and decisions open to evaluation and criticism. The anticult polemicists fend off such critique by denying that anyone in his or her "right mind" would join a "cult." Moreover, because affiliation is itself evidence of aberrant behavior, cultbusters can easily dismiss the diagnoses of American society that such groups offer and the remedies that they propose. They act as if they have nothing to learn and much to fear from the intruder. Their general response to "cults" is exemplified by the unheeding responses that government officials made to Koresh's religious pronouncements during the siege at Mount Carmel. When Koresh spoke *his* truth, they heard only "Bible babble." Where the Branch Davidians saw a religious community prepared for the end of the world, the authorities saw an armed compound full of "hostages."

The cultbusters' opposition to new and unconventional religious groups depends not only on an image of a passive self but also on an image of a broadly *uniform society* whose values and ethical codes are commonly agreed upon. They see an American consensus and claim to speak for it. In their view, the uniformity of social values guarantees the integrity of the family, harmonious interpersonal relations, and overall social stability. Despite their emphasis on common values, however, cultbusters see their society as extremely fragile and besieged from without. Cult members also see the problems and weaknesses in contemporary American society, but they do not see the remedy in espousing a vaguely defined uniform set of core values without any secure links to a specific social group. Instead, they locate the remedy in the creation of an *ideal society,* a select voluntary association founded on intense commitment to explicit religious values. Their vision is often exclusive; it offers a path toward perfection for those willing to pursue it. That exclusivity, however, allows them to sharpen their critique of American society. Cults typically offer a closed system of internally consistent doctrine, such as Koresh's biblical interpretation, that is passionately espoused by the members of the elect and contributes to their distinctive individual and social identities. The exclusivity, passion, and sheer differentness that mark cult life have the potential to create considerable friction between members of the group and those outside. The Mount Carmel community maintained a sometimes uneasy, often bemused, and generally comfortable peace with its neighbors over the course of its sixty-year history. The introduction of actors who had neither personal nor doctrinal familiarity with the Branch Davidians was a scenario that presaged conflict.

THE PROBLEM WITH THE CULTBUSTERS

Opposition to so-called cults enables many Americans to condemn much of what they find wrong in their society by attributing it to the influence of an alien "other." That strategy allows opponents to draw clear and sharp lines between right and wrong, good and evil, and legitimate and illegitimate religion. It is based from the outset, however, on an unexamined reaction that presumes that one's own position is self-evidently true and unassailable. In that sense it represents a flight from self-examination, a refusal to think hard about one's own values and commitments, and an authoritarian willingness to impose one's views on others. It is a form of intellectual, spiritual, and social isolationism that denies the possibility of learning anything new or valuable from those significantly different from oneself. When such an attitude is adopted in defense of the fundamental values of American society, as it is by the cultbusters, it is out of tune with the demands of a democratic society, particularly one that is rapidly becoming more diverse. It provides constricting and oppressive answers to serious questions about how Americans should deal with any minority groups, however they are defined. At the same time, it raises the issue of whether those whose beliefs or way of life is unconventional should receive the same protection of the law that other minority groups enjoy. In sum, the cultbusters' appeal to a supposed consensus of values expresses a nostalgia for a homogeneous society that never existed, which can have pernicious effects.

Government action against new or unorthodox religious groups, advocated by some anticult workers, bodes ill not only for such movements but also for everyone in our society. It arrogates to the state a power that all must oppose and depends on a very restricted reading of the constitutional guarantee of free exercise of religion. New and unconventional religions provide some of the most vivid examples of nay-saying in contemporary American society. To enlist the state in an effort to control or eradicate such groups is to deprive our common life of an invigorating diversity, as well as to sanction its immense power to enforce conformity. The anticult activists' claim to support the fundamental values of American democratic society is undermined by their willingness to suppress the exercise of religious freedom and, moreover, to engage the state in that campaign. If the purpose of the First Amendment is to protect religions from the state, rather than the state from religion, there is no constitutional basis for enlisting the power of the state in the campaign against so-called cults. That does not mean that the state is impotent to punish illegal acts done in the name of religion, but that the intervention must be carried out through normal legal channels. A wholesale government crusade against "destructive cults," such as that championed after Waco, is illegitimate and unconstitutional.

THE PROBLEM WITH "CULTS"

Much of the polemic against "cults" in America has taken an inappropriate form based on a constricted view of human abilities of self-determination, an intolerant attitude toward differences in belief and practice, and an inflated expectation of the role of the government. Also, despite the anticultists' success in shaping the negative public attitude toward "cults," their efforts to deter individuals from pursuing their chosen religious path has been surprisingly ineffective. The efforts of cultbusters can be depreciated on the basis of their own testimony. For all the small "victories" that they can count, they admit that the enemy is far from conquered. The reasons are found both in the weakness of the anticult position and in the promise of personal and social transformation held out by new and unconventional religious groups. How often that promise has actually been fulfilled is another question.

The body counts alone at Jonestown and Mount Carmel should give anyone pause. In addition, there are countless atrocity stories associated with so-called cults: tales of physical and psychological suffering, wasted opportunities and squandered fortunes, exploitation, and disillusionment. Even if the anticult forces have exaggerated the prevalence and misdiagnosed the cause of such experiences, they should not be ignored. There is no doubt that some people involved with new or unconventional religions suffer harm. Yet, so do many individuals who make personal choices outside the purview of the so-called cult. The important question is whether there is something *characteristic* about a given group that can *incontrovertibly* be shown to cause harm to its members or to others. Such a finding might provide justifiable cause for concern or even appropriate legal action against an entire group. The government prosecutor's assertion that Koresh preached a "theology of death" and his likening Koresh to Hitler and Stalin was an attempt to provide such a rationale for action against the Branch Davidians. But the question of the fundamental character of the whole religious group cannot be described by such facile comparisons.

In most instances, we believe, the damage attributed to "destructive cults" is not only peripheral to their avowed purposes but is also almost totally subjective. Common living conditions at the Mount Carmel center were often substandard and never luxurious; meals were simple at best; some of the work was physically draining, and the marathon Bible study sessions were undeniably arduous. Yet, those facts of Branch Davidian life were accepted and sometimes joyfully embraced by the faithful. Such conditions can be taken as evidence of damage done by Koresh only by ignoring his adult followers' professed commitment to their chosen way of life. Even where children are involved, our society allows a great measure of latitude and freedom to a family to follow its religious convictions, however strict or unconventional. In keeping with a proper concern over the issue of damage caused by cults, but in balance with our commitment to freedom of religion, a few simple principles of judgment are proposed.

Illegal actions should be evaluated according to the appropriate laws and pursued accordingly. The relevant criteria are explicit, public, and sanctioned by the force of the government and the will of the people it represents. The specific religious or ideological commitments of the perpetrators should be irrelevant to the process of assessing the legal status of their actions. With behavior that breaks religious or moral conventions, however, the waters become muddy. Despite cultbusters' claims to the contrary, their particular moral standards and religious convictions are not shared by the majority of the population, nor are they written into our laws. Our pluralistic society is intentionally designed to be hospitable to a wide range of moral persuasions and religious beliefs. Moral and religious judgments about cults are necessarily situated within specific subgroups of our society. Beyond the question of the legality of certain actions, where cult members must meet the same criteria as anyone else, the problem with so-called cults can only be articulated convincingly from a very specific standpoint in defense of very particular moral and religious values. By offering an alternative vision of individuals and society, cults deliberately provoke a conflict over values. Any opposition to such groups must itself offer a compelling alternative, not merely anxious alarms and exaggerated criticisms. Whatever the specific items at issue, the most effective critique of any cult would not only condemn its errors but also offer a path that the opponent would argue is closer to the truth. In other words, cults are most effectively encountered by committed representatives of other religious communities that set forth a comprehensive view of the world and the proper place of human beings in it, which they attempt to make convincing. In that sense, cults make a signal contribution to American life by raising questions of ultimate value, by offering paradigms of commitment, and by making principled challenges to the status quo. Their presence in our society is undeniably disruptive and intentionally so. They may fade in and out of the public view, but they will not disappear as the history of religions, and particularly those in America, makes clear. Our democratic society serves, however imperfectly, as a free marketplace of ideas. Intolerant government policies, and particularly antidemocratic and military tactics like those used at Waco, have no place in such a society. Rather than conduct a war against so-called cults, we can more profitably and pointedly ask ourselves what we believe in, how we are practicing our beliefs, and what is our level of participation in the open and ongoing exchange of ideas that our society affords.

APPENDIX

*An Unfinished Manuscript
by David Koresh on the Seven Seals of the
Book of Revelation*

EDITORIAL PREFACE

On Wednesday, April 14, just five days before the fire, David Koresh released what turned out to be his final letter through his lawyer, Dick DeGuerin. In this communication he joyfully reports that "his waiting period was over" and that upon completion of a manuscript containing the "decoded message of the Seven Seals" he would come out. He considered the composition of this manuscript a privilege allowed him by God, the direct answer to his prayers, which he had sought for the past seven weeks.

Although many questioned his intentions in producing this manuscript, we received this announcement with great relief. We had been urging him for several weeks through radio broadcasts and cassette tapes to exit Mount Carmel peacefully as he now proposed to do. We had based our case to him on interpretations of the book of Revelation that we felt he might find persuasive.

Whereas many doubted his ability to write such a document, we now know that Koresh did dictate this manuscript and took it most seriously. A computer disk containing his text was carried out of Mount Carmel by Ruth Riddle, a survivor of the fire. Indeed, Riddle tells us that she and Koresh worked for several hours on Sunday night, the last night of his life; he dictated while she typed out his thoughts. She reports that the Branch Davidians were calm and joyful that evening at the prospect of Koresh completing his work and their impending exodus.

Koresh's manuscript speaks for itself to those interested in his exegesis and understanding of the mysterious Seven Seals of the book of Revelation. Regardless of how the content is evaluated, one point is clear: in a short time, under most trying circumstances, Koresh produced a substantial piece of work. He completed the preface, which is a poem; the introduction to the work; and chapter 1, which discusses the First Seal. Judging from this work, we estimate that the finished manuscript would have run about 50–75 pages and might have taken him another week or more to write.

In his last letter, Koresh asks that the completed manuscript be given to his lawyer, Dick DeGuerin, then passed on to us. He had apparently come to trust our knowledge and integrity in discussing with him his interpretation of Revelation. He then authorized our release of copies to scholars, religious leaders, and the general public. Although Koresh died a few days later and did not finish this work, we still think it best to release this incomplete portion, following his instructions. Actually, his exposition of the First Seal is in itself vital to understanding his perspective regarding his mission, the reasons for the Waco siege, and what ultimately transpired.

The text is produced here precisely as it came to us from the computer disk, with minor changes in spacing. In the interest of accuracy we have also carefully consulted Ruth Riddle. For the sake of brevity she did not type all of Koresh's verbal quotations of Scripture since she planned to insert them later. We have added these citations, which are set in italics; all are from the King James Version.

Koresh's last sentence is suggestive: he urges readers and followers to be ready to "come out of our closet." He calls upon those of us on the outside to forsake our own dark closets and summons the Branch Davidians to "come out" of Mount Carmel and face the world as lovers of Christ. His first chapter concludes with two scriptural quotations that promise the reader that God will one day reestablish Koresh's fallen community.

J. Phillip Arnold
James D. Tabor
Rosh Hashanah 1993

THE SEVEN SEALS OF THE BOOK
OF REVELATION

David Koresh

EDEN TO EDEN

Search forth for the meaning here,
Hidden within these words
'Tis a song that's sung of fallen tears,
Given way for two love birds.

Love birds yet not of feathered creed
Shot down for gambled play,
And caged a far distance betweenst themselves
For the hunter felt it best that way.

"She bird is mine," the hunter said,
'Twas this bird I raised and faithfully fed."
'Twas he bird who released her from her cage,
Sought her womb in youthful age.

Love birds the name, these birds they call,
Two, plural, love bird, takes two.
'Twas not her womb of which he sought,
And certainly not her youth.

Love birds, the name these birds they call,
Two, plural, love bird, takes two,
It's just that he needed she,
To fly the skies of blue.

And now we see the hunter man,
Robbed without a prey,
The evil which he sought to do,
Caused the birds to pass away.

For loneliness and solitaire,
Is death to every soul.
For birds of God were meant to pair,
The two to complete the whole.

And now we see the final meaning
Of this rhyme and verse:
The pending judgment of the King
Who rules the universe.

For with Adam and his spirit Eve,
To share the kingdom fair;
But when they sinned they lost their crown
In exchange for shame to bear.

So Eve travailed and brought forth death,
And passed the crown to all;
For each to learn the lesson here,
The kingdom of the fall.

For virgins do not bring forth sons,
Until God does reverse,
The inner meaning of the law,
To remove man from the curse.

For in the Christ, we've seen a bride,
The water mixed with blood,
The wife with cloven tongues of fire,
Of whom the Christ has loved.

And now He's back to sing His song,
The life of every spring,
And love birds gather, each one with mate,
For the marriage of the King.

INTRODUCTION

John 18:33–38[:] *Then Pilate entered into the judgment hall again, and called Jesus, and said unto him, Art thou the King of the Jews? Jesus answered him, Sayest thou this thing of thyself, or did others tell it thee of me? Pilate answered, Am I a Jew? Thine own nation and chief priests have delivered thee unto me. What hast thou done? Jesus answered, My kingdom is not of this world; if my kingdom were of this world, then would my servants fight, that I should not be delivered to the Jews; but now is my kingdom not from here. Pilate therefore said unto him, Art thou a king, then? Jesus answered, Thou sayest that I am a king. To this end I was born, and for this cause came I into the world, that I should bear witness unto the truth. Everyone that is of the truth heareth my voice. Pilate saith unto him, What is truth? And when he had said this, he went out again unto the Jews, and saith unto them, I find in him no fault at all.*

Strange indeed for the judgment of man, for who knows within himself that his judgment be true?

Scripture tells us that Pilate was convicted of the truth in Christ, but failing to take heed thereto, he lost his soul, causing the blood of the innocent to be shed. How many of us since the dawning of time have committed such things? Who was this Jesus? Who was this Saviour that nearly a whole religious nation rejected?

Matthew told us. Mark, Luke, and John all recorded their side of the story of which remains unto this day, read and judged of all. Likewise, the Acts, the Book of Romans, Corinthians, Ephesians, Galatians and such books open for our learning this most unique mystery of judgment and justice undone. But of all the records the most awe inspiring remains to be the most misunderstood, that being the Revelation of Jesus Christ written by the Apostle John to the churches of Asia and left on record that all who follow may ask the question: "Who is this Christ and what remains to be the mystery of Him?"

In my work to unfold this mystery to you I will not use great techniques of scholarly display nor in-depth reasonings of philosophy, no sophisticated, congenial language shall be used, just simple talk and reason.

First of all, "the Revelation of Jesus Christ which God gave unto Him to show unto His servants things which must shortly come to pass" are to be seen just as that: a revelation of Jesus to reveal to men His wishes and His desires for those who make up His church. For the kingdom of God being that of heaven, and not of this world, is to be revealed unto this world by the means He has chosen—"the foolishness of preaching." John the Apostle while on the Isle of Patmos received the Lord's messenger and in obedience placed in written form all that he saw and all that he heard pertaining to the mysteries of Christ. And in good faith the Apostle stated, "Blessed is he that readeth, and they that hear the words of this prophecy, and keep those things which are written therein for the time is at hand" (Revelation 1:3).

Likewise John was commanded of the angel, "Write the things which thou hast seen, and the things which are, and the things which shall be hereafter" (Revelation 1:19). Simply, John's record contains the past, present, and future events that revolve around the Revelation of Jesus Christ. John in faithfulness sent his writings to the seven churches in Asia and the will of Christ for these churches is plainly revealed from chapter 2 to chapter 4 of Revelation. Therefore on record, all may read and see how Christ has dealt with His churches of old.

Our subject of interest will be taken up from chapters 4–22, for these passages entail the events that are to be after John's time. For it is written (Revelation 4:

entire chapter): *After this I looked, and, behold, a door was opened in heaven: and the first voice which I heard was as it were of a trumpet talking with me; which said, Come up hither, and I will show thee things which must be hereafter. And immediately I was in the spirit; and, behold, a throne was set in heaven, and one sat on the throne. And he that sat was to look upon like a jasper and a sardine stone: and there was a rainbow round about the throne, in sight like unto an emerald. And round about the throne were four and twenty seats: and upon the seats I saw four and twenty elders sitting, clothed in white raiment; and they had on their heads crowns of gold. And out of the throne proceeded lightnings and thunderings and voices: and there were seven lamps of fire burning before the throne, which are the seven Spirits of God. And before the throne there was a sea of glass like unto crystal: and in the midst of the throne, and round about the throne, were four beasts full of eyes before and behind. And the first beast was like a lion, and the second beast like a calf, and the third beast had a face as a man, and the fourth beast was like a flying eagle. And the four beasts had each of them six wings about him; and they were full of eyes within: and they rest not day and night, saying Holy, holy, holy, Lord God Almighty, which was, and is, and is to come. And when those beasts give glory and honour and thanks to him that sat on the throne, who liveth for ever and ever, the four and twenty elders fall down before him that sat on the throne, and worship him that liveth for ever and ever, and cast their crowns before the throne, saying, Thou art worthy, O Lord, to receive glory and honour and power: for thou hast created all things, and for thy pleasure they are and were created.*

John states that "that which must be hereafter"—sometime after his day there will be a God who sits on His throne. There will be a jury of twenty-four elders. God will be declared as "worthy to receive glory and honour and power," because unto Him and for Him all things were created.

John continues to say (Revelation 5: entire chapter): *And I saw in the right hand of him that sat on the throne a book written within and on the backside, sealed with seven seals. And I saw a strong angel proclaiming with a loud voice, Who is worthy to open the book, and to loose the seals thereof? And no man in heaven, nor in earth, neither under the earth, was able to open the book, neither to look thereon. And I wept much, because no man was found worthy to open and to read the book, neither to look thereon. And one of the elders saith unto me, Weep not: behold, the Lion of the tribe of Judah, the Root of David, hath prevailed to open the book, and to loose the seven seals thereof. And I beheld, and lo, in the midst of the throne and of the four beasts, and in the midst of the elders, stood a Lamb as it had been slain, having seven horns and seven eyes, which are the seven Spirits of God sent forth into all the earth. And he came and took the book out of the right hand of him that sat upon the throne. And when he had taken the book, the four beasts and four and twenty elders fell down before the Lamb, having every one of them harps, and golden vials full of odours, which are the prayers of saints. And they sung a new song, saying, Thou art worthy to take the book, and to open the seals thereof: for thou wast slain, and hast redeemed us to God by thy blood out of every kindred, and tongue, and people, and nation; and hast made us unto our God kings and priests: and we shall reign on the earth. And I beheld, and I heard the voice of many angels round about the throne and the beasts and the elders: and the number of them was ten thousand times ten thousand, and thousands of thousands; saying with a loud voice, Worthy is the Lamb that was slain to receive power, and riches, and wisdom, and strength, and honour, and glory, and blessing. And every creature which is in heaven, and on the earth, and under the earth, and such as are in the sea, and all that are in them, heard I saying, Blessing, and honour, and glory, and power, be unto him that sitteth upon the throne, and unto the Lamb for ever and ever. And the four beasts said, Amen. And the four and twenty elders fell down and worshipped him that liveth for ever and ever.*

Very clearly John tells of a judgment in which only one question is asked, "Who is worthy" to open or to reveal a book found in the right hand of God clearly sealed with seven seals. John states, "No man in heaven nor in earth, neither under the earth was able to open the book, neither to look thereon." Then John is pointed to the hope of all men: the Lamb that was slain. Here is a revelation of Christ as our High Priest in heaven. Here His work is revealed: the opening of the mysteries of God. These mysteries of which reveal Christ and His sufficiency to save all whose prayers are directed to God through Him. Likewise Paul the Apostle has stated: Hebrews 5:5; 7:19, 24–25; 8:6; 9:24; 10:12–14, 26, 29; 12:18–25.

So also Christ glorified not himself to be made a high priest; but he that said unto him, Thou art my Son, to-day have I begotten thee. [Heb. 5:5]

For the law made nothing perfect, but the bringing in of a better hope did; by the which we draw nigh unto God. [Heb. 7:19].

But this man, because he continueth ever, hath an unchangeable priesthood. Wherefore he is able also to save them to the uttermost that come unto God by him, seeing he ever liveth to make intercession for them. [Heb. 7:24–25]

But now hath he obtained a more excellent ministry, by how much also he is the mediator of a better covenant, which was established upon better promises. [Heb. 8:6]

For Christ is not entered into the holy places made with hands, which are the figures of the true; but into heaven itself, now to appear in the presence of God for us. [Heb. 9:24]

But this man, after he had offered one sacrifice for sins for ever, sat down on the right hand of God; From henceforth expecting till his enemies be made his footstool. For by one offering he hath perfected for ever them that are sanctified. [Heb. 10:12–14]

For if we sin willfully after that we have received the knowledge of the truth, there remaineth no more sacrifice for sins. [Heb. 10:26]

Of how much sorer punishment, suppose ye, shall he be thought worthy, who hath trodden under foot the Son of God, and hath counted the blood of the covenant, wherewith he was sanctified, an unholy thing, and hath done despite unto the Spirit of grace? [Heb. 10:29]

For ye are not come unto the mount that might be touched, and that burned with fire, nor unto blackness, and darkness, and tempest, And the sound of a trumpet, and the voice of words; which voice they that heard entreated that the word should not be spoken to them any more: (For they could not endure that which was commanded, And if so much as a beast touch the mountain, it shall be stoned, or thrust through with a dart: And so terrible was the sight, that Moses said, I exceedingly fear and quake:) But ye are come unto mount Sion, and unto the city of the living God, the heavenly Jerusalem, and to an innumerable company of angels, To the general assembly and church of the firstborn, which are written in heaven, and to God the Judge of all, and to the spirits of just men made perfect, And to Jesus the mediator of the new covenant, and to the blood of sprinkling, that speaketh better things than that of Abel. See that ye refuse not him that speaketh. For if they escaped not who refused him that spake on earth, much more shall not we escape, if we turn away from him that speaketh from heaven. [Heb. 12:18–25]

Clearly then, John is showing us of that very event of which Paul the Apostle so clearly writes. Christ is the mediator of the New Covenant and that New Covenant is contained in the seven seals. If we the church have been so long awaiting that which must be hereafter, why is it that so many of us in Christendom have not even heard of the seven seals?

Why is this Revelation of Jesus Christ which God gave to Him such a mystery? The Apostle Peter gives us a clue when he said (1 Peter 1:3–5): *Blessed be the God and Father of our Lord Jesus Christ, who, according to his abundant mercy, hath begotten us again unto a living hope by the resurrection of Jesus Christ from the dead to an inheritance incorruptible, and undefiled, and that fadeth not away, reserved in heaven for you, who are kept by the power of God through faith unto salvation ready to be revealed in the last time.*

Truly Christ is our only Saviour, our only Mediator between man and God. Likewise, it is true the opening of the seven seals by Christ is as much or more so important for our salvation as any other former gospels. If this salvation is "ready to be revealed in the last time," as Peter says, then we should hear another statement from the Apostle Peter (1 Peter 1:13): *Wherefore, gird up the loins of your mind, be sober, and hope to the end for the grace that is to be brought unto you at the revelation of Jesus Christ.*

So the question remains—What are the seven seals? And the answer remains— a Revelation of Jesus Christ which God gave unto Him to show unto His servants things which must shortly come to pass. If these things were to have shortly come to pass then surely they must have already been fulfilled, and if so, does that mean we are His servants if we know these things not? Or could it be that the things which must be hereafter pertaining to God's throne, the judgment, the book, and the Lamb receiving that book are events directed primarily to the last times or the last days? If that's the case are we in the last days? If so then it must be time for God's servants to know these things (Psalms 90:12–17; 91:1–4; 11:3–4).

So teach us to number our days, that we may apply our hearts unto wisdom. Return, O LORD, how long? and let it repent thee concerning thy servants. O satisfy us early with thy mercy; that we may rejoice and be glad all our days. Make us glad according to the days wherein thou hast afflicted us, and the years wherein we have seen evil. Let thy work appear unto thy servants, and thy glory unto their children. And let the beauty

of the LORD our God be upon us: and establish thou the work of our hands upon us;
yea, the work of our hands establish thou it. [Ps. 90:12–17]

He that dwelleth in the secret place of the most High shall abide under the shadow
of the Almighty. I will say of the LORD, He is my refuge and my fortress: my God; in
him will I trust. Surely he shall deliver thee from the snare of the fowler, and from the
noisome pestilence. He shall cover thee with his feathers, and under his wings shalt thou
trust: his truth shall be thy shield and buckler. [Ps. 91:1–4]

If the foundations be destroyed, what can the righteous do? The LORD is in his holy
temple, the LORD's throne is in heaven: his eyes behold, his eyelids try, the children of
men. [Ps. 11:3–4]

The servant of God will find as we continue in our searching of the scriptures
that every book of the Bible meets and ends in the book of Revelation. Gems of
most sacred truth are to be uncovered, golden promises never before seen are to
be brought to view, for when has grace ever been needed more than now in the
time of which we live?

CHAPTER I
THE FIRST SEAL

Although we, the servants of God, do not live in Asia, we are none the less [*sic*] to
be beneficiaries of their counsels; and they likewise, not being alive today are no
doubt to be a part of the grace which we are to receive.

Revelation 6:1–2. And I saw when the Lamb opened one of the seals, and I
heard, as it were the noise of thunder, one of the four beasts saying, Come and
see. And I saw, and behold a white horse: and he that sat on him had a bow; and
a crown was given unto him: and he went forth conquering, and to conquer.

Here in our Heavenly Zion we see the Lamb loose the first seal. This preview of
God's revelation of His Son is to be of our utmost interest, for not only will it
more clearly reveal the nature of Christ, but it will likewise unfold more clearly
the Divine nature of God who is the Author of this revelation.

Now let's turn to Psalms 45: *My heart is inditing a good matter: I speak of the*
things which I have made touching the king: my tongue is the pen of a ready writer.
Thou art fairer than the children of men: grace is poured into thy lips therefore God
hath blessed thee for ever. Gird thy sword upon thy thigh, O most mighty, with thy
glory and thy majesty. And in thy majesty ride prosperously because of truth and meek-
ness and righteousness; and thy right hand shall teach thee terrible things. Thine arrows
are sharp in the heart of the king's enemies; whereby the people fall under thee. Thy
throne, O God, is for ever and ever: the sceptre of thy kingdom is a right sceptre. Thou
lovest righteousness, and hatest wickedness: therefore God, thy God, hath anointed thee
with the oil of gladness above thy fellows. All thy garments smell of myrrh, and aloes,
and cassia, out of the ivory palaces, whereby they have made thee glad. Kings' daughters
were among thy honourable women: upon thy right hand did stand the queen in gold
of Ophir. Hearken, O daughter, and consider, and incline thine ear; forget also thine

own people, and thy father's house; So shall the king greatly desire thy beauty: for he is thy Lord; and worship thou him. And the daughter of Tyre shall be there with a gift; even the rich among the people shall entreat thy favour. The king's daughter is all glorious within: her clothing is of wrought gold. She shall be brought unto the king in raiment of needlework: the virgins her companions that follow her shall be brought unto thee. With gladness and rejoicing shall they be brought: they shall enter into the king's palace. Instead of thy fathers shall be thy children, whom thou mayest make princes in all the earth. I will make thy name to be remembered in all generations: therefore shall the people praise thee for ever and ever.

Verse 1: "My (God's) heart is inditing a good matter: I (God) speak of the things which I (the Creator of all things) have made touching the King (Christ), my (God's) tongue is the pen of a ready writer." Here we see God not only creates all things by His Word but in His wisdom, He has chosen some things to be written that by the power of His word He may bring to pass in His own time. Here we see God by His written Word foretelling his determined purpose for His Son, Christ.

Verse 2: "Thou art fairer than the children of men, grace is poured into thy lips; therefore God hath blessed thee forever, Gird thy sword upon thy thigh, O most mighty, with thy glory and thy majesty. And in thy majesty ride prosperously because of truth and meekness and righteousness; and thy right hand shall teach thee terrible things." Clearly in the Revelation Christ is fairer than the fairest. Those who receive the seals receive the grace found therein. Christ is capable of destroying his enemies for His majesty truly is great in heaven, for it is witnessed that all angels bow before him. What is it that Christ shall ride but the white horse because the book given to Him is the truth and He shall ride prosperously.

Verse 5: "Thine arrows are sharp in the heart of the king's enemies whereby the people fall under thee." Here we see the meaning of the bow of which the first seal speaks. Let us pray that none of us refuse "Him that speaks from heaven" and the Spirit of Truth that is now speaking from heaven for it is likewise written in verse 6: "Thy throne O God, is for ever and ever; the scepter of thy kingdom is a right scepter. Thou lovest righteousness, and hatest wickedness: therefore God (Christ), thy God (Father), hath anointed thee with the oil of gladness above thy fellows. All thy garments smell of myrrh, and aloes, and cassia, out of the ivory palaces, whereby they have made thee glad. Kings's [*sic*] daughters were among thy honourable women: upon thy right hand did stand the queen in gold of Ophir, Hearken, O daughter, and consider, and incline thine ear; forget also thine own people, thy father's house; so shall the King (Christ) greatly desire thy beauty; for he is thy Lord; and worship thou him."

How can any man deny that the first seal is a preview into the event spoken of by the 45th Psalm? How important is this insight? How important is it to God, or to Christ, or to the church? While on earth Christ spoke many parables regarding His kingdom and his bride. Let's hear one and see if we cannot more clearly understand the importance of these things. Matthew 22:1–14: *And Jesus answered and spake unto them again by parables, and said, the kingdom of heaven is like unto a certain king, which made a marriage for his son, and sent forth his servants to call them that were bidden to the wedding: and they would not come. Again, he sent forth other servants, saying, Tell them which are bidden, Behold, I have prepared my dinner: my oxen and my fatlings are killed, and all things are ready: come unto the marriage. But they made light of it, and went their ways, one to his farm, another to his merchandise: and the remnant took his servants, and entreated them spitefully, and slew them. But when the king heard thereof, he was wroth: and he sent forth his armies, and destroyed those murderers, and burned up their city. Then saith he to his servants, The wedding is ready, but they which were bidden were not worthy. Go ye therefore into the highways, and as many as ye shall find, bid to the marriage. So those servants went out into the highways, and gathered together all as many as they found, both bad and good: and the wedding was furnished with guests. And when the king came in to see the guests, he saw there a man which had not on a wedding garment: and he saith unto him, Friend, how camest thou in hither not having a wedding garment? And he was speechless. Then said the king to the servants, Bind him hand and foot, and take him away, and cast him into outer darkness; there shall be weeping and gnashing of teeth. For many are called, but few are chosen.*

Notice that in this parable of Matthew, Christ clearly teaches that those with indifferent attitudes who would not come to the Marriage Supper were to be slain. Their disinterest offended the King who we know is God. So, likewise, today if we disregard the truth of the first seal we really disregard Christ, who opened it and in so doing we disregard God who gave it. This indifference most surely will place one's salvation in jeopardy.

Matthew 21:42: Jesus saith unto them, Did ye never read in the scriptures, The stone which the builders rejected, the same is become the head of the corner; this is the Lord's doing, and it is marvelous in our eyes?

In this passage we see Christ pointing his hearers to the Rock (His God). We know in Revelation 4 God is pictured as one who appears to be as jasper and sardine stone. This one is the same stone to which Christ referred to. So again we are reminded that what the Father gives to Christ is a revelation of Jesus Christ that God gives to Him to show unto his servants.

Was it really David who wrote the Psalms or was it God who spoke through David? Was it really the prophets who wrote their books or was it God who spoke through the prophets? If it was God, we must conclude God claims the book as His and we should more earnestly take it as God's Word.

We find now in Revelation 19 a verification of the events we have just read.

Revelation 19:1–13. *And after these things I heard a great voice of much people in heaven, saying, Alleluia; Salvation, and glory, and honour, and power, unto the Lord our God: for true and righteous are his judgments: for he hath judged the great whore, which did corrupt the earth with her fornication, and hath avenged the blood of his servants at her hand. And again they said, Alleluia. And her smoke rose up for ever and ever. And the four and twenty elders and the four beasts fell down and worshipped*

God that sat on the throne, saying, Amen; Alleluia. And a voice came out of the throne, saying, Praise our God, all ye his servants, and ye that fear him, both small and great. And I heard as it were the voice of a great multitude, and as the voice of many waters, and as the voice of mighty thunderings, saying, Alleluia: for the Lord God omnipotent reigneth. Let us be glad and rejoice, and give honour to him: for the marriage of the Lamb is come, and his wife hath made herself ready. And to her was granted that she should be arrayed in fine linen, clean and white: for the fine linen is the righteousness of saints. And he saith unto me, Write, Blessed are they which are called unto the marriage supper of the Lamb. And he saith unto me, These are the true sayings of God. And I fell at his feet to worship him. And he said unto me, See thou do it not: I am thy fellow servant, and of thy brethren that have the testimony of Jesus: worship God: for the testimony of Jesus is the spirit of prophecy. And I saw heaven opened, and behold a white horse; and he that sat upon him was called Faithful and True, and in righteousness he doth judge and make war. His eyes were as a flame of fire, and on his head were many crowns; and he had a name written, that no man knew, but he himself. And he was clothed with a vesture dipped in blood: and his name is called The Word of God.

Notice how in verse 9 it says, "Blessed are they which are called unto the marriage supper of the Lamb!" And he said unto me, "These are the true sayings of God!" Being the true saying of God, the first seal of Revelation 6:1–2 must be true according to the saying of God in Psalms 45. And how can we be *blessed* if we know nothing about the *Marriage Supper of the Lamb* nor what it entails? [Emphasis on disk.]

Isaiah 33:17: Thine eyes shall see the king in his beauty; they shall behold the land that is very far off.

Are we starting to see the King a little more clearly? And how about that heavenly land very far off?

Isaiah 55:3–4: Incline your ear, and come unto me; hear, and your soul shall live, and I will make an everlasting covenant with you, even the sure mercies of David. Behold, I have given him for a witness to the people, a leader and commander to the people.

Has not David truly witnessed on behalf of God by God's own power this beautiful marriage of which all are called to receive the knowledge of.

Isaiah 61:8–10: For I the LORD love judgment, I hate robbery for burnt offering; and I will direct their work in truth, and I will make an everlasting covenant with them. And their seed shall be known among the Gentiles, and their offspring among the people: all that see them shall acknowledge them, that they are the seed which the LORD hath blessed. I will greatly rejoice in the LORD, my soul shall be joyful in my God; for he hath clothed me with the garments of salvation, he hath covered me with the robe of righteousness, as a bridegroom decketh himself with ornaments, and as a bride adorneth herself with her jewels.

We should surely at this moment realize the importance of learning more thoroughly the meaning of Christ according to the seals lest we be found without "the wedding garment" of God's judgment, for if we receive this enlightenment, this grace which comes from heaven, we shall surely be partakers of *the marriage of the Lamb* for we are the guests who will "Hearken and consider." [Emphasis on disk.]

Jeremiah 23:5, 6, 7, 8, 18, 19, 20: *Behold, the days come, saith the LORD, that I will raise unto David a righteous Branch, and a King shall reign and prosper, and shall execute judgment and justice in the earth. In his days Judah shall be saved, and Israel shall dwell safely: and this is his name whereby he shall be called, THE LORD OUR RIGHTEOUSNESS. Therefore, behold, the days come, saith the LORD, that they shall no more say, The LORD liveth, which brought up the children of Israel out of the land of Egypt; but, The LORD liveth, which brought up and which led the seed of the house of Israel out of the north country, and from all countries whither I had driven them; and they shall dwell in their own land. . . . For who hath stood in the counsel of the LORD, and hath perceived and heard his word? who hath marked his word, and heard it? Behold, a whirlwind of the LORD is gone forth in fury, even a grievous whirlwind: it shall fall grievously upon the head of the wicked. The anger of the LORD shall not return, until he have executed, and till he have performed the thoughts of his heart: in the latter days ye shall consider it perfectly.*

This beautiful prophecy, the Desire of Ages, entails of Christ the Lord our Righteousness and also warns us of the latter days should we be found not standing in the counsel of the Lord. If we, the church of God, stand in the counsel of Christ, especially in the light of the seven seals, shall we not be a part of that beautiful bride spoken of in Jeremiah 33?

Jeremiah 33:14–16: *Behold, the days come, saith the LORD, that I will perform that good thing which I have promised unto the house of Israel and to the house of Judah. In those days, and at that time, will I cause the Branch of righteousness to grow up unto David; and he shall execute judgment and righteousness in the land. In those days shall Judah be saved, and Jerusalem shall dwell safely; and this is the name of which she shall be called, THE LORD, OUR RIGHTEOUSNESS.*

She, the city, she, the saints, those who are clothed with the righteousness of Christ and His Word, for it is also promised in verse 17, "David shall never want a man to sit upon the throne of the house of Israel." For Christ remains a King "forever." (Psalm 45:6)

Ezekiel 37:24–25[;] Daniel 12:1: *And David my servant shall be king over them; and they all shall have one shepherd: they shall also walk in my judgments, and observe my statutes, and do them. And they shall dwell in the land that I have given unto Jacob my servant, wherein your fathers have dwelt; and they shall dwell therein, even they, and their children, and their children's children for ever: and my servant David shall be their prince for ever. [Ezek. 37:24–25]*

And at that time shall Michael stand up, the great prince which standeth for the children of thy people: and there shall be a time of trouble, such as never was since there was a nation even to that same time: and at that time thy people shall be delivered, every one that shall be found written in the book. [Dan. 12:1]

If we are to be found written in the book, surely we should be found in the first seal for where Christ is revealed, shall not we also be revealed as one who "hearkens and considers" for is not He "our Lord" and shall not we "worship" him "in spirit and in truth" (John 4:24).

In Hosea 2:14 we read, "Therefore, behold I will allure her and bring her into the wilderness, and speak tenderly unto her." The Christian Church being scattered from Jerusalem went throughout all nations. Being amongst the Gentiles, the gospel was to impart unto the Gentiles the riches of God's mercy.

Verse 15: "And I will give her her vineyards from thence, and the Valley of Achor for a door of hope; and she shall sing there, as in the days of her youth, and as in the day when she came up out of the land of Egypt." Here it is promised that once the unfaithful ones as Achan are taken from amongst God's people we will definitely have a deliverance as all the prophets agree.

Verse 16: ["]And it shall be at that day, saith the LORD, that thou shalt call me Ishi, and shalt call me no more Baali. ["] If we are to call God by such an endearing term, we are to know Him a little better and what better [way] [Riddle's interpolation] to know him than in the revelation of Jesus Christ.

Verse 17: ["]For I will take away the names of Baalim out of her mouth, and they shall no more be remembered by their name.["] All false teachers and false prophets are to be forgotten for there is one God, and one Lamb and one seven seal truth.

Verse 18: ["]And in that day will I make a covenant for them with the beasts of the field, and with the fowls of the heavens, and with the creeping things of the ground; and I will break the bow and the sword and the battle out of the earth, and will make them to lie down safely.["] Just as Isaiah 11 has promised, so Hosea also promises, peace for those who are called to the Marriage Supper of the Lamb.

Verses 19 and 20: ["]And I will betroth thee unto me forever; yea, I will betroth thee unto me in righteousness, and in judgment, and in loving-kindness, and in mercies. I will even betroth thee unto me in faithfulness; and thou shalt know the LORD.["] So again, here we see the importance of this opportunity of learning these seven seals and the complete entailment of what that includes.

Verse 21: ["]And it shall come to pass in that day, I will hear, saith the LORD, I will hear the heavens, and they shall hear the earth.["] Are we not a part of this event by faith? Is not heaven in total unity to the receiving of these seals from God? Is not God's word supreme in heaven? And it being the Word which reveals Christ now is the time like never before to pray that we may be worthy to understand these things more clearly.

Verse[s] 22 and 23: ["]And the earth shall hear the corn and the wine, and the oil; and they shall hear Jezreel. And I will sow her unto me in the earth; and I will have mercy upon her that had not obtained mercy; and I will say to them who were not my people, Thou art my people; and they shall say, Thou art my God.["] We will not go at this point into the in depth meaning of the book of Hosea in every particular for our primary subject at this point is the first seal and the Marriage is that subject. This should inspire us to look into the meaning of Hosea 3:5: "Afterward shall the children of Israel return, and seek the LORD, their God, and David, their king, and shall fear the LORD and his goodness in the latter days".

Joel 2:15, 16: ["]Blow the trumpet in Zion, sanctify a fast, call a solemn assembly. Gather the people, sanctify the congregation, assemble the elders, gather the children, and those that nurse at the breasts; let the bridegroom go forth from his chamber, and the bride out of her closet.["] Yes, the bride is definitely to be revealed for we know that Christ is in the Heavenly Sanctuary anticipating His Marriage of which God has spoken. Should we not eagerly ourselves be ready to accept this truth and come out of our closet and be revealed to the world as those who love Christ in truth and in righteousness.

Amos 9:11, 14, 15: *"In that day will I raise up the tabernacle of David that is fallen, and close up the breaches of it; and I will raise up his ruins, and I will build it as in the days of old. . . . And I will bring again the captivity of my people of Israel, and they shall build the waste cities, and inhabit them; and they shall plant vineyeards, and drink their wine; they shall also make gardens, and eat the fruit of them. And I will plant them upon their land, and they shall no more be pulled up out of their land which I have given them, saith the LORD, thy God."*

Obadiah 21: *"And saviors shall come up on Mount Zion to judge the mount of Esau; and the kingdom shall be the LORD's."*

COMMENTARY ON THE KORESH MANUSCRIPT

James D. Tabor and J. Phillip Arnold

Through his lawyer, Dick DeGuerin, David Koresh asked that his completed manuscript be given to us. Evidently, Koresh expected that we would read it with sensitivity and offer some reaction and evaluation based on our academic study of biblical texts and our knowledge of the history of the interpretation of the book of Revelation. The following preliminary comments will help the reader not technically trained in these esoteric texts to follow Koresh's rather involved thinking and interpretation.

The key to understanding Koresh and his perception of his identity and mission clearly centers on one question from the book of Revelation: "Who is worthy to open the scroll and to loose its seals?" (Rev. 5:2). The text identifies a figure known as the Lamb, or "Root [Branch] of David," who alone is able to open this mysterious book sealed with Seven Seals (Rev. 5:5). Traditional Christianity has, of course, always understood this figure as Jesus Christ. Hence, the endless confusion as to whether or not Koresh actually claimed to be Jesus, or even God himself. This manuscript makes it clear that he claimed to be neither despite all the confused and misleading reports about his self-understanding. However, he certainly *did* claim to be the Lamb who opens the sealed scroll, as well as the figure who rides the White Horse when the First Seal is opened and who appears at the end of the book, still mounted on the same White Horse, when the "marriage of the Lamb" takes place (Rev. 6:1–2; 19:7–19).

Part of the confusion has to do with the use of the term "Christ," from the Greek word *christos,* which is not a proper name but a title. It means "anointed one" or, to use the original Hebrew word, "messiah." Since all the ancient high priests and kings of Israel were "anointed," in that sense they can be called "Christ" or "Messiah," which is standard biblical usage. However, the Prophets focus on the specific and ideal Christ, or Messiah, who is to come. This one was to be a "Branch of David," that is, a descendant of King David, and would rule as a king in Jerusalem, bringing peace to Israel and all nations (Isa. 11:1; Jer. 23:5). This Christ, like David of old, is also called the "Son of God" (Ps. 2:6; 2 Sam. 7:14). Koresh clearly believed that Jesus of Nazareth was this Christ. However, he also maintained that the Prophets foretell that another "Christ," a Branch of David, would appear at the end of time and open the Seven Seals.

Psalm 45 is the key to the First Seal according to Koresh's interpretation. Here the king is anointed, that is, made "Christ," and rides his horse triumphantly (v. 1–7). This parallels Revelation 6:1–2 and 19:7–19, and this figure is identified with the Lamb. After the conquest of his enemies, the marriage feast takes place. This Lamb marries virgin "daughters" and has many children who are destined to rule with him over the earth (Ps. 45:10–17). Jesus of Nazareth, though anointed, never fulfilled this prophecy, since he never married and had children, as this text requires. Accordingly, Koresh believed that Psalm 45, along with several other key messianic texts, could not apply to this appearance of Jesus Christ of the first century. Psalm 40 also speaks of the same figure: "Then said I, Lo, I come; in the scroll of the book it is written of me, I delight to do thy will, O my God, yea thy law is within my heart" (v. 6–7). The text then characterizes this one as having "iniquities more than the hairs of mine head" (v. 12). This "sinful Messiah" is nonetheless the one written of in the scroll, which Koresh connected to the seven-sealed scroll of Revelation 6. The same figure is mentioned in Isaiah 45:1 and called by name: "Thus says the LORD, to his anointed [Christ], to Cyrus ["Koresh" in Hebrew], whose right hand I have held, to subdue nations before him." This Cyrus, or Koresh, is called "Christ," and his mission is to destroy Babylon. Historians have understood the reference to be to the ancient Persian king Cyrus, who destroyed ancient Babylon. But there is a deeper spiritual and prophetic meaning according to Koresh and, for that matter, the book of Revelation. The whole religious-political system is called "mystery Babylon the Great." As the text says, "Babylon is fallen, is fallen" (Rev. 18:2). Koresh took the repetition of the verb to indicate a *double* meaning and fulfillment, that is, not only the fall of ancient Babylon but also the fall of her counterpart at the end of history. This last Babylon, Western society, is to be defeated by the last Christ/King/Koresh, who is also the Branch of David, according to Koresh.

Koresh found his role described in great detail in Isaiah 40–66. He interpreted some passages in Isaiah quite personally, as if the Scriptures had been written just for him, and found them encouraging. For example, "Assemble yourselves and hear, which among them has declared these things, Yahweh has *loved him:* he will do his pleasure on Babylon, and *his arm* shall be on the Chaldeans" (emphasis added) (Isa. 48:14). This verse was of particular importance to Koresh as a succinct statement of his mission: he was loved by God, and as the arm of Yahweh, he would bring down Babylon. God speaks in the first person about this figure: "I, even I, have spoken, yes I have *called him,* I have brought *him* and he shall make *his way* prosperous. Come near to me, and hear this: I have not spoken in secret from the beginning; from the time that it was, there am I: and now the Lord Yahweh and his *Spirit has sent me*" (emphasis added). (Isa. 48:15–16) This verse was instrumental in Koresh's understanding of the notion of Christ, which we explained above. Here Yahweh sends one with his Spirit, that same Christ Spirit, that was with him from the beginning. It is as if that Spirit, speaking through Isaiah, takes up the first person but then switches to the third person; in other words, the prophetic "I," who is with Yahweh in the beginning, embodies the "him" who is sent. The text continues: "Go forth from Babylon, flee from the Chaldeans" (v. 20), which the Davidians understood as yet another reference to their upcoming flight to Israel.

There are dozens of references to a mysterious "servant" of Yahweh in Isaiah 40–55. Most often, biblical scholars agree, these references are to the nation of Israel, which is called metaphorically God's servant (Isa. 42:21). However, there are five sections of Isaiah, which are called the "Servant Songs" in biblical scholarship, that appear to address an *individual* (Isa. 42:1–4; 49:1–6; 50:4–11; 52:13–53:12). This figure is, in fact, contrasted with the servant nation, which is said to be deaf and blind (Isa. 42:19). The New Testament applies each of these songs to Jesus. Koresh tried to demonstrate that these songs refer to a subsequent or final Christ figure, namely Cyrus, conqueror of Babylon, who will appear before the end of history. This teaching was of enormous influence upon his students, who became convinced that these texts did not and could not apply to Jesus. Given their unfaltering faith in the inspiration of the Bible, they found it easy to believe that Koresh was indeed the final Christ or "servant" of Yahweh. Koresh argued, for example, that the servant mentioned in Isaiah 49:1–4 is actually introduced in the previous chapter as the one who will lead God's people out of Babylon and eventually even destroy the Babylonians (48:14–20). The text also says this figure will "raise up the tribes of Jacob, and restore the preserved of Israel" (Isa. 49:6). Since Jesus never fulfilled this prophecy, Koresh connected such a task with Revelation 7, where the "messenger from the east" gathers his 144,000 from the twelve tribes of Israel. He maintained that Jesus never did any of these things, but they would be accomplished by this final messenger.

Koresh found every detail of the origin and mission of this figure meticulously described in Scripture. For example, this one is to come from the north and the east (Isa. 41:1–2, 25; 46:11). The one who comes from the north is the one who comes from God's throne, which is said to be in the northern part of the heavens (Ps. 48:2; Isa. 14:13; Job 26:7). When John has his vision in Revelation 4, he is told to "come up hither" to heaven, which would be to ascend to the north. Koresh believed that he too had been before the throne of God in the north and had now returned with the sealed book in his hand. Koresh claimed that the reference to the "east" prophesied his own revelation in Israel in 1985, a far country to the east of the United States. Since the United States, in his view, was the very "seat of modern Babylon," this figure comes from Israel to the United States to deliver his message. Koresh connected these references in Isaiah to Revelation 7:2: "And I saw another angel ascending *from the east,* having the seal of the living God" (emphasis added). This one from the east was to come to "Babylon" and call out the faithful, first spiritually and later physically. Koresh expected that his followers, who would eventually number 144,000, would someday move to Israel and actually participate in the final events set forth in Daniel 11:40–45, which he often called the most important prophecy in the Bible. This passage describes a wicked "king of the north," who will come into Palestine shortly before the end of the age but will ultimately be overthrown by God. The Davidians interpreted these prophecies literally and constantly discussed them in great detail. They often referred to Isaiah 2 and Micah 4, and the actual kingdom or government that God was to set up in Jerusalem, in the Land of Israel, following the events of Daniel 11.

Koresh found reference to this second "Christ" figure, who is called a "ravenous bird from the east" in Isaiah 46:11, in other biblical texts that appear to have nothing to do with prophetic apocalypticism. For example, Ecclesiastes 12 contains a number of poetic images such as the sun being darkened, the "keepers of the house" trembling, the "strong men" being bent, and the "grinders" ceasing because they are few (12:2–3). These have traditionally been understood as references to old age: dimming eyes, trembling hands, stooped legs, and loss of teeth. However, in verse 4 there is a reference to one "rising up at the voice of the bird," which Koresh equated to the "bird from the east" in Isaiah. On this basis Koresh saw the entire chapter as an apocalyptic poem about the end of the age. The "evil days" of verse 1 he took to be the tribulations of the end of history, rather than old age. The heavenly signs, the darkened sun and falling stars, mentioned in verse 2, he paralleled to the Sixth Seal and to Jesus' Olivet prophecy in which he predicted these very things (Rev. 6:13; Matt. 24:29). The "keepers of the house trembling" then refers to the kings and rulers who will tremble with fear when the great Day of Judgment is manifested as described in Revelation 6:15–17: And the kings of the earth, and the great men, and the rich men, and the chief captains, and the mighty men . . . hid themselves in the dens and in the rocks of the mountains and said to the mountains and rocks, Fall on us, and hide us from the face of him that sits on the throne and from the wrath of the Lamb. Koresh also saw the phrase in Ecclesiastes "they will be afraid of that which is high" (v. 12:5) as prefiguring this very passage in Revelation.

Koresh further expanded this concept, pulling in what he felt were parallel images throughout the Bible. For example, this "bird" or messenger from the east (Isa. 46:12) is also called the "arm of Yahweh" in related passages such as Isaiah 52:10–12 and Isaiah 40:10–11. In other words, he is the instrument who gathers this remnant people from Babylon and takes them to the land of Israel (Isa. 52:10–12). To establish that this metaphor the "arm of Yahweh" refers to a specific individual, Koresh incorporated other texts, particularly from the Psalms. Psalm 80:17 says: "Let your hand be upon the *man of your right hand*, upon the son of man whom you made strong for yourself" (emphasis added). Psalm 89, verses 13 and 27, directly speaks of this Davidic ruler or messiah: "You have a *mighty arm*, strong is your hand, and high is your right hand. . . . Also I will *make him* my first born, higher than the kings of the earth" (emphasis added). In this interpretation, this "man of the right hand" is the son of David, the Messiah, or Koresh, conqueror of Babylon.

This figure is also called the Branch, or sprout, of David. Isaiah 11 gives a sketch of his career (vv. 1–2). This Branch is also mentioned in Isaiah 4:2, Jeremiah 23:5, and Zechariah 3:8. In each of these contexts Koresh attempted to show that the accomplishments of the figure were not those of Jesus but would be those of the final Christ. To connect this Branch with the "arm of Yahweh" in other texts, Koresh used Psalm 80:15, which speaks of the "branch that you have made strong for yourself" and in the following verses of the "man of your right hand." The name "Branch Davidian," of course, is connected to these ideas; that one from the line of King David will actually reign in Jerusalem. Ben Roden, as we have described, applied some of these texts to himself when, in 1970, he added "Branch" to the group's name. However, Koresh took Roden's essential formulation and developed it beyond anything his predecessor could have imagined. It was unnecessary for Koresh to claim actual biological lineage from King David, which is the historical meaning of this reference to the Branch figure. In Isaiah 11:1 the "Branch" comes from the line of Jesse, the father of King David of Israel. This is why the New Testament writers go to such pains to demonstrate that Jesus of Nazareth is of this lineage (Matt. 1; Luke 3).

In his manuscript Koresh begins to discuss the many texts of the Prophets that herald this "Davidian" figure (Jer. 23:5–8; 19–20; 33:14–16; Ezek. 37:24–25; Hos. 3:5). He makes the point repeatedly that this Christ comes in the *latter* times and that Jesus of Nazareth, who came two thousand years ago, never fulfilled these prophecies. The Lamb who comes and opens the seals right before the end is humiliated and maligned and, like Jesus, offers God's truth to the world. As stated at the start of this commentary, Koresh believed he was the actual, final manifestation of the Lamb who will fulfill these prophecies regarding the Messiah.

According to this perspective, the Waco standoff and "waiting period" was a test for all humanity, but it did not have to end as it did. Koresh believed that the world was being offered a chance to listen to this last Christ/Koresh, who could open the seals and thus show the way of repentance to our society. He was offering the actual decoding of the Seven Seals in written form to all who wanted to hear. In the present Branch Davidian view, this opportunity to repent was lost, and the rejection and death of Koresh at thirty-three, close to Passover, was a repetition of the past. They assert that the Fifth Seal, which allowed for a time of repentance while the message went forth, ended with the "rest killed" as predicted (Rev. 6:11). The Branch Davidians now believe that the probation period is over, and the Sixth Seal of the Judgment of God is pending.

The manuscript indicates that those who respond to the message of repentance, who turn to God and follow the Law of God, through accepting the Lamb/Koresh/Christ/King, will be invited to the "marriage" feast. They are the elect who make up the Bride of the Lamb. As Koresh ends his discourse on the First Seal, this is his main point. Those who are truly part of the "Bride" are to come out of the "closet" and be revealed.

The manuscript also carefully maintains the distinction between God the Father and his Lamb, or the Messiah. In that sense Koresh never said he was God. However, like the Hebrew prophets of old and like Jesus of Nazareth, he did claim to speak the words of Yahweh God (the Father) directly and in that sense could use, as they did, the first person mode of discourse.

The poem "Eden to Eden" contains Koresh's more mystical teachings. Like the apostle Paul, Koresh implies that the "marriage of the Lamb" is a mystery that somehow rectifies what happened at Eden in the Fall (Eph. 5:31–32). The physical sexual union ("the two shall become one flesh") has a deeper meaning and involves the perfect bonding of "Adam and his spirit Eve" in the "new Man" to come. Koresh taught the importance of the feminine side of the Divine and implies that Adam was created to express this dual image. However, through sin, Adam and his descendants were separated from the spiritual, feminine side and remain so. Through the revelation of Christ in the person of the Lamb, people are reunited with their fragmented selves and gathered as lovers of God for the ultimate union, which will restore Eden.

The manuscript on the Seven Seals also suggests Koresh's state of mind the night before he died. We know that the first chapter of this work was completed on Sunday evening, the night before the fire, and was typed onto a computer disk by Ruth Riddle. This disk survived the fire, carried out by Riddle in her jacket pocket.

The existence of the manuscript itself, as well as internal evidence within the text, appears to confirm that Koresh was keeping his promise to produce an interpretive document and supports the view that Koresh intended to lead his group out peacefully. The form and structure of the manuscript indicate that Koresh did intend to write a substantive piece of work. After conceptualizing the project over that last weekend, Koresh dictated to Riddle, on Sunday evening, April 18, in one long sitting of approximately four hours. The printed-out text consists of about twenty-eight double-spaced pages. The work begins with a preface consisting of Koresh's poem "Eden to Eden," which is reproduced above. His next section, the "Introduction," sets forth the interpretive principles and general themes that underlie the main body of the envisioned work. In "Chapter One," Koresh turns his attention to the meaning of the First Seal. This chapter ends with two biblical quotations, offering a sense of closure regarding the First Seal and expectancy concerning his discussion of the Second Seal in the following chapter, which would have been dictated at the next sitting—probably on the day of the fire.

Throughout the work Koresh appears to direct his words to those outside Mount Carmel, assuming an audience who would not know the meaning of the Seven Seals. His vocabulary style, and approach show that he expects his words will be read by nonbelievers, whom Koresh hoped to persuade. Ironically, the very last words we have from him in this manuscript read: "Should we not eagerly ourselves be ready to accept this truth and come out of our closet and be revealed to the world as those who love Christ in truth and in righteousness?" Koresh not only expects some readers to accept his teaching but also prepares his followers inside Mount Carmel to "come out" of the center. This is seen further in his reference to Joel 2, verses 15 and 16, which is cited immediately before the sentence quoted above. This passage orders those in Zion (Mount Carmel) to "gather the people

. . . assemble the elders, gather the children" and infants and follow the bridegroom (Koresh) "from his chamber and the bride out of her closet." The Davidians understood other passages from Isaiah to refer to their refuge at Mount Carmel as a "chamber" where they could wait for God's intervention. This choice of the term "come out"—drawn from Scripture and used in Koresh's April 14 letter to Dick DeGuerin, as well as in the manuscript—offers the best evidence of what he had on his mind that last evening before the fire.

NOTES

CHAPTER I

1. According to David Thibodeau and other survivors, group members did not formally refer to themselves as Branch Davidians but rather understood themselves as "students of the seven seals." Those who came to Mount Carmel in the late 1980s were not organized into any official denomination. They were attracted to the teachings of David Koresh and came to the center to study the Bible, coming and going as they were willing or able. As we will discuss in the following chapter, the name "Davidian" goes back to Victor Houteff, who founded the original Mount Carmel community in 1935. The designation "Branch" was introduced in 1970 by Ben Roden, a subsequent leader of the group. Koresh identified himself with these leaders; and in his taped messages to his students around the world, he often addressed them as "Branches." We use the term "Branch Davidian" in this book as a convenient designation for the Mount Carmel movement in the 1980s and 1990s.

2. We use quotation marks to highlight the pejorative force that terms like "cult" and "cult" leader have in anticult polemics.

3. Koresh recounts his story later that day in a telephone interview with Charlie Serafin broadcast live on the Dallas radio station KRLD.

4. The official BATF account of what happened that day is in the *Report of the Department of the Treasury on the BATF Investigation of Vernon Wayne Howell also Known as David Koresh* (Washington, D.C.: U.S. Government Printing Office, 1993), hereafter, *Dept. of Treasury Report.* It is worth noting that the surviving videotape footage of the shoot-out shows BATF agents firing heavily and randomly at the building, but the cars and trucks behind which they are crouched show no signs of return fire—windshields are intact, no dust is being kicked up around them. Also, the windows in the front of the building are curtained, and no one is visible. Obviously, since BATF agents were wounded and killed, the Branch Davidians did return some fire; however, survivors insist it was minimal and that most of them were on the floor, terrified of being hit by the bullets coming from all directions, including from the helicopters overhead. On the 911 audiotapes, Wayne Martin, the Branch Davidian lawyer who made the call minutes after the raid, keeps insisting that they are not returning fire and demanding that the BATF agents be called off. He repeatedly says, "Tell them to back off, there are women and children in here."

5. In testimony at the trial, the BATF agent Ken King, who was severely wounded, testified that his orders were to forcefully enter the building on the south side within thirty seconds after arrival with no contingency plans for surrender or peaceful entry contemplated (Jack DeVault [special correspondent], unpublished notes of trial testimony, January 24, 1994). The *Dept. of Treasury Report* candidly discusses the forceful "raid" tactics, rejecting a peaceful serving of the search warrant as an option; see pp. 133–42.

6. See *United States Department of Justice Report to the Deputy Attorney General on the Events at Waco, Texas, February 28 to April 19, 1993*, Redacted Version (Washington, D.C.: U.S. Government Printing Office, 1993), pp. 280–94, for a detailed account (hereafter, *Dept. of Justice Report*). This is the main volume, 348 pages plus appendixes, of the official Department of Justice report on Waco.

7. The total cost of the Waco operation has not been disclosed and would be difficult to calculate; however it clearly ran into the millions of dollars. On any given day there were a minimum of 719 law enforcement officers involved in the Waco operation. The FBI alone committed 668 personnel to the standoff, with approximately 217 agents and 41 support personnel present each day of the siege. In addition, there were personnel from the BATF, Texas Rangers, Waco police, McLennan County Sheriff's Office, U.S. Customs, Texas National Guard, Texas Department of Public Safety, and the United States Army (See *Dept. of Justice Report*, pp. 8–10). The involvement of U.S. military personnel and equipment, including Bradley fighting vehicles, raises questions about possible violations of the *posse comitatus* act that forbids the use of United States armed forces against citizens.

8. See *Dept. of Justice Report*, pp. 102–104, for names and details of the injuries. The six Branch Davidians officially listed as dead do not include Koresh's eighteen-month-old daughter who, in his interviews over KRLD radio and CNN television the day of the raid, Koresh tearfully claimed was killed. Surviving Branch Davidians express puzzlement over this statement and deny knowledge of this child. Whereas the medical examiner concluded that seventy-five persons died in the fire on April 19, the Davidians only list seventy-four names, leaving one unaccounted for. This remains one of the many unsolved mysteries connected with the events at Waco.

9. Two of the women who died were pregnant. Some bodies cannot be identified although DNA testing continues. The total Branch Davidian community in the Waco area on the day of the initial raid numbered approximately 130. Fifty-one days later, 80 had been killed, 35 had been sent out before April 19, 9 survived the fire, and 6 or more had been outside Mount Carmel on February 28. Most died from smoke inhalation, a few from falling debris, and some from gunshot wounds, apparently self-inflicted as the heat from the fire became unbearable.

David Koresh's body was identified by the chief medical examiner, based on dental records in an autopsy completed on May 5, 1993 (Tarrant County Case no. 930009). He died from a gunshot wound to the midforehead. He was buried at a private gathering attended by his mother and four relatives in Tyler, Texas, in Memorial Park Cemetery on May 27. No clergy were present, and no ceremony was conducted. His coffin was draped with an Israeli flag procured from Congregation Ahavath Achim, the local Conservative Jewish temple. Rabbi Lawrence Finkelstein reported to James Tabor that Bonnie Haldeman, Koresh's mother, had come to his office and had asked how she could obtain an Israeli flag for the burial. He related that one had been recently found discarded on a Texas highway by a passerby and had been brought to the synagogue in Tyler. The rabbi had it cleaned and stored it away, having no immediate use for it. He gave the flag to Mrs. Haldeman for Koresh's burial.

10. On October 29, 1994, a full twenty months later, it was reported that the two BATF agents who had led the initial raid, Charles Sarabyn and Phillip Chojnacki, had also been dismissed from the agency. It was charged that they were guilty of poor judgment and subsequent lying to investigators (Bill Hirschman, "ATF Fires Agents Who Led Raid on Waco Compound," *Fort Lauderdale Sun-Sentinel*, October 29, 1994, p. 1A). Sarabyn and Chojnacki were subsequently rehired on December 21, 1994, with full back pay and benefits. Both had threatened lawsuits, which this settlement by the BATF sought to avoid.

11. These calls were initiated by Koresh in an attempt to tell his side of the situation to the public. Koresh had spoken over CNN with the anchorman David French at 7:25 P.M. on Sunday, the day of the raid. He subsequently called in and spoke with the KRLD station manager Charlie Serafin at 10:05 P.M. for about twenty minutes and then again at 1:50 A.M. for about twenty-five minutes. The FBI was upset over these contacts and requested that no further interviews be conducted. At 1:30 P.M. on Monday, March 1, all but two telephone lines in Mount Carmel were cut off. The remaining two lines could only be used to reach the federal negotiators (*Dept. of Justice Report*, pp. 26–28).

12. See Department of Justice, *Evaluation of the Handling of the Branch Davidian Stand-off in Waco, Texas* (Washington, D.C.: U.S. Government Printing Office, 1993), pp. 42 (hereafter *Evaluation*). In addition to the main volume of the *Dept. of Justice Report*, there were three smaller volumes produced by the Department of Justice review dealing with related aspects of the Waco events: *Recommendations of Experts, Evaluation of the Handling of the Branch Davidian Stand-off*, and *Lessons of Waco*.

13. See the interview with Koresh's attorney Dick DeGuerin, by Peter Maas in his article, "What Might Have Been," *Parade*, February 27, 1994, pp. 4–6.

Also, note the insightful reports of Nancy Ammerman and Lawrence Sullivan, both of whom offer a religious studies perspective, in the official Department of Justice report, *Recommendations of Experts for Improvements in Federal Law Enforcement after Waco* (Washington, D.C.: U.S. Government Printing Office, 1993), hereafter, *Recommendations.*

14. According to FBI records, over the fifty-one-day period negotiators spoke by telephone with over fifty individuals inside Mount Carmel, logging in a total time of over two hundred hours. However, 80 percent of this time was spent talking with Schneider and Koresh. There were 459 conversations with Schneider, which took up ninety-six hours, or nearly half the time; and Koresh had 117 conversations that took up another sixty hours (*Dept. of Justice Report,* pp. 10–11).

15. Ibid., pp. 57–58.

16. Ibid., pp. 54–55.

17. Lee Hancock, "Another Delay at Waco," *Dallas Morning News,* March 5, 1993, pp. 1A, 15A.

18. *Dept. of Justice Report,* p. 237. On March 1, President Clinton spoke with Acting Attorney General Gerson about the Waco situation.

19. Ibid., p. 70.

20. Ibid., p. 79.

21. We are using *apocalypticism* here to refer to the view that the End Time is imminent, with the signs of the end unfolding according to a set sequence of events revealed in the prophetic texts of Scripture.

22. According to surviving Davidians, the change in location for some of these events from Israel to Texas was increasingly discussed as Koresh became more and more convinced that an initial confrontation at Mount Carmel was likely.

23. See interview with Henry McMahon, by James L. Pate, in "Waco: Behind the Cover-up," *Soldier of Fortune,* November 1993, pp. 36–41, 71–72; also Livingstone Fagan, "Mt. Carmel: The Unseen Reality," p. 12.

24. *Dept. of Justice Report,* p. 75.

25. "And there shall be signs in the sun, and in the moon, and in the stars; and upon the earth distress of nations, with perplexity; the sea and the waves roaring; men's hearts failing them for fear, and for looking after those things which are coming on the earth: for the powers of heaven shall be shaken" (Luke 21:25–26). The gospel of Matthew speaks of "the sign of the Son of man in heaven" (Matt. 24:30).

26. David Thibodeau, conversations with James Tabor, Guilford College, Greensboro, N.C., June 22–23, 1994.

27. Phillip Arnold attended the March 7 FBI press briefing and introduced himself to the spokesperson, Agent Bob Ricks. He later went to the FBI Command Center in Waco and offered his services.

28. As it turned out, Arnold and Tabor were never allowed to communicate directly with Koresh. The FBI negotiators only made use of their expertise in the few conversations that Arnold had with several midlevel agents.

29. *Dept. of Justice Report,* appendix C, and p. 186.

30. At one point, early in March, Engleman asked the Branch Davidians to move their satellite dish to a specific position if they were listening. They responded a few minutes later. Also, David Thibodeau, one of those who survived the fire, reports that Engleman's show was avidly followed by the group each day.

31. David Thibodeau, conversations with James Tabor, Washington, D.C., November 15, 1993.

32. A full account of Arnold and Tabor's involvement is published in *From the Ashes: Making Sense of Waco,* ed. James R. Lewis (Lanham, Md.: Rowman & Littlefield Publishers, 1994), pp. 13–32.

33. As we will explain in chapter 2, the Branch Davidians observed the Sabbath on Saturday and other Jewish annual holy days mentioned in the Bible.

34. A facsimile of this letter is found in *Dept. of Justice Report,* appendix E.

35. *Dept. of Justice Report,* p. 105. In this official report, the only place this April 14 letter is mentioned is the chronological log for April 9, five days *before* it was even written. Koresh released his first letter that day, and the log notes that "Koresh sent out four additional letters." It is unlikely that anyone reading the Department of Justice report would notice its existence or realize that it was a direct response to the audiocassette from Arnold and Tabor that the FBI allowed Dick DeGuerin to carry into Mount Carmel on April 4.

36. This is also the conclusion of Brad Bailey and Bob Darden, *Mad Man in Waco: The Complete Story of the Davidian Cult, David Koresh and the Waco Massacre* (Waco, Tex.: WRS Publishing, 1993), pp. 218–30.

37. See *Evaluation,* pp. 41–42.

38. *Dept. of Justice Report,* p. 175.

39. Ibid., p. 176.

40. As it turns out, quite the opposite is the case. Apparently, Miron is an anticult activist. He was involved in the 1970s with the Citizens' Freedom Foundation, the anticult group that became CAN. The very week he was offering his evaluation to the FBI, he published an article in the *Syracuse New Times* called "The Mark of a Cult," which simply echoed standard, uninformed slander of new religious movements. Few scholars in the academic study of religion or in the field of sociology accept the category or label "cult" for such new religious movements. Dr. Miron appears to lack academic qualifications in the fields of religious studies, biblical studies, or the sociology of religion. Although the FBI denies that it was influenced by so-called cult experts, the evidence shows otherwise (*Dept. of Justice Report,* pp. 190–93).

41. *Dept. of Justice Report,* pp. 263–79.

42. See *Dept. of Justice Report,* pp. 263–76, for documentation on the following sequence of events.

43. We have a copy of the transcript of a phone conversation between Koresh and Joyce Sparks, a supervisor from the Texas Children's Protective Services office, taped on April 2, 1992, discussing the investigation. The tone of the conversation is extremely cordial, and Koresh effectively presents the perspective of the group. See the discussion of this point by Lawrence Lilliston, "Who Committed Child Abuse at Waco?" in *From the Ashes,* pp. 169–73.

44. *Dept. of Justice Report,* p. 217.

45. Paul Anderson, in his recent biography of Janet Reno, *Janet Reno: Doing the Right Thing* (New York: John Wiley & Sons, 1994) perpetuates this false story. As part of his justification of Reno's decision to move against Mount Carmel with the tanks, he claims that Koresh had promised to surrender after writing his Seven Seals manuscript, "but he wasn't writing" (p. 188).

46. DeGuerin, "Interview," p. 6.

47. Ruth Riddle, telephone conversations with Phillip Arnold, October 1993, reported to James Tabor; and Thibodeau, conversations with Tabor, June 22–23, 1994.

48. For the text of Koresh's manuscript, "The Seven Seals of the Book of Revelation," and the commentary by James Tabor and Phillip Arnold, see the appendix. The computer disk is actually listed as Lab Item 20D in the "Fire Investigation Report," see *Department of Justice Report,* appendix D, p. vii. It is described as a Maxell MF2-DD floppy disk marked "Seven Seals." It was subsequently released to the attorneys of Ruth Riddle, passed on to Dick DeGuerin, and finally to Arnold and Tabor for analysis. Tabor and Arnold prepared a printed edition with commentary, in consultation with Ruth Riddle, who was being held in jail in San Antonio. Dick DeGuerin authorized the release of the manuscript to *Newsweek* magazine and the Associated Press in October 1993. The manuscript was formally presented by Arnold and Tabor to interested scholars at the American Academy of Religion, Annual Meeting, Washington, D.C., November 22, 1993.

49. The government position is summarized in the *Dept. of Justice Report,* pp. 295–307, and appendix D, which contains the "Fire Investigation Report."

50. In the taped conversation between Koresh and Joyce Sparks of the Texas Children's Protective Services made on April 2, 1992, he discusses in detail the charge that the group might commit suicide, denying it categorically. Koresh repeatedly told FBI negotiators that suicide was not a possibility (*Dept. of Justice Report,* pp. 50, 210–14). See James R. Lewis, "Fanning the Flames of Suspicion: The Case against Mass Suicide at Waco," in *From the Ashes,* pp. 115–20; and Ron Cole, *Sinister Twilight,* 2d ed. (privately published, 1994), pp. 65–79.

CHAPTER 2

1. *Dept. of Justice Report*, p. 205.
2. *Seventh-Day Adventist Yearbook, 1994* (Hagerstown, Md.: Review and Herald Publishing Assoc., 1994), p. 4.
3. Thibodeau, conversations with Tabor, June 22–23, 1994.
4. They mailed out the literature and distributed it at Adventist gatherings. One tract from the 1980s is titled "Divided We Stand-Divided We Fall." Directly addressed to the Seventh-Day Adventist reader, it offers a survey of church history up through Ellen G. White, then catalogues the apostasy of the Adventist movement since her time. The concluding paragraph captures the flavor of the essential message: "The Seventh-day Adventists were given a divine commission to warn the world of these events, but they themselves rejected truth from Heaven in 1929, 1955, and 1977, when divinely inspired messengers bearing the 4th, 5th, and 6th angels messages of Revelation 14:14–18 were sent to them. Now God calls the world to witness what He will do to His rebellious children in the Seventh-day Adventist church. Read Amos 3:7–10. The prophetic voice of the Seventh Angel of Revelation 10:7 is speaking to you. The seventh and last prophetic movement of the Reformation has been raised up by God with a prophet to call you to repentance and to bring the Reformation to a grand, glorious climax of unity amongst God's children of all denominations and religions (Eph 4:13). "SURELY THE LORD GOD WILL DO NOTHING, BUT HE REVEALETH HIS SECRET UNTO HIS SERVANTS THE PROPHETS (LIVING TODAY).' Amos 3:7." This tract is undated, but it gives a post office box in Palestine, Texas, indicating that it comes from the period 1985–1990 when Koresh's followers were located there. Koresh is not mentioned in this tract. The messengers in 1929, 1955, and 1977 are of course his predecessors, Houteff and Ben and Lois Roden, respectively. Despite this prediction of a completion of the Protestant Reformation and the appeal to "all denominations and religions," it is obvious that the audience is in fact limited to Seventh-Day Adventists, who would be familiar with the idea of the angelic messages of Revelation 14, and who would have identified the third angel with their own prophet Ellen G. White.
5. For example, the opening of "Judge What I Say" (April 2, 1985), audiocassette.
6. "Study on Joel and Daniel 11" (1987), audiocassette.
7. See Marc Breault's autobiographical account, co-written by Martin King, in *Inside the Cult: A Member's Chilling, Exclusive Account of Madness and Depravity in David Koresh's Compound* (New York: Signet Books, 1993), pp. 46–70.
8. "Confusion" (July 18, 1987), audiocassette transcript, p. 21.

9. The following material is taken from a transcript of an interview with Rita Riddle, by Professor Stuart Wright of Lamar University, Waco, Texas, December 17, 1993.

10. Rita Riddle, interview transcript, Wright, p. 1.

11. Ibid., pp. 2–3.

12. James Tabor had extensive conversations with Rita Riddle, Catherine Matteson, David Thibodeau, Clive Doyle, and Wally Kennett on various occasions from fall 1993 through summer 1994.

13. Fagan, "Mount Carmel," p. 7.

14. Ibid., p. 8.

15. "Ancient of Days," audiocassette transcript, June 14, 1986, p. 7.

16. Ibid., p. 2.

17. This material is taken from conversations between Catherine Matteson and James Tabor, Waco, Texas, April 17–19, 1994; and from the transcript of an interview with Catherine Matteson by Professor Stuart Wright of Lamar University, Waco, Texas, September 10, 1993.

18. Matteson, interview by Wright, p. 1.

19. Ibid., p. 1.

20. Fagan, "Mt. Carmel," p. 7.

21. "Ancient of Days," pp. 15, 25.

22. Fagan, "Mt. Carmel," pp. 8–9.

23. This is confirmed in James Tabor's conversations with Sheila Martin, Rita Riddle, and Catherine Matteson, Waco, Texas, April 17–19 1994.

24. Houteff's name is pronounced HOT-eff. Sources on the Houteff Davidians are varied. The most valuable original sources are his own prolific writings, which run thousands of pages and are bound in two volumes, *Shepherd's Rod* and *Timely Greetings,* and the extensive interviews conducted in 1975 by Dan McGee of Baylor University with George Saether, who joined the community in 1936 (George W. Saether, "Oral Memoirs" [Institute for Oral History, Baylor University, 1975]). Houteff wrote numerous tracts that survive, some of which are still circulated by his followers. We also have copies of his periodical, *The Symbolic Code,* which was published in the late 1930s and 1940s. The best scholarly account is by the Baylor University professor William Pitts, in *Syzgy: Journal of Alternative Religion and Culture,* vol. 2, nos. 1–2 (1993), pp. 39–54, as well as his short summary "The Davidian Tradition," in *From the Ashes,* pp. 33–39. A more popular narrative account by Bob Darden and Brad Bailey runs through the book *Mad Man in Waco.* Also, see the short entry in *The Encyclopedia of American Religions,* 3d ed., p. 514. Our summary of Houteff's life is based on the Saether material, and our discussion of his doctrinal beliefs is based on his own published writings.

25. See Ellen G. White, *The Great Controversy* (Washington, D.C.: Review and Herald Publishing Assoc., 1911), pp. 424–25. Ellen G. White maintained that a "special work of purification, of putting away of sin, among God's people

upon earth," was necessary, but in her time she obviously viewed her own followers as the purified who had left their more mainstream Christian churches.

26. Ibid., pp. 653–61.
27. See "Davidian Seventh-Day Adventists-Shepherd's Rod," *Seventh-Day Adventist Encyclopedia* (Washington, D.C.: Review and Herald Publishing Assoc., 1966), p. 329. The Seventh-Day Adventists later published a refutation of Houteff's theology in an official church document titled *Some Teaching of the Shepherd's Rod Examined* (Washington, D.C.: Review and Herald Publishing Assoc., 1956).
28. See Victor Houteff, "The Judgment and the Harvest," *Shepherd's Rod,* vol. 1, tract 3 (1933), p. 72.
29. Houteff quotes such texts as Ezekiel 36–38, Isaiah 11, and Jeremiah 31 in this regard. See his "Mount Zion at the Eleventh Hour," tract 8 (1947), pp. 8–28.
30. See Houteff's tract, "Mount Sion at 'The Eleventh Hour' " (1937), pp. 8–17.
31. Early life at Mount Carmel was documented by Mary Elizabeth Power in her master of arts thesis done at Baylor University in 1940, "A Study of the Seventh-Day Adventist Community, Mount Carmel Center, Waco, Texas." She did interviews with Victor Houteff and most of the community's principals of this period. In addition to the oral memoirs of George Saether, there are also those of Bonnie Smith, who lived at Mount Carmel at the time ("Oral Memoirs" [Institute for Oral History, Baylor University, 1989]).
32. Saether, "Oral Memoirs," pp. 171–72.
33. Ibid., p. 123.
34. The *Waco Tribune-Herald* ran some interesting stories during late April and early May 1959 on events at Mount Carmel, including interviews with some of the residents who had come from around the country. Other Davidian groups who remained loyal to the Houteff message have survived. One is now located in Exeter, Missouri, and another in Salem, South Carolina. See *Encyclopedia of American Religions,* 3d ed., p. 514.
35. We are indebted to Catherine Matteson, who served for years as Lois Roden's secretary and able assistant, for insight into this aspect of Roden's theology. We also have tapes of Lois Roden's sermons, a small book she wrote titled *As an Eagle: The Holy Spirit Mother* (1981), and copies of her magazine, *SHEkinah,* which she began to publish in late 1980.
36. Lois Roden relied on passages in both the Hebrew Bible and the New Testament, which she said had not been accurately translated; for example, she maintained that Psalm 113:4–6 should read: "High above the nations is the LORD, above the heavens is His glory. Who is like unto the LORD our God, she that is enthroned on high, she that looks down low upon the earth."

37. See the account in Kenneth Samples, et al., *Prophets of the Apocalypse* (Grand Rapids, Mich.: Baker Books, 1994), pp. 17–28, which is based on interviews with Koresh's mother, Bonnie Haldeman, née Clark, and others.

38. Teresa Moore, telephone interview by Phillip Arnn, June 2, 1994, quoted in Phillip Arnn, "The Rod and the Branch: From Victor Houteff to David Koresh," *The Watchman Expositor,* vol. 11 (1994), pp. 21–22.

39. See Breault and King, *Inside the Cult,* pp. 41–45; and the documented account in Samples, et al., *Prophets of the Apocalypse,* pp. 38–43.

40. David Koresh, interview by Martin King, *A Current Affair,* January 5, 1992. This Australian program has no connection with the American show of the same name.

41. See Samples, et al., *Prophets of the Apocalypse,* p. 42. This account is based on interviews with David Bunds, who was at Mount Carmel at the time.

42. The best account to date of this period is in Bailey and Darden, *Mad Man in Waco,* pp. 60–94.

43. The Branch Davidians owed a total of $62,660 in back taxes to McLennan County and the Axtell Independent School District. Apparently, taxes had not been paid since 1968. See Bailey and Darden, *Mad Man in Waco,* p. 81.

44. See Cari Haus and Madlyn Hamblin, *In the Wake of Waco* (Hagerstown, Md.: Review and Herald Publishing Assoc., 1993). This thoroughly negative portrayal of Koresh, published by the official Seventh-Day Adventist publishing house, goes to great lengths to demonstrate that Koresh was a "cult" leader with no signifcant ties to the larger movement.

45. Miller's interpretation centered on the 2,300-day period of Daniel 8:14, after which, the prophet declares, "The sanctuary will be cleansed." Using the principle of "a day for a year" based on Ezekiel 4:6, and interpreting the language in a symbolic, Christianized way, he understood this period as 2,300 *years,* following which Christ would exit the heavenly sanctuary and return to earth. This idea that Christ has entered a heavenly temple or sanctuary, modeled on the Mosaic tabernacle, is found in Hebrews 9:24–28. There, in the inner room of the holy of holies, which represents the presence of God himself, he makes atonement for sins with his own blood. The prophecy originally referred to the defilement of the Jewish temple in 164 B.C.E. by the Syrian king Antiochus Epiphanes, as described in 1 Maccabees. Miller's problem was to pinpoint the terminus a quo to begin this prophetic countdown. Here, Miller turned to the mysterious "Seventy Weeks" prophecy of Daniel 9:24–27, which most Christian interpreters had understood to refer to a 490-*year* period (7 × 70), following the Babylonian Exile and terminating with the appearance of Jesus as the Messiah. Significantly, this prophecy contains an explicit beginning point, "from the going forth of the commandment to restore and rebuild Jerusalem" (v. 25), which Miller took to be the year 457 B.C.E. when Ezra returned to Jerusalem during the reign of the Persian ruler Artaxerxes I. The text goes on to say that the Messiah is

to arrive, and subsequently be "cut off," precisely sixty-nine weeks, or 483 years (69 × 7), from this date. The result of this computation is the year 26 C.E. when Jesus of Nazareth was baptized by John and began his public ministry. The precision of this prophecy impressed Miller. He reasoned that if the first coming of Jesus had been predicted by the prophet Daniel to the exact year, then why not the Second Coming as well? He concluded that the two prophecies, the 2,300 years of Daniel 8 and the 490 years of Daniel 9, should be viewed as one extended revelation. He found his key in Daniel 9:24, which speaks of "putting an end to sin" and "atoning for iniquity." He concluded that the 2,300 years would begin in the year 457 B.C.E. and end in the fateful year 1843. In fact, Miller made a mathematical mistake. From 457 B.C.E. to 1843 C.E. is 2,299 years, not 2,300. Since there is no year zero, one must add a year to the sum when counting from before the common era to the common era. Apparently, the Millerites never discovered this error. Although this remained the main evidence for the 1843 date, it was by no means the only argument Miller used. He gradually developed twelve additional "secondary proofs" for the date—all based on history and biblical prophecy, which precisely correlated with his argument from Daniel 8 and 9 that the end would come in 1843. These are listed in Francis D. Nichol, *The Midnight Cry,* appendix L (Washington, D.C.: Review and Herald Publishing Assoc., 1944), pp. 507–10. For example, Miller understood the "seven times" punishment upon Israel mentioned in Leviticus 26:21 to refer to a prophetic period of 2,520 years (360 × 7), which began in 677 B.C.E. with the Babylonian invasion of Judea and would end in 1843 C.E. This dovetailing of seemingly disparate evidence from so many sources seemed to Miller to offer irrefutable evidence that he was correct in his understanding.

46. He later describes his search and his main conclusion: "Finding all the signs of the times and the present condition of the world, to compare harmoniously with the prophetic descriptions of the last days, I was compelled to believe that this world had about reached the limits of the period allotted for its continuance. As I regarded the evidence, I could arrive at no other conclusion. . . . I was thus brought, in 1818, at the close of my two years study of the Scriptures, to the solemn conclusion, that in about twenty-five years from that time all the affairs of our present state would be wound up. I need not speak of the joy that filled my heart in view of the delightful prospect, nor of the ardent longings of my soul, for a participation in the joys of the redeemed. The Bible was now to me a new book" (William Miller, *Apology and Defense* [Boston: Joshua V. Himes, 1845], pp. 9–13). Miller published this thirty-six-page formal account of his quest after the "Great Disappointment" of 1843–44 when Christ failed to come. He never lost his faith that he was, somehow, essentially correct in his interpretations. This general sketch is based on the original source material preserved in Nichol, *Midnight Cry;* and George R. Knight, ed., *1844 and the Rise of Sabbatarian Adventism* (Ha-

gerstown, Md.: Review and Herald Publishing Assoc., 1994). Although Nichol's account is still quite valuable, George R. Knight has recently published an updated definitive history, *Millennial Fever and the End of the World* (Boise, Idaho: Pacific Press Publishing Assoc., 1993). Other recent useful studies of the Millerite movement include David L. Rowe, *Thunder and Trumpets: Millerites and Dissenting Religion in Upstate New York, 1800–1850* (Chico, Calif.: Scholars Press, 1985); Michael Barkun, *Crucible of the Millennium: The Burned-over-District of New York in the 1840s* (Syracuse, N.Y.: Syracuse University Press, 1986); Ruth Alden Doan, *The Miller Heresy, Millennialism, and American Culture* (Philadelphia: Temple University Press, 1987); and Ronald L. Numbers and Jonathan M. Butler, eds., *The Disappointed: Millerism and Millenarianism in the Nineteenth Century* (Bloomington: Indiana University Press, 1987).

47. The largest body to develop from this movement is the Seventh-Day Adventist Church, which numbers 7,724,760 adult members worldwide as of June 1993 with over 750,000 in the United States (*Seventh-Day Adventist Yearbook 1994,* p. 4). Neither figure includes unbaptized children, so the total family membership is much higher. The "Adventist family," that is, churches that have historical ties to the Millerite movement, numbers as many as eighty-four groups and sects including numerous Seventh-Day Church of God, Jehovah's Witnesses, and Sacred Name groups (*Encyclopedia of American Religions,* 3d ed., pp. 511–54). If these are counted, one can speak loosely of at least 10 million "Adventists" worldwide with as many as 2 million in the United States. In contrast, the Mormons number around 4 million in the United States and 6.5 million worldwide.

48. The Millerite movement marks the inauguration of a tremendous public interest in what Paul Boyer calls "Prophecy Belief" in American culture. Beyond that, it shares close parallels with other important movements within fundamentalist and evangelical Christianity that have focused on a literal, premillennial interpretation of Bible prophecy and brought it to the forefront of American society, particularly since World War II (see Paul Boyer, *When Time Shall Be No More: Prophecy Belief in Modern American Culture* [Cambridge: Harvard University Press, 1992], pp. 1–18, 46–79).

49. Miller did not immediately go public with his astounding discovery. He did speak privately about it to friends and acquaintances, but without much positive response. Most took it as a bit too complicated and somewhat eccentric. He continued his fervent study of the Bible, now determined to formulate for himself a "clear-cut belief on every Bible doctrine that affected salvation" (*Apology and Defense,* p. 16). It was not until the summer of 1831, when he was nearly fifty years old, that he began to experience an overwhelming conviction that he must go forth and tell the world what he had learned. He writes: "My distress became so great, I entered into a solemn covenant with God, that if He would open the way, I would go and perform my duty to

the world" (*Apology and Defense*, p. 17). Miller never claimed to be a prophet or to have received any direct revelation from God; he was more lecturer than preacher. He was not a dynamic speaker, but, through the use of charts and a detailed discussion of history and prophecy, he stressed the inescapable "logic" of his conclusions.

50. *Signs of the Times,* January 31, 1844, p. 196. Many thousands of copies of his printed lectures, numerous pamphlets, and several periodicals, such as *Signs of the Times* and the *Midnight Cry,* carried the Millerite message throughout the United States and to England and Europe. Gradually, Miller gathered around himself a band of highly capable men, who became loyally dedicated to the message. Three hundred copies of his lecture chart were printed so that others could go forth and offer similar presentations all over the country. Although the mainstream clergy denounced the Millerites, and the popular press found him a worthy subject for endless satire and caricature, he did touch the hearts and minds of thousands of listeners who became captivated by his logical presentation.

51. Luke 21:25. See Nichol, *Midnight Cry,* pp. 135–36, for a discussion of the comet and its impact at the time.

52. He systematically set forth fourteen "Rules of Interpretation" in his publication the *Midnight Cry* and urged others to follow them in their own study of the Bible. For the relevant documents, see Knight, *Rise of Sabbatarian Adventism,* pp. 66–82.

53. His method was to meticulously compare every reference in the Bible to a given word, term, concept, or figure of speech until the full meaning became clear. Miller insisted that nothing in Scripture would remain hidden from those who diligently sought the truth through rigorous study. In other words, with Bible and concordance in hand, any man or woman could uncover biblical truths long hidden from the Christian world at large.

54. See the discussion in Boyer, *When Time,* pp. 83–86.

55. This is one of the most repeated assertions in the surviving tapes of Koresh's Bible study sessions.

56. William Miller to Joshua Himes, March 25, 1844, in *Advent Herald,* April 10, 1844, p. 77.

57. Miller had allowed his calculations and arguments to be published in the *Midnight Cry,* March 20, 1844, p. 53. Why the Millerites opted to use the Karaite calendar, rather than the standard Jewish date for Yom Kippur that year, is unclear.

58. When their opponents countered by insisting that Jesus had taught that no one would know the "day or the hour of his coming," the Millerites insisted that this statement applied to prior centuries but not to the final time once it drew close. They argued that Daniel was told, "Seal the book even *to the time of the end*" (emphasis added), implying that a time would come when the prophetic mysteries would be "unsealed." They coupled this with the

phrase in Habakkuk 2:3 that speaks of a "delay," after which "at the end it [the vision] shall speak," as well as the text in Revelation 10:4 that tells of the "mystery" God spoke to the prophets being "finished." Koresh and the Branch Davidians later used the very same texts in the same way to justify their own calculations of the end.

59. Adventist writers have sought to refute such charges; see Nichol, *Midnight Cry,* pp. 303–453. The oft-repeated tale that Millerites wore special "ascension robes" and waited on rooftops was apparently concocted and passed on by the hungry print media, eager to poke fun at these people.

60. Since the time of Augustine (fourth century C.E.), the 1,000-year reign of Christ, mentioned in Revelation 20, had been understood to refer to the triumph of the Christian Church, which would gradually establish God's Kingdom on earth. This view became known as postmillennialism, meaning that the Second Coming was expected only *after* the 1,000-year reign of the Church. The Millerites were the first to popularize the premillennial doctrine, standard among evangelical Christians today, that the Second Coming could arrive at any moment, suddenly and without warning, and would be followed by the 1,000-year reign of Christ.

61. The first issue of the Millerite newsletter, the *Midnight Cry,* published in February 1844, contained a long article on "Babylon." In the September 1844 issue, Miller and all the leaders were united in calling their followers to leave their churches. Joshua Himes wrote: "We are agreed in the *instant* and [call for] final separation from all who oppose the doctrine of the coming and kingdom of God at hand. . . . It is death to remain connected with those bodies that speak lightly of, or oppose the coming of the Lord. . . . We therefore now say to all who are in any way entangled in the yoke of bondage, 'Come out from among them, and be you separate, says the Lord' " (*Midnight Cry* [September 1844], p. 3).

62. Hiram Edson, one of Miller's close associates, wrote: "Our fondest hopes and expectations were blasted, and such a spirit of weeping came over us as I never experienced before. It seemed that the loss of all earthly friends could have been no comparison. We wept, and wept, till the day dawn." Only a portion of this undated manuscript survives; it is reproduced in Knight, *Rise of Sabbatarian Adventism,* pp. 123–26. Later in the year, the December 1844 issue of the *Midnight Cry* published a long letter from William Miller himself. Although Miller had no ready explanation for the failure, he remained firm in his faith: "I have been waiting and looking for the blessed hope, and in expectation of realizing the glorious things which God has spoken of Zion. Yes, and although I have been twice disappointed, I am not yet cast down, or discouraged" (p. 179).

63. The Greek word *angelos,* translated "angel," simply means "messenger" and can be applied to human beings as well as heavenly agents of God.

64. These Adventists organized themselves through a series of conferences, working first in New England but gradually spreading to other areas, reaching both former Millerites and the general public. They distributed thousands of tracts and booklets, and in July 1849, they began publication of a new periodical, the *Present Truth*. This was quickly followed in 1850 by the *Advent Review*. The former was geared to address the ongoing insights and revelations of the group whereas the latter reprinted many of the most important of the Millerite articles from the 1840s to impress followers with the logic and necessity of the 1844 date. In late 1850, the two were combined into the *Review and Herald*, which became the lifeline of scattered believers in the "message" for decades to come. In 1855, they set up their headquarters in Battle Creek, Michigan, and by 1860 had formally adopted the name Seventh-Day Adventist. In 1903 their headquarters was moved to Washington, D.C. Over the years, Ellen G. White became the spiritual and administrative leader of the growing denomination, and her dreams and revelations were understood to be the living prophetic voice for the church in the last days.

65. In Revelation 11:15–19, there is a scene associated with a seventh angel sounding a trumpet, which Bates took to be a message to the world at the end of time. The temple in heaven is opened, and the ark of the covenant is revealed, followed by "lightnings, voices, thunderings, an earthquake, and great hail." The ark, of course, held the tablets of stone upon which were written the Ten Commandments. So, Bates concluded, as Christ entered the heavenly sanctuary, on October 22, 1844, the Law of God in its original and pure form was revealed to his people. He also relied on Revelation 12:7, which identifies the End Time remnant people of God as those who "keep the commandments of God," which he claimed included the seventh-day Sabbath. These and other related arguments are set forth in Joseph Bates, *The Seventh Day Sabbath, a Perpetual Sign* (New Bedford, Mass.: Benjamin Lindsey, 1846).

66. In 1847 the three published jointly a small twenty-four-page document titled *A Word to the "Little Flock"* to encourage Adventists to hold to their 1844 faith and continue to seek greater light.

67. See Revelation 19:10. References abound in her writings; but see her best-known work, *The Great Controversy*, pp. 143–44, 408.

68. White, *Great Controversy*, p. 408.

69. As Marc Breault has explained in an unpublished manuscript that he was gracious enough to share with us, Koresh found this seventy-year period prophesied in a number of places in the Bible. Isaiah 23:15–17 speaks of "Tyre" being forgotten by God: "And it shall come to pass in that day, that Tyre shall be forgotten seventy years. . . . after the end of seventy years shall Tyre sing as an harlot. . . . And it shall come to pass after the end of seventy years that the LORD will visit Tyre, and she shall turn to her hire, and shall

commit fornication with all the kingdoms of the world upon the face of the earth." He connected this with a passage from Hosea that speaks of Ephraim, one of the major tribes of Israel, as Tyre (Hos. 9:13). Koresh argued that this prophecy did not apply literally to the ancient city of Tyre on the coast of Palestine but rather "spiritually" to God's people as "Tyre," indicating that they had sold themselves to commerce and worldly power. A related passage to which Koresh appealed was Psalm 90, which he took to be speaking of the "age of humankind," not that of any individual: "The days of our years are threescore years and ten; and if by reason of strength they be fourscore years, yet is their strength labor and sorrow; for it is soon cut off, and we fly away" (v. 10). He would point out that, here again was a seventy-year period, followed by a ten-year period of labor and sorrow.

70. Koresh also quoted Isaiah 42:1–2 to make the same point: "Behold my servant, whom I uphold, my elect, in whom my soul delights. I have put my Spirit upon him, he shall bring forth judgment to the Gentiles. He shall not cry, *nor lift up his cause in the street*" (emphasis added).

CHAPTER 3

1. The following account of Koresh's message is based upon a combination of sources. Readily available are the following: the February 28, 1993, KRLD live radio interviews; the February 28, 1993, CNN live interview; the March 2, 1993, fifty-eight-minute address; the 1992 documentary by Martin King aired on the Australian television program *A Current Affair*; a one-hour address by Koresh to a potential convert released on compact disc with two of his songs; a 1985 taped message by Koresh titled "What Is Truth?" which was geared to the public; and Koresh's incomplete manuscript, "Seven Seals" (see appendix). However, from these more public presentations, one is only able to derive a bare outline of the group's understanding. One of our most valuable sources is an eight-hour collection of tapes made in 1987 (hereafter, Instruction audiotapes, 1987), in which Koresh informally instructs a potential convert, painstakingly moving through the most important Scriptures line by line. We also have tapes and transcripts of eight lengthy Bible study sessions, in which Koresh teaches his followers various aspects of his theology. These were recorded from 1985 through 1989. We have carried on extensive conversations with some of the key surviving students of Koresh, namely Rita Riddle, David Thibodeau, Catherine Matteson, Janet Kendrick, Janet McBean, Wally Kennett, and most notably Livingstone Fagan, who has a master of arts degree in theology from Newbold College and a thorough understanding of the Branch Davidian theology. Mr. Fagan has written a draft of a formal presentation of Branch Davidian theology and has provided a copy to us. Finally, in an effort to present a balanced picture, we have carried on extensive communications with Marc Breault, a former Davidian

who remains highly critical of both Koresh's behavior and his exegesis of Scripture.

2. The best published explanation of Koresh's view of the Seven Seals is James Trimm, "David Koresh's Seven Seals Teaching," *Watchman Expositor,* vol. 11 (1994), pp. 7–8. We also have the unpublished one hundred-page exposition of Livingstone Fagan, "Mount Carmel," which is largely on the Seven Seals.

3. He pointed out that, according to the book of Hebrews, such a Christ figure had also appeared two thousand years before Jesus in the person of the enigmatic priest Melchizedek, in the time of Abraham (Heb. 7:1–4).

4. The Dead Sea Scrolls community also had such an exalted view of Melchizedek and actually expected him to return as a Messiah; see James Tabor and Michael Wise, "The Messiah of Qumran," *Biblical Archaeology Review,* November/December 1992, pp. 58–59.

5. On their history and theology, see H. J. Schoeps, *Jewish Christianity* (Philadelphia: Fortress Press, 1969), pp. 68–73.

6. *Pseudo-Clementine Recognitions* 2.22, in Wilhelm Schneemelcher, *New Testament Apocrypha,* vol. 2 (Philadelphia: Westminster Press, 1964), p. 538.

7. See Koresh, "Seven Seals," p. 191, in the appendix.

8. This comes out clearly in Koresh, Instruction audiotapes, 1987, where he is teaching a potential student who has been drawn to the movement. Koresh takes him verse by verse, hardly skipping a word, through whole books of the Bible: Isaiah 40–61, many of the Psalms, Micah, Nahum, Obadiah, and so forth. He constantly makes the point to this student that this is never done "in the churches" and that no other Bible teacher can possibly do what he is doing—explain the entire Bible, line by line, in "perfect harmony."

9. Bailey and Darden, *Mad Man in Waco,* pp. 75–77.

10. Others before Koresh had picked up on this idea. Moshe Guibbory, a self-proclaimed prophet and mystic who lived in Israel in the 1920s, used Isaiah 45:1 in the same way: to identify a specific figure who would come before the End Time, a new Cyrus, or Koresh, who would conquer a modern Babylon. He, of course, claimed to be such a one. For his specific claim, see Moshe Guibbory, *The Bible in the Hands of Its Creators* (New York: Society of the Bible in the Hands of Its Creators, 1943), pp. 425–28. Also, Cyrus R. Teed changed his name to Koresh in 1869 and founded a community of Koreshians in Chicago and Florida. He was a mystic and Bible student who also claimed in his extensive writings to "open the Seven Seals." He died in 1906 after a violent confrontation with a marshal in Fort Myers, Florida. See Robert S. Fogarty, " 'Cults,' Guns and the Kingdom," *The Nation,* April 12, 1993, pp. 485–87; and Robert S. Fogarty, "Cyrus Teed Koresh and Benjamin Purnell: Forerunners of Koresh and the Branch Davidians," in *Armageddon in Waco,* ed. Stuart A. Wright (Chicago: University of Chicago Press, forthcoming, 1995).

11. In Judaism this is referred to as the *omer*.

12. For example, Judy Schneider introduces herself as "Judy Koresh" in the March 8, 1993, videotape made inside Mount Carmel.

13. See the appendix for a fuller discussion of the technical aspects of Koresh's biblical exegesis.

14. He describes the experience in an audiotape when discussing Isaiah 44 (Instruction audiotapes, 1987).

15. This was reported by Clive Doyle to Phillip Arnold in a series of interviews in Houston in late 1993 and was relayed to James Tabor by Arnold. Koresh also told the FBI negotiators a bit about this experience. He claimed to have gone past the constellation Orion and actually entered into a UFO, a heavenly "vehicle." We know from Lois Roden's publication *SHEkinah* that she had studied material related to the *merkabah* tradition. The word *merkabah* refers to the throne-chariot upon which God sits as described in Ezekiel 1 and 10, and some popular interpreters have likened it to the descriptions of modern UFOs. Ancient Jewish mystics sought to ascend to heaven and behold that throne-vehicle. The apostle Paul reports such an experience in 2 Corinthians 12:1–10. On the historical background, see James Tabor, *Things Unutterable* (Lanham, Md.: University Press of America, 1986), pp. 113–22.

16. Clive Doyle and Catherine Matteson, conversations with James Tabor, Waco, Texas, April 17–19, 1994.

17. This is clearly expressed by Livingstone Fagan in his unpublished paper titled "Christ."

18. The only parallel we have found to this very detailed exegetical focus on such a figure is in the writings of Moshe Guibbory, mentioned in note 10 of this chapter. Guibbory was also a master at detailed exposition of Scripture and used most of the same texts that Koresh interpreted in precisely the same way. As a Jew, he also tried to prove explicitly that none of these texts could refer to Jesus, though for obviously different reasons. Although it is possible that Koresh had read Moshe Guibbory's book, *The Bible in the Hands of Its Creators,* when he was in Israel in 1985, we find that unlikely. The close similarity between the two can probably be attributed to the nature of the texts themselves. Once one begins to look for this figure, he does emerge rather clearly throughout the prophetic texts. The best ancient parallels to this way of reading the Hebrew Prophets are found among the early followers of Jesus and the Dead Sea Scrolls community. Both groups identified their Teacher as this figure found in Isaiah and elsewhere though neither, to our knowledge, specifically made use of Isaiah 45:1 and the name "Koresh."

19. See Cole, *Sinister Twilight,* p. 30.

20. Reported by Ken Fawcett, correspondent at the trial, in Dispatch 1, February 15, 1994. Judge Smith was referring to Texas Penal Code, subchapter C, Article 9, 31 on Self-defense: "The use of force to resist an arrest or search is

justified; if, before the actor offers any resistance, the peace officer uses, or attempts to use, greater force than necessary to make the arrest or search, and; when and to the degree the actor reasonably believes the force is immediately necessary to protect himself against the peace officer's use of or attempted use of greater than necessary force."

21. Breault and King, *Inside the Cult,* p. 283.

22. There were seven "wives," who had borne him twelve children, inside Mount Carmel at the time of the raid: (1) Rachel Howell, his legal wife, with the children Cyrus (8) and Star (6) and the infant Bobbie Lane; (2) Michelle Jones, Rachel's sister, with the child Serenity (4) and the twins Chica and Latwan (22 months); (3) Nicole Gent with the child Dayland (3) and the infant Paige; (4) Katherine Andrade with daughter Chanel (14 months); (5) Aisha Gyarfas with daughter Startle (1); (6) Judy Schneider, former wife of Steve Schneider, with daughter Mayanah (2); (7) Lorraine Sylvia, former wife of Stan Sylvia, with daughter Hollywood (2). Apparently, four of Koresh's children have survived. Three were born to women who had left the group before the fire: Shaun, Robyn Bunds's son; Sky and Scooter, Dana Okimoto's sons. He also had a daughter prior to joining the Mount Carmel group.

23. Koresh, interview by King.

24. Fagan, "Christ," p. 9.

25. Fagan, quoted in Bailey and Darden, *Mad Man in Waco,* p. 103.

26. This explanation comes from Marc Breault, who was in the group when these ideas were first presented as New Light.

27. *Dept. of Justice Report,* p. 51.

28. Ibid., p. 59.

29. We have not revealed the name of this woman for the sake of her privacy although we note that she was not someone else's wife at the time. The complete text of the interview is published in Samples, et al., *Prophets of the Apocalypse,* pp. 182–89.

30. Apparently, the only outsider to whom this has been explained is Phillip Arnold, who got it from Livingstone Fagan and passed it on to us. Marc Breault, who left the group in 1989, says he never heard this explanation for the children and suggests it was part of Koresh's ever-evolving justification for his behavior.

31. See, for example, the New Revised Standard Version or the New Jerusalem Bible.

32. Fagan, "Mt. Carmel," p. 11.

33. Chuck Lindell, "Waiting for the Return of a Messiah," *Austin American-Statesman,* February 27, 1994. See also the interviews and analysis of Dick Reavis, "The World Is Over," *Dallas Observer,* March 31–April 6, 1994, pp. 13–19.

CHAPTER 4

1. Breault and King, *Inside the Cult,* p. 49.
2. Ibid.
3. Ibid., p. 208.
4. Marc Breault to James Tabor, June 12, 1994. Concerning a Bible study session given by Koresh in October 1989, Breault writes, "Whoever has listened to this tape has no doubt that Vernon was fast descending into, if not already arrived at, madness. The sad thing is, some of Vernon's stuff, even at this stage, is really profound. I just wish he would have gotten off his power trip. He would have been a great asset if only he could have done that."
5. Breault and King, *Inside the Cult,* pp. 195–96.
6. Marc Breault to James Tabor, May 30, 1994.
7. Breault and King, *Inside the Cult,* p. 198.
8. Marc Breault to James Tabor, June 14, 1994.
9. Breault and King, *Inside the Cult,* p. 206.
10. Ibid., p. 208.
11. Ibid., p. 210.
12. Ibid., p. 227.
13. Ibid., p. 12.
14. Ibid., p. 254.
15. Breault's testimony quoted in Tim Madigan, *See No Evil: Blind Devotion and Bloodshed in David Koresh's Holy War* (Fort Worth, Tex.: Summit Group, 1993), p. 109.
16. Ibid., p. 117.
17. Ibid., p. 116.
18. Ibid., p. 121.
19. Breault and King, *Inside the Cult,* p. 295.
20. Breault to Tabor, May 30, 1994.
21. Bob Lott, "About Our Series on Mount Carmel," *Waco Tribune-Herald,* March 1, 1993, p. 4A.
22. Ibid.
23. Pam Lambert and Joe Treen, "Thirteen Who Died," *People,* May 3, 1993, p. 44.
24. Breault and King, *Inside the Cult,* p. 51.
25. Mark England and Darlene McCormick, "The Sinful Messiah," *Waco Tribune-Herald,* February 27, 1993, p. 11A; and March 1, 1993, p. 6A.
26. England and McCormick, "Sinful Messiah," March 1, 1993, p. 6A.
27. Breault and King, *Inside the Cult,* pp. 271–82.
28. Breault to Tabor, June 14, 1994.
29. Breault to Tabor, May 30, 1994.
30. Breault to Tabor, June 14, 1994.
31. In an addendum to her report to the deputy attorney general, Nancy Ammer-

man is sharply critical of the FBI for relying on Ross without considering his considerable ideological and financial stake in opposing any cult and "the numerous legal challenges to the tactics employed by Mr. Ross in extricating members from the groups he hates" (Nancy T. Ammerman, "Waco Report-Addendum," September 10, 1993). The *Waco Tribune-Herald,* July 9, 1993, pp. 1C, 6C, reports on Ross's arrest for unlawful imprisonment in connection with a deprogramming attempt in the state of Washington.

32. Madigan, *See No Evil,* p. 91.
33. Ibid., p. ix.
34. Ibid., p. x.
35. Ibid., p. 90.
36. Madigan has changed the Davidian's name and deleted his surname for purposes of confidentiality; see ibid., p. 77.
37. Ibid., p. 89.
38. Ibid., p. xv.
39. Ibid., pp. xi–xii.

CHAPTER 5

1. 911 Audiotapes, in the authors' possession. "Waco 911," *Nightline,* June 9, 1993 (transcript, Journal Graphics), pp. 3–4.
2. See *Dept. of Justice Report,* pp. 114–50.
3. We have a copy of this February 25, 1993, search warrant in our files.
4. "Probable Cause Affidavit," par. 2. Actually, the Aguilera affidavit slightly misquotes the law, whether intentionally or not. The affidavit quotes the key phrase in the above paragraph: "including any combination of parts, *either* designed or intended for use in converting any firearm into a machine gun"; whereas the law actually says, "including any combination of parts designed *and* intended for use" (emphasis added). There is a significant difference related to demonstrating intent and probable cause for a search.
5. Ibid., par. 30.
6. Ibid., par. 31.
7. See *Dept. of Treasury Report,* pp. 211–14. The United States military is forbidden to act against citizens by the *posse comitatus* act (*U.S. Code,* title 18, sec. 1385). However, the secretary of defense is authorized to provide military support to law enforcement agencies engaged in counterdrug operations (*U.S. Code,* title 10, sec. 371).
8. *Dept. of Treasury Report,* pp. B-40, B-48.
9. McMahon's account is published in "Waco: Behind the Cover-Up," pp. 36–41, 71–72.
10. Jamar reported directly to FBI Assistant Director Larry Potts, who reported to Associate Deputy Director Douglas Gow, Deputy Director Floyd Clarke, and Director William S. Sessions. See *Dept. of Justice Report,* p. 116.

11. Ibid., pp. 8–9.
12. Ibid., p. 114.
13. *Evaluation*, p. 42, n. 16.
14. *Dept. of Justice Report*, p. 205.
15. Ibid., p. 119.
16. Ibid., pp. 160–61.
17. See the summary in ibid., pp. 164–65.
18. Ibid., p. 170.
19. See DeGuerin, "Interview," p. 6.
20. See the section on "negotiation team themes," *Dept. of Treasury Report*, pp. 128–29.
21. At the daily FBI press briefing, when asked why Tibetan chants were included, the agents asserted that they intended them to be irritating to those inside Mount Carmel.
22. *Dept. of Justice Report*, pp. 139–40.
23. See ibid., pp. 141–42.
24. Department of Justice, negotiation transcript, March 2, 1993, 4 P.M.
25. *Dept. of Justice Report*, pp. 167–68.
26. See, for example, ibid., p. 207.
27. Press briefing at the release of the Department of Justice's final report, October 8, 1993.
28. *United States v. Branch, et al.*, W-93-CR-046 (trial transcript), Opening Statements, vol. 1, p. 8. Volume numbers for the trial are preliminary and are cited as provided to us by the court clerk.
29. Ibid., vol. 1, p. 8.
30. Ibid., vol. 2, p. 313.
31. Ibid., vol. 1, p. 8.
32. Ibid., vol. 1, p. 19.
33. Ibid., vol. 1, p. 59.
34. Ibid., vol. 1, p. 61.
35. Ibid., vol. 1, p. 66.
36. Clive Doyle (53), an Australian, and Woodrow Kendrick (63) were freed; Ruth Riddle (30), a Canadian, and Norman Washington Allison (29) of Great Britain were acquitted but held for immigration violations.
37. See Pierre Thomas, "Verdicts Bring a Long, Painful Year for ATF to a Bitter End," *Washington Post*, February 27, 1994.
38. Renos Avraam (29) of Great Britain; Brad Branch (34); Jaime Castillo (25); Livingstone Fagan (34) of Great Britain; and Kevin Whitecliff (32).
39. Paul Fatta (35) received fifteen years and a $50,000 fine; Graeme Craddock (32) of Australia received twenty years; and Ruth Riddle, who had originally been acquitted, was sentenced to five years for use of a firearm in the commission of a crime.

CHAPTER 6

1. Shortly after the April 19 tragedy, a vast international bad-joke enterprise went into full gear. A forty-page sample of this sick humor recently circulated over the Internet, for example: *What does WACO stand for?* We All Cremated Ourselves; When Attacked, CookOut; We're All Crunch Omelets; We Are Clinical Outpatients; *What kind of pants do Branch Davidian's wear?* Charred-Ash Jeans; *What were David KorASH's last words?* No, Bud Light!; Just kidding, I'm not really God; OW!!!; *What is David KorASH wearing right now?* His best Sunday soot. *What do you call Asian Branch Davidians?* Rice Crispies.

2. Gustave Niebuhr and William Hamilton, "Cult's Isolation from Society Seen As Factor in Violence," *Washington Post,* March 2, 1993, p. A4.

3. "Child Speaks out and Other Waco Cult Insiders," *Donahue,* March 10, 1993 (transcript, Journal Graphics), p. 2.

4. Ibid., p. 4.

5. Ibid., p. 10.

6. Ibid., p. 17; see pp. 12, 16.

7. Ibid., p. 18.

8. Ibid., p. 16.

9. Ibid., p. 19.

10. "Inside Waco and Other Cults," *Oprah: The Oprah Winfrey Show,* March 25, 1993 (transcript, Burrelle's), p. 18.

11. Ibid., p. 20.

12. Ibid., p. 14.

13. Ibid., p. 23.

14. Ibid., pp. 4–5.

15. "The Koresh Cult and Its Children," *Larry King Live,* May 11, 1993 (transcript, Journal Graphics), p. 5.

16. Ibid., p. 6.

17. "Waco: The Decision to Die," ABC News Special, April 20, 1993 (transcript, Journal Graphics), p. 3.

18. Ibid., p. 8.

19. Ibid., p. 5.

20. Ibid.

21. Ibid., p. 13.

22. Ibid.

23. Ibid.

24. Ibid., p. 14.

25. Ibid.

26. The 93-minute film was directed by Dick Lowry and produced by Republic Pictures. It is now widely available in video-rental stores.

27. Lee Hancock, "Waco Tale Is Effective, Engrossing," *Dallas Morning News,* Sunday, May 23, 1993 (wire story).

28. Bailey and Darden, *Mad Man in Waco,* p. 135.

29. Ibid., p. xi.

30. Ibid., p. xii.

31. Ibid., p. 113.

32. Ibid., p. 131.

33. Ibid.

34. Ibid., p. 206.

35. James L. Pate, "Gun Gestapo's Day of Infamy," *Soldier of Fortune,* June, 1993, p. 48.

36. Michael Barkun, "Reflections after Waco: Millennialists and the State," *The Christian Century,* vol. 110 (June 2–9, 1993), p. 597. Barkun's article is reprinted in Lewis, *From the Ashes,* pp. 41–49.

37. Karl Meyer, " 'Cults,' Deconstructed," *New York Times,* March 7, 1993, sec. 4, p. 16.

38. James L. Pate, "A Blundering Inferno," *Soldier of Fortune,* July 1993, p. 38.

39. For a summary of Thompson's argument and the critical responses to it, see the series of articles in the *Waco Tribune-Herald:* Mark England, "Where Does the 'Lie' Lie?" December 26, 1993, pp. 1A, 10A; John Young, "Building a Bigger Lie," January 9, 1994, p. 1A; and Mark England, "Think Tank Chief Adds Fuel to Cult-Fire Fire," January 16, 1994, p. 1A.

40. Mike Menichini, "Attorney Intends to Subpoena Reno in Cultists' Trial," *Waco Tribune-Herald,* January 8, 1994, p. 1C.

41. Teresa Talerico, "Jury Selected in Cultist Trial," *Waco Tribune-Herald,* January 12, 1994, pp. 1A, 6A.

42. During his closing argument the attorney John Phinizy, representing the prosecution, argued that the BATF agents on February 28 "went up against an armed camp; not a home, not a church, but an armed camp." See *United States v. Branch, et al.,* vol. 2, p. 275.

43. Ibid., p. 237.

44. Ibid., pp. 133–34.

45. England and McCormick, "Sinful Messiah," March 1, 1993, p. 6A.

46. Ibid., p. 9A.

47. Ibid., p. 8A.

48. Amy Walton, "A New Awareness of 'Cults,' " *Waco Tribune-Herald,* February 27, 1994, p. 11.

49. David J. Bardin, "Psychological Coercion & Human Rights: Mind Control ("Brainwashing") Exists," *Cult Abuse Policy & Research* (distributed by the American Family Foundation and the Cult Awareness Network, 1994), p. 1.

50. "CAN: Cult Awareness Network" (Chicago: Cult Awareness Network, 1990), p. 1.

51. See, for example, Billy Graham's judgment that Jim Jones was "a slave of a diabolical supernatural power," quoted in Jonathan Z. Smith, "The Devil

in Mr. Jones," in *Imagining Religion: From Babylon to Jonestown* (Chicago: University of Chicago Press, 1982), p. 110.

52. S. N. Eisenstadt, ed., *Max Weber: On Charisma and Institution Building* (Chicago: University of Chicago Press, 1968), p. 46.

53. Ibid.

54. Ibid.

55. Ibid., p. 49.

56. Susan J. Douglas, "Of Deviance and Conformity," *The Progressive,* June 21, 1993, p. 21.

57. Stephen L. Carter, *The Culture of Disbelief: How American Law and Politics Trivialize Religious Devotion* (New York: Basic Books, 1993), pp. 105–6.

CHAPTER 7

1. See Catherine Collins and Douglas Frantz, "Let Us Prey," *Modern Maturity,* June 1994, pp. 22–32.

2. "CAN: Cult Awareness Network," rev. ed. (Chicago: CAN, 1993), p. 1.

3. "Explanation of Position" (Chicago: CAN, 1984).

4. "Cult Proofing" (Toronto: COMA, n.d.), p. 2.

5. "Cult Proofing."

6. For a critical evaluation of one aspect of the influence of the anticult polemic on law enforcement, see Robert D. Hicks, *In Pursuit of Satan: The Police and the Occult* (Buffalo, N.Y.: Prometheus Books, 1991); and Gerald Arenberg, "The Rise and Fall of Deprogramming," *Chief of Police,* vol. 8 (March/April 1993), pp. 59–60.

7. CFF of New York and New Jersey, "Prevention Is the Message!" (New York: CFF, n.d.), p. 3.

8. David G. Bromley and Anson D. Shupe, Jr., *The New Vigilantes: Deprogrammers, Anti-Cultists, and the New Religions* (Beverly Hills, Calif.: Sage, 1980), p. 173.

9. Cynthia Kisser, "Cult Awareness and Education Must Be Taught," *Los Angeles Daily News,* March 7, 1993, sec. V, p. 1.

10. Ibid.

11. Ibid.

12. Eric Brazil, "Waco: Another Deadly Ending to Cult Episode," *San Francisco Examiner,* April 19, 1993, p. A15.

13. Kisser, "Cult Awareness," sec. V, p. 1.

14. Ibid.

15. Brazil, "Waco," p. A15.

16. Walton, "A New Awareness of 'Cults,'" p. 11.

17. Ibid.

18. Walter Martin, the late dean of Christian "cultbusters," quoted in Samples, et al., *Prophets of the Apocalypse,* p. 161. Samples is on the staff of the Califor-

nia-based CRI, which is heir to Martin's cult-exposing enterprise. Samples and his associates, however, seem to have adopted a less narrowly theological definition of a "cult" than did Martin.

19. Masthead text, *The Watchman Expositor,* the publication of Watchman Fellowship, Inc., which is a nonprofit organization.
20. Samples, et al., *Prophets of the Apocalypse,* pp. 133–34.
21. Ibid., p. 134.
22. "Our Response to Allegations of Mind Control and Brainwashing" (Zurich: World Services, 1993), pp. 1,2.
23. *United States v. Branch, et al.,* vol. 2, p. 314.
24. "A Criminal Assault on Religious Freedom: The Anti-Religious Movement" (Hollywood, Calif.: Church of Scientology International, 1993), p. 3.
25. Ted Patrick with Tom Dulack, *Let Our Children Go!* (New York: Ballantine Books, 1976), p. 10.
26. "CAN: Cult Awareness Network," p. 1.
27. "CAN at a Glance" (Chicago: CAN, 1990), p. 1.
28. See Eugene V. Gallagher, *Expectation and Experience: Explaining Religious Conversion* (Atlanta, Ga.: Scholars Press, 1990).
29. Eileen Barker, *The Making of a Moonie: Choice or Brainwashing?* (Oxford: Basil Blackwell, 1984), p. 147.
30. Bromley and Shupe, *New Vigilantes,* p. 208.
31. See *Dept. of Justice Report,* pp. 30, 33.
32. "Clinton Defends Action in Waco," *Congressional Quarterly Weekly Report,* April 24, 1993, p. 1041.
33. Koresh, "Seven Seals," p. 191, in the appendix.
34. Quoted in John R. Hall, *Gone from the Promised Land: Jonestown in American Cultural History* (New Brunswick, N.J.: Transaction Books, 1987), p. 31.
35. Quoted in David Chidester, *Salvation and Suicide: An Interpretation of Jim Jones, the Peoples Temple, and Jonestown* (Bloomington: Indiana University Press, 1988), p. 61.
36. Ibid.
37. Ibid., p. 107.
38. Ibid.
39. Ibid., p. 64.
40. Koresh, "Seven Seals," p. 191, in the appendix.
41. Ibid.
42. Smith, "Devil in Mr. Jones," p. 115.
43. Quoted in ibid., p. 116.
44. Melinda Liu and Todd Barrett, "Hard Lessons in the Ashes," *Newsweek,* May 3, 1993, p. 31.
45. David Gelman, "An Emotional Moonscape," *Newsweek,* May 17, 1993, p. 52.
46. For example, the clinical psychologist Margaret Singer, a major contributor

to the anticult position, is quoted at length about the problem of widespread sexual abuse within "cults." Nowhere is it mentioned, however, that Singer's views have been strongly challenged and that in some instances her testimony as an expert witness has been rejected by skeptical judges. In disqualifying Singer as an expert witness in the 1989 case of *United States vs. Fishman,* concerning a former member of the Church of Scientology who was being prosecuted for mail fraud, the presiding judge stated that "although the record before the Court is replete with declarations, affidavits and letters from reputable psychologists and sociologists who concur with the thought reform theories propounded by Dr. Singer and Dr. Ofshe, the government has submitted an equal number of declarations, affidavits and letters from reputable psychologists and sociologists who disagree with their theories. . . . A more significant barometer of prevailing views within the scientific community is provided by professional organizations such as the American Psychological Association ('APA') and the American Sociological Association ('ASA'). The evidence before the Court, . . . shows that neither the APA nor the ASA has endorsed the views of Dr. Singer and Dr. Ofshe on thought reform. . . . At best, the evidence establishes that psychiatrists, psychologists, and sociologists disagree as to whether or not there is agreement regarding the Singer-Ofshe thesis. The Court therefore excludes the defendants' proffered testimony" (743 F. Supp. 713 [1990]).

47. Carter, *Culture of Disbelief,* p. 276.

48. Mary Zeiss Stange, "The 'Crazy' Label Was Lethal," *Los Angeles Times,* April 21, 1993, p. B7.

49. *Dept. of Justice Report,* pp. 164, 165.

50. Ibid., p. 175.

51. Ibid., p. 176.

52. Ibid., p. 170.

53. James A. Beckford, *Cult Controversies: The Societal Response to the New Religious Movements* (London: Tavistock, 1985), p. 282.

54. "CAN: Cult Awareness Network," p. 2.

55. "Explanation of Position," p. 1.

CHAPTER 8

1. See Jeff Sheler, "Waiting for the Messiah," *U.S. News & World Report,* December 19, 1994, pp. 62–71. A *U.S. News* poll found that 61 percent of Americans say they believe in the Second Coming of Christ, 34 percent of those think he will come within a few decades, and 53 percent believe some world events of this century have fulfilled biblical prophecy.

2. Illinois State Senate, Res. 448.

3. Ibid.

4. Ibid.
5. Office of Illinois State Senator Frank C. Watson, press release, February 16, 1994, p. 2.
6. See David G. Bromley and James T. Richardson, eds., *The Brainwashing/ Deprogramming Controversy: Sociological, Psychological, Legal, and Historical Perspectives* (Lewiston, N.Y.: Edwin Mellen Press, 1983).
7. Bardin, "Psychological Coercion & Human Rights," p. 1.
8. For a fuller treatment of ways of explaining religious conversion, see Gallagher, *Expectation and Experience.*

A NOTE ON SOURCES

Of the wide variety of sources on which we have drawn for this book, the most important have been the surviving members of the Mount Carmel community, especially Catherine Matteson, Rita Riddle, and David Thibodeau, with whom we have had extensive conversations. The former member Marc Breault was also quite gracious and helpful in answering our many questions. Livingstone Fagan kindly allowed us to examine his book-length manuscript, "Mt. Carmel: The Unseen Reality," as well as a half dozen of his theological papers—all written from jail since the April 19, 1993, fire. We also had access to over two dozen audiotapes by David Koresh in which he teaches his message in both public and private situations during the years 1985–1992, several videotapes, and an hour-long compact disc that contains an address by Koresh and two of his songs. Along with his fragmentary manuscript on the Seven Seals of Revelation, all of these materials provide essential sources for recovering his theology. The footage shot for the Australian television news program *A Current Affair* offers a rare and valuable glimpse of David Koresh as a Bible teacher. Similarly, the two videotapes sent from the Mount Carmel center during the prolonged siege help to put human faces on the residents, particularly the children. William Pitts of Baylor University has published the best material on the history of the Mount Carmel residents ("The Mount Carmel Davidians: Adventist Reformers, 1935–1959," *Syzgy: Journal of Alternative Religion and Culture,* vol. 2, nos. 1–2 [1993], pp. 39–54). In addition, there are extensive archives being developed on the Branch Davidians by both Baylor University and the city of Waco; they contain much important information.

The *Waco Tribune-Herald* provided the most detailed coverage of Mount Carmel from before the initial BATF raid through the 1994 trial and its aftermath. Most of what appeared in other newspapers was also covered by the *Tribune-Herald.* Mark England and Darlene McCormick's reporting remains the benchmark against which other news coverage should be measured. The articles that appeared in other newspapers throughout the United States are far too numerous to be catalogued. Our extensive sampling of the press reports, however, suggests that they rarely depart from common patterns of presentation and interpretation. Coverage in the mainstream newsweeklies, particularly *Newsweek,* was also extensive.

Journals of opinion and other specialty publications covered Waco from their own distinctive viewpoints. We found the articles in the *Nation,* the *New Republic,* and *Soldier of Fortune* to be particularly helpful. As with the newspapers, any electronic search service will quickly yield mounds of reading material to the interested researcher.

The national office of the Cult Awareness Network in Chicago provides free copies of its brochures and pamphlets, and it will also compile packets of news stories on particular groups for a nominal fee.

The official reports produced by the Treasury and Justice departments, available from the Government Printing Office, are fascinating documents. They are as interesting for what they don't say as for what they do. Both the reports released to the public were heavily "redacted" in order to protect the government's case in the 1994 trial of eleven surviving Branch Davidians. The Justice Department report is particularly complicated. It does not include either the expert report of Alan Stone or an addendum submitted by Nancy Ammerman. We hope that fuller versions of both reports will soon be made available to the public. Transcripts of the trial proceedings in San Antonio are also very revealing. They are available from the court reporter, Morris Bowen.

Waco was also widely discussed in the electronic news media. The transcript services Burrelle's and Journal Graphics provide helpful transcripts of a variety of television shows. As in the newspaper and newsmagazine accounts of Waco, both the content and the interpretive stance of the television programs seem to conform to a few common patterns.

Quite a lot of information and opinion about David Koresh and the Branch Davidians circulated outside established channels. Material was widely available on the Internet, circulated through ad hoc systems such as the American Patriot Fax Network, copied and passed on through the mail. Once we scratched the surface, one source quickly led to another. We hope that the aforementioned archives will include as much of this type of material as possible.

Given the current nature of our topic, standard sources such as scholarly books and articles played a relatively small part in our research though several books have made valuable contributions to our thinking about David Koresh and Mount Carmel. Paul Boyer's *When Time Shall Be No More: Prophecy Belief in Modern American Culture* provides a captivating view of the subculture in which David Koresh developed his distinctive ideas. Stephen L. Carter's *The Culture of Disbelief: How American Law and Politics Trivialize Religious Devotion* raises important and difficult questions about religion, including new or unconventional religious groups. *The New Vigilantes: Deprogrammers, Anti-Cultists, and the New Religions,* by David G. Bromley and Anson D. Shupe, Jr. provides a challenging critique of the mission and practices of cultbusters. The analyses of the Peoples Temple in David Chidester's *Salvation and Suicide: An Interpretation of Jim Jones, the Peoples Temple, and Jonestown,* John R. Hall's *Gone from the Promised Land: Jonestown in American Cultural History,* and Jonathan Z. Smith's "The Devil in Mr. Jones," in his *Imagining Religion: From Babylon to Jonestown,* provide important comparative contexts for the Mount Carmel community and a solid introduction to new religious movements in contemporary America.

INDEX

Biblical references are listed by book, with the chapter and verse in bold type, for example: Psalms, Book of, **49:2–4;** 143; **51:15,** 61.

Chojnacki, Phillip, 215n10
Christ: the final, 55, 56–57, 71, 75, 207, 76-77; as a title, 55, 205. *See also* Jesus of Nazareth; Messiah
Christ Spirit, 72, 206
Christendom, "paganized" customs in, 27, 47, 49, 50
Christian Century, The (Michael Barkun), 130
Christian Research Institute (CRI), 152–53, 238n18
Christians: critical of cults, 37–38n18, 122, 152–53; evangelical, 152–53, 172
Citizens' Freedom Foundation, 148
Clark, Bonnie (Haldeman), 58, 215n9, 222n37
Clinton, Bill, President, 6, 100, 216n18, 238n32
CNN interview with Koresh, 3, 4, 19, 214n8
Columbia Journalism Review, 131
COMA (Council on Mind Abuse), 147, 148, 170, 179
comets, 12, 45, 216n25
Committee on Waco Justice, 132
conversion, religious, 89, 135, 140, 155–58, 165, 178–79, 240n7
Corinthians, Letters of Paul to: **1 Cor. 7,** 71; **7:29,** 68; **7:32–33,** 72; **10:4,** 76; **2 Cor. 5:17,** 68
Council on Mind Abuse (COMA), 147, 148, 170, 179
CRI (Christian Research Institute), 152–53, 238n18
CS gas attack, 2, 15, 17, 77–78, 111
Cult Awareness Network (CAN), 105, 125, 140, 146, 155–56, 170, 171–72, 177, 179, 236n50
"cult" defectors, 82–83, 89, 95, 101, 138
"cult leader" stereotype, 90, 102, 112,

121–24, 129, 141, 144, 150, 179–80
"cult" life, 182
"cult" member: self-determination of, 113, 137–38, 177–79; stereotype of, 90, 139. *See also* conversion, religious
"cultbusting." *See* anticult activism; anticult polemics
"cults": considered social problem, 149–52; offering alternative perspectives, 175–76; popular image of, 95, 96, 101, 119, 122, 123, 150–51, 166–67, 170–71, 213n2; and society, 180–83; threatening established views, 175–77; "dangerous," 153, 166, 171, 217n40. *See also* new religious movements
Culture of Disbelief, The (Stephen L. Carter), 145, 168, 169, 172, 237n57, 243
Current Affair, A, 84, 124, 222n40, 228n1, 241
custody hearing, 85–86
Cyrus, 42, 59–60

Daly, Tim, 127
Daniel, Book of, 9, 44, 225–26n58; **8:14,** 222n45; **9:24–27,** 222n45; **11:40–45,** 207; **12:1,** 201; **12:7–12,** 79
Darden, Bob, and Brad Bailey, *Mad Man in Waco,* 128–30, 217n36, 222n42
David, star of, 63
"Davidian," meaning of, 35
Davidian groups, 221n34. *See also* Branch Davidians
Davidic kingdom, 35
Davidic figure, 39, 54, 63, 209
Day of Atonement, 46

184, 186; as "Babylon," 4, 11, 51, 207. *See also* BATF; FBI

Great Controversy, The (Ellen G. White), 220–21n25, 227n67

"Great Disappointment," 47

great whore, 199–200

Green, Dennis, Judge, 100

Guibbory, Moshe, 229n10, 230n18

gun business, 64

guns. *See* firearms allegations

Guns & Ammo, 131

Guyana. *See* Jonestown

Gyarfas, Aisha, 82

Habakkuk, Book of, **2:3,** 226n58

Haldeman, Bonnie (Clark), 58, 215n9, 222n37

Harvey, Paul, 12

Harwell, Jack, 11

Hebrews, Letters of Paul to: **5:5, 7:19,24–42, 8:6, 9:24, 10:12–14, 26, 29,** 195; **7:1–4,** 195, 229n3; **7:3–4,** 55; **9:24–28,** 222n45; **12:18–25,** 194–95

Henry, Zilla, 24

Hermanson, Florence, 37

Higgins, Stephen, 3

Holy Spirit, as feminine, 40, 50, 221n5

Hosea, Book of: **2:14–23,** 202; **3:5,** 203; **9:13,** 228n69

Hossack, Geoffrey, 84

Hostage Rescue Team (HRT), 3, 53, 103

"Hostage / Barricade rescue situation," 4, 99–100, 103

Houteff, Victor, 33–38, 49, 213n1, 220n24, 221n31; *The Shepherd's Rod,* 35

Howell, Vernon. *See* Koresh, David

HRT. *See* Hostage Rescue Team

Hughes, Anna, 43

Illinois Senate Education Committee, resolution of, 173–74, 175

In the Line of Duty: Ambush in Waco (ABC), 126–27

Inside the Cult (Marc Breault and Martin King), 81, 84, 85, 91, 92, 127

Isaiah, Book of: **2,** 8, 35, 75, 208; **2:19–22,** 68; **11,** 35, 209; **23:15–17,** 227–28n69; **25,** 207; **33:17,** 200; **40:11,** 75; **40–54,** 60; **40–61,** 9; **40–66,** 61, 206; **41:1–2,** 207; **42:1–2,** 228n70; **44:26–28,** 61; **45,** 59; **45:1,** 206, 229n10; **45:4,** 60; **46:11,** 52, 207; **46:12,** 208; **48:14–16,** 206; **49:1–4,** 207; **50:4,** 61; **52:11–12,** 75; **52:14,** 77; **53,** 51, 76; **53:10,** 75; **55:3–4,** 200; **61:8–10,** 200–201

Israel: Koresh's trip to, 43, 58–59, 61, 207; role in apocalyptic scenario, 10, 38, 39–40, 76, 207, 216n22

Jahn, W. Ray, 112–13, 155

Jamar, Jeff, 3–4, 6, 19–20, 108, 233n10

Jarriel, Tom, 124–25

Jennings, Peter, 124, 126

Jeremiah, Book of: **23:5,** 208; **23:5–8,18,19–20,** 201; **33:14–16,** 201

Jesus of Nazareth, 8, 63, 205, 206, 209, 223n45, 225n58

Jewell, David, 85, 86

Jewell, Kiri, 120, 85–86

Jewell, Sherri, 86

Joel, Book of: **2:15–16,** 20, 203, 210; **2:23,** 28

John, Gospel of: **1:1,** 55; **4:24,** 202; **15:1–3,** 39; **18:33–38,** 192; **18:36,** 65

Ross, Rick, 93–96, 100, 120–21, 138, 139, 177, 232–33n31
Ryan, Patricia, 150

Samples, Kenneth, 152–53, 237–38n18
Samuel, Book of, **10:1**, 60
San Antonio trial, 64–65, 112–16, 133–35, 234nn36–39
Sarabyn, Charles, 215n10
Schneider, Judy, 67, 230n12
Schneider, Mayanah, 67
Schneider, Steve, 5, 25, 26, 27, 42, 64, 91, 104, 107
Schroeder, Mike, 64
Scientology, Church of, 155
Scriptural interpretation: Branch Davidian's interest in, 90–92, 143–44; as context for events, 52, 61–62, 82; Koresh's skill in, 29–30, 31, 53, 62, 90–91, 162, 182
Second Coming, 44–46, 63
See No Evil (Tim Madigan), 96, 127
self-defense, 64–65
self-determination of cult members, 177–79, 184
Serafin, Charlie, 3, 52, 58, 65, 213n3
"Servant, the," 61, 207
Seven Seals: biblical, 8, 16, 29, 53–58, 58, 75, 90, 98, 99, 108, 196, 209; message of the, 15–16, 77
Seven Seals manuscript, 20, 65, 78, 187–90, 228n1; on computer disk, 189, 210, 218n48; suggesting Koresh's state of mind, 210; text of, 191–203
seven Spirits of God, 194
"Seventh angel's message," 25
Seventh-Day Adventists, 24–27, 34, 143, 163, 219n4; Adventist tradition,

43–48; Branch Davidians and, 35–36, 40–41, 221n27, 222n44; founding of, 48–49; Koresh and, 25, 26–28, 50
seventh-day Sabbath, 47, 48, 217n33
seventh messenger, 56, 62
seventh Prophet, 56
"Seventy Weeks" prophecy, 222n45
sexual harassment allegations, 103
sexual practices, 2, 66, 83, 101; celibacy, 66, 68–69, 71–72; Koresh's relations with minors, 16, 41, 42–43, 66, 82, 85, 101–2, 231n22; polygamy, 41, 42, 63, 66–68, 72–75, 231n22
SHEkinah, 40, 72, 230n15
Shepherd's Rod, The (Victor Houteff), 35
Shupe, Anson, 149, 158
siege, fifty-one-day. See standoff period
"sinful Messiah," 57, 80, 96
"Sinful Messiah" series, 2, 7, 93, 105, 117–19, 232n25
Singer, Margaret, 238–39n46
Sixth Seal, 77, 208
Slawson, Barbara, 135
Smith, Walter, Federal Judge, 116, 134, 230n20
Snow, Samuel, 46
society and cults, 180–83
Soldier of Fortune, 130
Sparks, Joyce, 218n43, 218n50
"Spirit of prophecy," 48–49, 55
standoff period, 6–7, 64, 103, 110, 216; Koresh's state of mind during, 7, 15, 77–78, 110–11, 217n35, 218n45
Stange, Mary Zeiss, 168, 239n48
Stone, Alan, 242
"stress escalation" tactics, 6, 107–8

Compositor:	Maple-Vail Book Mfg. Group
Text:	12/14.5 Garamond
Display:	Perpetua
Printer:	Maple-Vail Book Mfg. Group
Binder:	Maple-Vail Book Mfg. Group

Died in February 28 raid

Winston Blake
Peter Gent
Peter Hipsman
Perry Jones
Michael Schroeder
Jaydean Wendel

Exited during siege (adults)

Brad Branch
Livingstone Fagan
Oliver Gyarfas
Victorine Hollingsworth
Margaret Lawson
James Lawter
Sheila Martin
Catherine Matteson
Gladys Ottman
Anetta Richards
Rita Riddle
Ofelia Santoya
Kathryn Schroeder
Kevin Whitecliff

Exited during siege (children)

Neharah Fagan
Renea Fagan
Heather Jones
Kevin Jones
Mark Jones
Christyn Mabb
Jacob Mabb
Scott Mabb
Daniel Martin
James Martin
Kimberly Martin
Natalie Nobrega
Bryan Schroeder
Angelica Sonobe
Crystal Sonobe

Joshua Sylvia
Joann Vaega
Juanessa Wendel
Landon Wendel
Patron Wendel
Tamarae Wendel

Died in April 19 fire (adults)

Catherine Andrade
Jennifer Andrade
Alrick George Bennett
Susan Benta
Mary Jean Borst
Pablo Cohen
Abedowalo Davis
Shari Doyle
Beverly Elliot
Doris Fagan
Evette Fagan
Lisa Farris
Raymond Friesen
Nicole Elizabeth Gent
Aisha Gyarfas
Sandra Hardial
Diana Henry
Pauline Henry
Phillip Henry
Stephen Henry
Vanessa Henry
Zilla Henry
Novellette Sinclair Hipsman
Floyd Houtman
Rachel Jones Howell (Koresh)
Sherri Jewell
David Michael Jones
Michelle Jones
David Koresh
Jeffery Little
Livingstone Malcolm
Anita Martin
Diane Martin
Douglas Wayne Martin
Wayne Martin
Juliet Santoyo Martinez
John Mark McBean
Alison Bernadette Monbelly

Rosemary Morrison
Sonia Murray
Theresa Nobriega
James Riddle
Rebecca Saipaia
Judy Schneider
Steve Schneider
Cliff Sellors
Floracita Sonobe
Scott Sonobe
Gregory Summers
Lorraine Sylvia
Margarida Joann Vaega
Neil Vaega
Mark Wendel

Died in April 19 fire (children)

Chanel Andrade, 1
Dayland Gent, 3
Paige Gent, 1
Cyrus Howell (Koresh), 8
Star Howell (Koresh), 6
Chica Jones, 2
Latwan Jones, 2
Serenity Sea Jones, 4
Bobbie Lane Koresh, 2
Lisa Martin, 13
Sheila Martin, 15
Abigail Martinez, 11
Audry Martinez, 13
Crystal Martinez, 3
Isaiah Martinez, 4
Joseph Martinez, 8
Melissa Morrison, 6
Mayanah Schneider, 2
Startle Summers, 1
Hollywood Sylvia, 2
Rachel Sylvia, 13

Survived fire

Renos Avraam
Jaime Castillo
Graeme Craddock
Clive Doyle
Misty Ferguson

Derek Lovelock
Ruth Riddle
David Thibodeau
Marjorie Thomas

Outside Mount Carmel on February 28

Norman Allison
Donald Bunds
Paul Fatta
Mary Jones
Janet Kendrick
Woodrow Kendrick

Totals

Died in February 28 raid   6
Died in April 19 fire   74
Total dead   80

Survived fire   9
Exited during siege   35
Outside on February 28   6

Total Branch Davidians   130
Men   41
Women   46
Children   43